KB218663

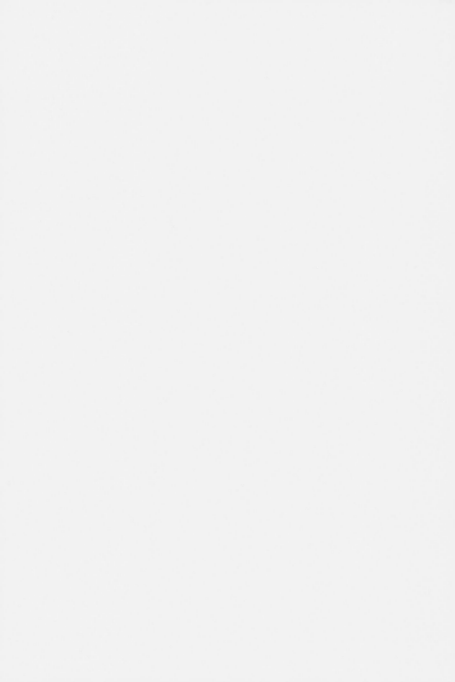

직독직해로 읽는

걸리버 여행기

Gulliver's Travels

직독직해로 읽는

걸리버 여행기

Gulliver's Travels

개정판 1쇄 발행 2020년 11월 20일
초판 1쇄 발행   2010년 11월 20일

원작	조나단 스위프트
역주	더 콜링(김정희, 박윤수, 조윤빈)
디자인	DX
일러스트	정은수
발행인	조경아
발행처	랭귀지북스
주소	서울시 마포구 포은로2나길 31 벨라비스타 208호
전화	02.406.0047 **팩스** 02.406.0042
이메일	languagebooks@hanmail.net
MP3 다운로드	blog.naver.com/languagebook
등록번호	101-90-85278 **등록일자** 2008년 7월 10일
ISBN	979-11-5635-146-7 (13740)
가격	12,000원

© LanguageBooks 2010

「이 도서의 국립중앙도서관 출판예정도서목록(CIP)은 서지정보유통지원시스템 홈페이지(http://seoji.nl.go.kr)와
국가자료공동목록시스템(http://www.nl.go.kr/kolisnet)에서 이용하실 수 있습니다.(CIP제어번호: CIP2020044002)」

직독직해로 읽는

걸리버 여행기
Gulliver's Travels

조나단 스위프트 원작
더 콜링 역주

Language Books

머리말

"어렸을 때 누구나 갖고 있던 세계명작 한 질.
그리고 TV에서 하던 세계명작 만화에 대한 추억이 있습니다."

"친숙한 이야기를 영어 원문으로 읽어 봐야겠다고 마음 먹고 샀던 원서들은
이제 애물단지가 되어 버렸습니다."

"재미있는 세계명작 하나 읽어 보려고 따져 보는 어려운 영문법,
모르는 단어 찾느라 이리저리 뒤져 봐야 하는 사전.
몇 장 넘겨 보기도 전에 지칩니다."

영어 독해력을 기르려면 술술 읽어가며 내용을 파악하는 것이 중요합니다. 현재 수능 시험에도 대세인 '직독직해' 스타일을 접목시킨 〈직독직해로 읽는 세계명작 시리즈〉는 세계명작을 영어 원작으로 쉽게 읽어갈 수 있도록 안내해 드릴 것입니다.

'직독직해' 스타일로 읽다 보면, 영문법을 들먹이며 따질 필요가 없으니 쉽고, 끊어 읽다 보니 독해 속도도 빨라집니다. 이 습관이 들여지면 어떤 글을 만나도 두렵지 않을 것입니다.

명작의 재미를 즐기며 영어 독해력을 키우는 두 마리의 토끼를 잡으세요!

〈직독직해로 읽는 세계명작 시리즈〉와 함께해 준 윤수와 번역하느라 고생한 윤빈 씨, 좋은 디자인으로 예쁜 책이 될 수 있도록 마음 써 주시는 디자인 DX, 빠듯한 스케줄에도 잘 맞춰주시는 일러스트레이터 은수 씨, 그리고 이 책이 출판될 수 있도록 언제나 든든하게 지원해 주시는 랭귀지북스에 감사의 마음을 전합니다.

마지막으로 내 삶의 주관자 되시는 하나님께 영광을 올려 드립니다.

더 콜링 김정희

목차

CONTENTS

1

The author gives some account / of himself and family.
저자는 설명한다 그 자신과 가족에 관해.

His first inducements / to travel. He is shipwrecked, / and
그의 첫 동기를 여행하는. 그는 난파당했고,

swims for his life. Gets safe / on shore in the country of
살기 위해서 헤엄친다. 무사히 도착해 릴리펏 나라의 해안에;

Lilliput; / is made a prisoner, / and carried up the country.
릴리펏; 포로가 되어, 그 나라로 압송된다.

My father had a small estate / in Nottinghamshire: / I was
아버지에게는 작은 토지가 있었다 노팅엄셔에; 나는

the third of five sons. He sent me / to Emanuel College in
나는 5형제 중 셋째였다. 아버지는 나를 보냈다 캠브리지 대학의 엠마뉴엘 대학에

Cambridge / at fourteen years old, / where I resided three
14살 때, 그곳에서 나는 3년 동안 살았고,

years, / and applied myself close to my studies; / but the
학업에 전념했다;   그러나

charge of maintaining me, / although I had a very scanty
학업을 유지하는 비용이,   비록 용돈은 매우 적게 받았지만,

allowance, / being too great / for a narrow fortune, / I
    너무 많이 들어서 적은 재산으로는,

was bound apprentice / to Mr. James Bates, / an eminent
나는 견습생으로 보내졌다 제임스 베이츠 씨에게,

surgeon in London, / with whom I continued four years.
런던에서 유명한 의사인. 그리고 그의 밑에서 나는 4년 동안 계속 있었다.

My father now and then / sending me / small sums of
아버지는 가끔 내게 보냈고 적은 돈을,

money, / I laid them out / in learning navigation, / and other
나는 그것을 썼다 항해술을 배우는데,

parts of the mathematics, / useful to those who intend to
그리고 수학의 다른 분야도, 여행하는 사람에게 필요한

estate 토지 | reside 살다 | apply oneself close to 전념하다, 몰두하다 | maintain 유지하다 | scanty 적은,
얼마 안 되는 | apprentice 견습생 | eminent surgeon 유명한 외과의사 | navigation 항해술

travel, / as I always believed / it would be, / some time or
나는 항상 믿었기 때문이다   그럴 것이라고,   언젠가는,

other, / my fortune to do.
여행을 할 운명이라고.

When I left Mr. Bates, / I went down to my father: /
내가 베이츠 씨를 떠나서,   아버지에게 내려갔을 때:

where, / by the assistance of him and my uncle John, and
그곳에서,   아버지와 존 삼촌, 그리고 다른 친척의 도움으로,

some other relations, / I got forty pounds, / and a promise
나는 40파운드를 받았다,   그리고 약속도

/ of thirty pounds a year / to maintain me at Leyden: /
1년에 30파운드씩 주겠다는   라이덴에서 지내는 비용으로:

There / I studied physic / two years and seven months, /
그곳에서   나는 의학을 공부했다   2년 7개월 간,

knowing / it would be useful / in long voyages.
알았기 때문에   그것이 유용할 것이라는 사실을   긴 항해에서.

Key Expression ❓

apply oneself to~ : ~에 전념하다

apply oneself to~는 '~에 전념하다'라는 뜻을 가진 숙어로 apply 대신 devote를 써도 같은 의미가 됩니다.
이처럼 재귀대명사를 목적어로 사용하는 동사+재귀대명사+전치사 형태의 숙어는 'be동사+형용사+전치사'의 형태로 바꾸어 쓸 수 있는 경우가 많습니다. 각각의 동사와 함께 쓰이는 전치사를 외워두고 전치사 뒤에는 명사나 동명사만 온다는 사실도 기억하세요.

▶ devote oneself to : 전념하다 (=be devoted to)
▶ absorb oneself in : 몰두하다 (=be absorbed in)
▶ absent oneself from : 결석하다 (=be absent from)
▶ present oneself at : 출석하다 (=be present at)
▶ pride oneself on : 자랑스러워 하다 (=be proud of)
▶ acquaint oneself with : 익숙하다 (=be acquainted with)
▶ accustom oneself to : 익숙해지다 (=be accustomed to)
▶ convince oneself of : 확신하다 (=be convinced of)
▶ content oneself with : 만족하다 (=be contented with)

ex) ···where I resided three years, and applied myself close to my studies.
그곳에서 나는 3년을 살았고 학업에 전념했다.

Soon after my return from Leyden, / I was recommended
라이든에서 돌아오자 마자,   나는 스승인, 베이츠 씨의 추천으로

by my good master, Mr. Bates, / to be surgeon to the
                                        스왈로우 호의 의사가 되었고,

Swallow, / Captain Abraham Pannel, commander; / with
            에이브라함 판넬 선장이, 지휘하는;

whom / I continued three years and a half, / making a
그와 함께   3년 반을 지냈다,

voyage or two / into the Levant, and some other parts.
한두 번 항해하면서   동부 지중해 연안, 그리고 다른 지방으로.

When I came back / I resolved to settle in London; / to
돌아왔을 때   나는 런던에 정착하기로 결심했다;

which Mr. Bates, my master, encouraged me, / and by him
스승인, 베이츠 씨도, 나를 격려해 주었고,   그리고 그에게

/ I was recommended / to several patients. I took part of
   추천받았다   몇몇 환자들을.   나는 작은 집을 마련했다

a small house / in the Old Jewry; / and being advised / to
                 올드 쥬리에;   그리고 충고를 받아

alter my condition, / I married Mrs. Mary Burton, / second
생활을 바꿔 보라는,   나는 매리 버튼 양과 결혼했다,

daughter to Mr. Edmund Burton, / hosier, in Newgate-
에드먼드 버튼 씨의 둘째 딸인,   뉴게이트 거리의 속옷 상인인,

street, / with whom / I received four hundred pounds / for
            그녀와 함께   나는 400파운드를 받았다

a portion.
결혼 지참금으로.

Key Expression

접속사 for의 해석

for는 '~을 위해, ~ 로' 등 다양한 의미를 가진 전치사로 쓰입니다. 그런데 for가
쉼표 뒤에서 완전한 문장을 동반하고 등장할 경우 접속사 for로 해석합니다.
접속사 for는 '왜냐하면(그 이유는)~이니까'라는 의미로 회화체에서는 거의 쓰
이지 않고 문학작품에 주로 등장합니다.

ex) I having few friends, my business began to fail; for my conscience would not
    suffer me to imitate the bad practice.
    내가 아는 사람이 거의 없었기 때문에, 내 사업은 기울기 시작했다; 왜냐하면 내
    양심상 잘못된 의료 행위를 흉내 내는 일은 도저히 할 수 없었기 때문이다.

But my good master Bates dying / in two years after, /
그러나 베이츠 선생님이 돌아가시자   2년 후,

and I having few friends, / my business began to fail; /
나는 아는 사람이 거의 없었기 때문에,   내 사업은 기울기 시작했다;

for my conscience would not suffer me / to imitate the
양심상 도저히 할 수 없었기 때문에   잘못된 의료 행위를

bad practice / of too many among my brethren. Having
흉내 내는 것은   수많은 동료 의사들이 하고 있던.

therefore consulted / with my wife, and some of my
그래서 상담한 후,   아내, 그리고 몇몇 아는 사람들과,

acquaintance, / I determined to go again to sea. I was
     나는 다시 배를 타기로 결심했다.

surgeon successively in two ships, / and made several
나는 계속해서 두 척의 배의 선상 의사가 되어,   몇 차례의 항해를 했다.

voyages, / for six years, / to the East and West Indies, /
     6년 동안,   동인도 및 서인도로,

by which I got some addition to my fortune. My hours of
그것으로 재산을 약간 불렸다.   여가 시간 동안

leisure / I spent in reading / the best authors, ancient and
나는 독서하며 시간을 보냈다   고대와 현대의 훌륭한 작가들의.

modern, / being always provided with a good number
     항상 많은 책이 있었기 때문에;

of books; / and when I was ashore, / in observing the
     그리고 상륙하게 되면,

manners and dispositions of the people, / as well as
사람들의 관습과 기질을 관찰했다,

learning their language; / wherein I had a great facility, /
그들의 언어를 배웠을 뿐만 아니라;   그런 점에서 나는 뛰어났다,

by the strength of my memory.
기억력이 좋아서.

recommend 추천하다 | commander 선장 | resolve 결심하다 | encourage 격려하다 | patient 환자 |
brethren 동업자들 | acquaintance 아는 사람 | successively 계속적으로, 연속해서 | ashore 물가에, 해안에 |
wherein 그런 점에서

The last of these voyages / not proving very fortunate, /
이 항해들 중 마지막은   그다지 운이 좋지 않아서,

I grew weary of the sea, / and intended to stay at home /
나는 바다에 싫증을 냈고,   집에 머물기로 했다

with my wife and family. I removed from the Old Jewry
아내와 가족이 있는.   나는 올드 주리를 떠나 페터 레인으로 이사했다,

to Fetter Lane, / and from thence to Wapping, / hoping
          그리고 다시 그곳에서 와핑으로,

to get business among the sailors; / but it would not turn
선원들을 상대로 개업하겠다는 희망으로;   그러나 이는 돈이 되지 않았다.

to account. After three years expectation / that things
          3년 동안 기대한 끝에   상황이 나아질 것이라는,

would mend, / I accepted an advantageous offer / from
          나는 유리한 제안을 받아들였다

Captain William Prichard, / master of the Antelope, / who
윌리엄 프릿처드 선장으로부터의,   엔틸로프 호의 선주인,

was making a voyage to the South Sea. We set sail from
남대양으로 항해할 예정이었던.   우리는 브리스톨에서 출항했고,

Bristol, / May 4, 1699, / and our voyage was at first / very
          1699년 5월 4일에,   처음에는 항해가

prosperous.
매우 순조로웠다.

It would not be proper, / for some reasons, / to trouble the
적절한 일이 아닐 것이다,   여러 가지 이유에서,   독자를 지루하게 하는 것은

reader / with the particulars of our adventures / in those
          우리의 모험을 상세하게 말하는 것으로   그 해상에서 경험한;

seas; / let it suffice to inform him, / that in our passage from
독자에게 알리는 것으로 충분할 것이다,   그곳(브리스톨)에서 동인도로 가는 중에,

thence to the East Indies, / we were driven/ by a violent
          우리가 밀렸다는 것을   사나운 폭풍 때문에

storm / to the north-west of Van Diemen's Land. By an
반 디멘즈 랜드의 북서부까지.

grow weary 지친,~에 싫증남 | turn to account 돈이 되다 | prosperous 순조로운 | particular 상세한 |
suffice 충분하다 | immoderate 지나친 | hazy 안개 짙은 | seaman 선원, 뱃사람 | spy 발견하다 | row 노를 젓다
| computation 계산 | overset 뒤집히다 | flurry 돌풍, 강풍 | companion 동료

12   Gulliver's Travels

observation, / we found ourselves / in the latitude of 30
관측해 보고,　　　　우리는 알았다

degrees 2 minutes south. Twelve of our crew were dead /
남위 30도 2분에 있다는 것을.　　　　선원 중 12명이 숨졌고

by immoderate labor and ill food; / the rest were in a very
과로와 영양 실조로;　　　　나머지도 매우 허약한 상태였다.

weak condition. On the 5th of November, / which was the
11월 5일에,

beginning of summer in those parts, / the weather being
그 지역에서 여름이 시작되는,　　　　안개가 짙은 날씨 속에서,

very hazy, / the seamen spied a rock / within half a cable's
선원들이 암초 하나를 발견했다　　　배에서 반련(鏈) 거리에 있는:

length* of the ship; / but the wind was so strong, / that we
그러나 바람이 너무 강해서,

were driven directly upon it, / and immediately split. Six
우리는 그쪽으로 밀렸고,　　　　곧바로 배가 산산조각이 났다.

of the crew, / of whom I was one, / having let down the
6명의 선원들은,　　　나를 포함한,　　　보트를 바다에 내리고,

boat into the sea, / made a shift to get clear / of the ship
벗어나기 위해 방향을 틀었다

and the rock. We rowed, / by my computation, / about three
배와 암초로부터.　　우리는 노를 저었다, 내 짐작으로,

leagues**, / till we were able to work no longer, / being
3리그 정도,　　　더 이상 움직일 수 없을 때까지,

already spent with labor / while we were in the ship. We
이미 기력을 다하여　　　배에 있는 동안.

therefore trusted ourselves / to the mercy of the waves, / and
그래서 우리는 운명을 맡겼다　　　파도에,

in about half an hour / the boat was overset / by a sudden
그런데 약 30분 후　　　보트가 뒤집혔다　　　갑작스러운 돌풍에

flurry / from the north. What became of my companions
북쪽에서 불어온.　　배에 있던 내 동료들이 어떻게 되었는지,

in the boat, / as well as of those who escaped on the rock,
암초로 피난한 사람들과,

*1련(鏈), 해상 거리를 나타내는 단위; 미해군에서는 720피트(약 219m), 영해군에서는 608피트(약 185 m)

**리그, 옛날 거리의 단위. 약 3마일 또는 약 4,000미터에 해당

/ or were left in the vessel, / I cannot tell; / but conclude
혹은 본선에 남았던 이들이,　　　나는 알 수 없다;　　　그렇지만 모두 죽었다고

they were all lost. For my own part, / I swam as fortune
짐작된다.　　　내 경우는,　　　운명이 가리키는 쪽으로 헤엄쳤고,

directed me, / and was pushed forward / by wind and tide.
　　　앞으로 밀려 나아갔다　　　바람과 조수에 의해.

I often let my legs drop, / and could feel no bottom; / but
나는 자주 발을 아래로 뻗었는데,　　　바닥이 느껴지지 않았다;

when I was almost gone, / and able to struggle no longer,
그러나 거의 기운이 다해서,　　　더 이상 몸부림을 칠 수 없었을 때,

/ I found myself within my depth; / and by this time / the
나는 발이 바닥에 닿는 것을 알았다;　　　그리고 그 즈음

storm was much abated. The declivity was so small, / that
폭풍도 많이 누그러져 있었다.　　　경사가 매우 완만해서,

I walked near a mile / before I got to the shore, / which I
나는 1마일 가량 걸어서　　　해변에 도착했다.

conjectured was / about eight o'clock in the evening.
내 짐작으로　　　저녁 8시 경에.

I then advanced forward / near half a mile, / but could not
그리고 나서 더 걸었으나　　　약 반 마일을,

discover any sign / of houses or inhabitants; / at least / I
어떤 흔적도 보이지 않았다　　　집이나 주민의;　　　혹은 적어도

was in so weak a condition, / that I did not observe them.
내가 너무 허약한 상태라서,　　　보지 못했다.

I was extremely tired, / and with that, / and the heat of the
나는 매우 피곤했고,　　　게다가　　　더운 날씨와,

weather, / and about half **a pint*** of brandy / that I drank /
　　　약 반 파인트의 브랜디 때문에　　　마셨던

as I left the ship, / I found myself much inclined to sleep.
배를 떠날 무렵에,　　　너무 자고 싶은 상태였다.

I lay down on the grass, / which was very short and soft,
나는 풀밭에 누웠는데,　　　풀밭이 매우 짧고 부드러워서,

/ where I slept sounder / than ever I remembered to have
거기에서 단잠을 잤다　　　내 기억에 그 어느 때보다,

done / in my life, / and, as I reckoned, / about nine hours; /
평생　　　그리고, 내 계산으로,　　　9시간 가량;

for when I awaked, / it was just day-light.
왜냐하면 깨어났을 때,　　　막 동이 트고 있었으니까.

I attempted to rise, / but was not able to stir: / for, / as I
나는 일어나려고 했지만,   꼼짝할 수 없었다: 왜냐하면,

happened to lie on my back, / I found my arms and legs were
등을 땅에 댄 채 누워 있었고,   팔과 다리는 단단히 묶여 있었기 때문에

strongly fastened / on each side to the ground; / and my hair,
양쪽 모두 땅에;   그리고 머리카락도,

/ which was long and thick, / tied down in the same manner.
길고 숱이 많은,   같은 방식으로 묶여져 있었다.

I likewise felt / several slender ligatures across my body, /
마찬가지로 느꼈다   여러 개의 가느다란 끈이 몸을 묶고 있는 것을 .

from my arm-pits to my thighs. I could only look upwards; /
겨드랑이로부터 허벅지에 이르기까지.   나는 위쪽 밖에 볼 수 없었는데:

the sun began to grow hot, / and the light offended my eyes.
태양이 뜨거워지기 시작했고,   햇빛이 시야를 방해했다.

I heard a confused noise about me; / but in the posture I lay,
나는 요란한 소리를 들었지만;   누워 있는 자세로는,

/ could see nothing except the sky.
하늘 밖에 볼 수 없었다.

In a little time / I felt something alive / moving on my left
얼마 후에   나는 살아있는 무언가를 느꼈다   왼쪽 다리 위에서 움직이는,

leg, / which advancing gently forward / over my breast,
그리고 그것은 살며시 다가와서   가슴 위로,

/ came almost up to my chin; / when, / bending my eyes
거의 턱까지 올라왔다: 그 때,   시선을 아래로 내리자

downwards / as much as I could, / I perceived it to be a
할 수 있는 한,   그것이 사람임을 알아차렸다

human creature / not six inches high, / with a bow and arrow
키는 6인치가 안 되고,   손에 활과 화살을 들고,

in his hands, / and a quiver at his back. In the mean time, / I
등에 화살통을 맨.   그러는 동안,   나는

felt / at least forty more of the same kind / (as I conjectured)
느꼈다 그와 같은 사람이 40명이나 더 있음을 느꼈다   (내 추측으로는)

/ following the first.
처음 사람을 따라오고 있는.

*파인트, 부피의 단위, 영국에서는 0.568리터, 일부 국가와 미국에서는 0.473리터, 8파인트가 1갤런
vessel 본선, 배 | tide 조수 | struggle 몸부림치다 | abate 누그러지다 | declivity 경사 | conjecture 짐작하다
| inhabitant 주민 | incline 하고 싶은 | sleep sounder 숙면하다 | reckon 계산하다 | stir 움직이다 | likewise
마찬가지로 | slender 가느다란 | ligature 끈 | arm-pit 겨드랑이 | thigh 넓적다리 | posture 자세 | gently
살며시 | perceive 알아차리다 | quiver 화살통

I was in the utmost astonishment, / and roared so loud, /
나는 극도로 놀랐고,   크게 소리치자,

that they all ran back in a fright; / and some of them, / as
그들은 겁에 질려 달아났다: 그 중 몇 명은,

I was afterwards told, / were hurt with the falls they got
나중에 들었지만,   떨어지는 바람에 다쳤다

/ by leaping / from my sides upon the ground. However, /
/ 뛰어 내리다가   내 허리에서 땅으로.   그러나,

they soon returned, / and one of them, / who ventured so
그들은 곧 되돌아왔고,   그들 중 한 명이   대담하게 가까이 와서

far as / to get a full sight of my face, / lifting up his hands
         내 얼굴 전체를 보려고,   그의 두 손과 눈을 들고

and eyes / by way of admiration, / cried out in a shrill but
           감탄의 표시로,   날카롭지만 분명한 목소리로 외쳤다.

distinct voice, / HEKINAH DEGUL: / the others repeated
'헤키나 데굴'이라고: 다른 이들도 같은 말을 되풀이 했다

the same words / several times, / but then / I knew not /
                여러 번,   하지만 그때   나는 몰랐다

what they meant. I lay all this while, / as the reader may
그것이 무슨 뜻인지 몰랐다. 그 동안 내내 나는 누워 있었다,   독자 여러분도 짐작하겠지만,

believe, / in great uneasiness.
          매우 불안해 하며.

At length, / struggling to get loose, / I had the fortune to /
마침내,   풀려나려고 버둥거리자,   다행스럽게도

break the strings, / and wrench out the pegs / that fastened
줄을 끊을 수 있었다,   그리고 말뚝을 뽑았다

my left arm to the ground; / for, / by lifting it up to my
내 왼팔을 땅에 고정시켰던;   왜냐하면, 팔을 얼굴로 들어 올려보니

face, / I discovered the methods / they had taken to bind
        방법을 알게 되었기 때문에   그들이 나를 묶어 놓은,

me, / and at the same time with a violent pull, / which gave
      그래서 즉시 세게 잡아 당겨서,

me excessive pain, / I a little loosened the strings / that tied
몹시 아프기는 했으나,   약간 끈을 느슨하게 했다

down my hair on the left side, / so that I was just able to
왼쪽 머리카락을 묶고 있던,   그래서 나는 겨우 고개를 돌릴 수 있게 되었다

turn my head / about two inches. But the creatures ran off
2인치 가량.　　　　　　　　　　그러나 소인들은 도망쳤다

/ a second time, / before I could seize them; / whereupon
또 다시,　　　　　내가 그들을 잡기도 전에;

there was a great shout / in a very shrill accent, / and
그러자 큰 고함 소리가 났다　　매우 날카로운 어조로,

after it ceased / I heard one of them cry aloud / TOLGO
그리고 그 소리가 그치자　그 중 한 명이 외치는 것을 들었다

PHONAC; / when in an instant / I felt / above a hundred
'톨고 포낙'이라고;　그 순간　　　　나는 느꼈다　100여 개의 화살이

arrows discharged / on my left hand, / which, / pricked me
발사되어　　　　　내 왼손에 꽂히는 것을.　그리고, 그것은, 따끔거렸다

/ like so many needles; / and besides, / they shot another
마치 수많은 바늘처럼;　게다가,　　　　그들은 또 화살을 날렸다

flight / into the air, / as we do bombs in Europe, / whereof
공중에,　　유럽에서 우리가 폭탄을 던지듯,　　　그 많은 화살 중

many, / I suppose, / fell on my body, / (though I felt
대부분,　내 추측에,　몸 위로 떨어졌다　　　(느끼지는 못했으나),

them not), / and some on my face, / which I immediately
그리고 몇 개는 얼굴에 떨어져,　　즉시 가렸다

covered / with my left hand.
내 왼손으로.

Key Expression 🍖

have the fortune to~ : 다행스럽게도 ~하다
'have the fortune to~'는 부사 fortunately로 바꾸어 쓸 수 있습니다.
이처럼 fortune 대신에 다양한 추상명사를 넣어 같은 표현을 만들 수 있어요.

▶ have the + 추상명사(A) + to 동사원형(B) : A하게도 B하다

have the fortune to~	다행히도 ~하다(=fortunately)
have the luck to~	다행히도 ~하다(=luckily)
have the misfortune to~	불행히도 ~하다(=unfortunately)
have the cruelty to~	잔인하게도 ~하다(=cruelly)
have the foolishness to~	어리석게도 ~하다(=foolishly)
have the courage to~	용감하게도 ~하다(=courageously)

ex) At length, struggling to get loose, I had the fortune to break the strings.
마침내, 풀려나려고 버둥거리자, 다행스럽게도 줄을 끊을 수 있었다.

astonishment 놀람 | roar 소리치다 | fright 겁먹은 | leap 뛰어넘다 | venture 대담하게도 ~하다 | excessive
지나친, 과도한 | whereupon 그러자, 그 때문에 | prick 따끔하게 찌르다

When this shower of arrows was over, / I fell a groaning
이 소나기 같은 화살이 끝나자,   나는 슬픔과 통증으로 신음했다;

with grief and pain; / and then / striving again to get loose,
                        그리고 나서   끈을 풀기 위해 몸부림쳤다,

/ they discharged another volley / larger than the first, /
그들은 또 다시 화살을 발사했다   처음보다 더 많이,

and some of them attempted / with spears / to stick me
그리고 그 중 몇 명은 시도했다   창으로   내 옆구리를 찌르려고;

in the sides; / but by good luck / I had on a buff jerkin, /
하지만 다행히도   나는 가죽 조끼를 입고 있었고,

which they could not pierce. I thought / it the most prudent
그들은 뚫을 수 없었다.   나는 생각했다   가장 신중한 방법은

method / to lie still, / and my design was / to continue so
가만히 누워 있는 것이라고,   그래서 내 계획은   계속 가만히 있는 것이었다

/ till night, / when, / my left hand being already loose, / I
밤까지,   그때는,   왼손이 이미 풀렸으니,

could easily free myself: / and as for the inhabitants, / I
쉽게 풀 수 있을 것이었다: 그리고 그 소인들로 말하자면,

had reason to believe / I might be a match for the greatest
나는 믿을 만한 이유가 있었다   대부대라도 상대할 수 있을 거라고

army / they could bring against me, / if they were all of the
그들이 몰고 오는,   만약 그 소인들이 모두 작다면

same size with him / that I saw.
                내가 보았던 것처럼.

But fortune disposed otherwise of me. When the people
그러나 운명은 나를 다른 상황으로 몰았다.   소인들은 보자

observed / I was quiet, / they discharged no more arrows; /
내가 가만히 있는 것을, 더 이상 화살을 발사하지 않았다;

but, by the noise I heard, / I knew their numbers increased;
그러나, 들리는 소음에 의해,   그들의 수가 많아졌음을 알았다;

/ and about four yards from me, / over against my right
그리고 4야드 가량 떨어져서,   오른쪽 귀 근처에서

ear, / I heard a knocking / for above an hour, / like that of
뭔가 두들기는 소리가 들렸다   한 시간 이상이나,   소인들이 작업을

people at work; / when turning my head that way, / as well
하는 듯이;   그쪽으로 고개를 돌리자,

as the pegs and strings would permit me, / I saw a stage
말뚝과 끈이 허용하는 범위 안에서,   나는 무대가 세워진 것을

erected / about a foot and a half from the ground, / capable
보았다   땅에서 1피트 반 높이에.

of holding four of the inhabitants, / with two or three
네 명의 주민(소인)을 수용할 수 있는 크기이며,   두세 개의 사다리가 걸쳐져 있는:

ladders to mount it: / from whence one of them, / who
                    그곳에서 한 사람이,

seemed to be a person of quality, / made me a long speech,
높은 신분으로 보이는,   내게 긴 연설을 했지만.

/ whereof I understood not one syllable. But I should have
    무엇에 대해서인지 나는 한 마디로 알아들을 수 없었다.   하지만 난 말했어야만 했다.

mentioned, / that before the principal person began his
            그 중요한 인물이 말을 하기 전에,

oration, / he cried out three times, / LANGRO DEHUL
            그는 세 번 외쳤다.   '랑그로 데훌 산'이라고

SAN / (these words and the former / were afterwards
        (이 말과 그 전에 한 말들은   나중에 세 번 반복하고 뜻을

repeated and explained / to me); / whereupon, immediately,
설명해 주었다   내게);   그러자, 곧,

/ about fifty of the inhabitants came / and cut the strings
    약 50명의 소인들이 나타나서   줄을 잘랐다

/ that fastened the left side of my head, / which gave me
    내 머리 왼쪽을 묶고 있던,

the liberty of turning it to the right, / and of observing the
그래서 오른쪽으로 고개를 돌릴 수 있게 되었고,   그 사람의 몸짓을 관찰할 수 있었다

person and gesture of him / that was to speak.
                            연설하려는.

buff 가죽 | jerkin 조끼 | pierce 뚫다, 관통하다 | prudent 신중한 | erect 세우다 | syllable 말 한 마디

He appeared to be of a middle age, / and taller than / any
그의 중년으로 보였고,　키가 컸다

of the other three who attended him, / whereof one was a
그를 시중 드는 다른 세 사람보다,　그들 중 한 명은 하인으로

page / that held up his train, / and seemed to be somewhat
그의 옷자락을 들고 있는,　약간 더 커 보였고;

longer / than my middle finger; / the other two stood one on
가운데 손가락보다;　나머지 둘은 양 옆에 서 있었다

each side / to support him. He acted every part of an orator,
그를 보좌하며.　그는 웅변가가 하는 모든 행동을 했고,

/ and I could observe / many periods of threatenings, / and
나는 볼 수 있었다　여러 차례의 협박과,

others of promises, pity, and kindness. I answered in a few
약속과, 연민과, 호의를.　나는 간단한 말로 대답했다.

words, / but in the most submissive manner, / lifting up my
그러나 아주 공손한 태도로,

left hand, / and both my eyes to the sun, / as calling him /
왼손을 들고,　두 눈을 태양으로 돌리며,　그에게 호소하듯이

for a witness; / and being almost famished with hunger, /
증인이 되어 달라고;　그리고 배가 고파 죽을 지경이었기에,

having not eaten a morsel / for some hours / before I left
아무것도 먹은 것이 없었기 때문에　몇 시간 동안　배를 떠나기 전,

the ship, / I found the demands of nature so strong upon
자연적인 욕구가 너무 커서,

me, / that I could not forbear showing my impatience /
참을 수 없음을 드러낼 수밖에 없었다

(perhaps against the strict rules of decency) / by putting
(아마도 엄격한 예절에는 어긋나겠지만)

my finger frequently to my mouth, / to signify / that I
입에 자주 손가락을 가져감으로써,　보여 주기 위해

wanted food. The HURGO / (for so they call a great lord,
음식을 원하고 있음을. 그 '후르고'는　(그들은 고관 대작을 그렇게 불렀다,

---

orator 웅변가 | submissive 공손한 | famished 몹시 배고픈 | impatience 참을수 없음 | decency 예절 | signify
보여 주다, 나타내다 | laden 가득한 | thither (고어) 그쪽에, 저쪽에 | distinguish 구별하다 | mutton 양고기 | lark
종달새 | mouthful 한 입 | loaf 빵 한 덩이 | bigness 크기 | musket 머스킷 총(과거 병사들이 쓰던 장총)

/ as I afterwards learnt) / understood me very well. He
나중에 알았지만)   내 말을 잘 알아들었다.

descended from the stage, / and commanded / that several
그는 무대에서 내려가서,   명령했다

ladders should be applied to my sides, / on which / above a
여러 개의 사다리를 내 옆구리에 놓으라고,   그 위로

hundred of the inhabitants / mounted and walked towards
백 명 이상의 소인들이   올라와서 내 입 쪽으로 걸어왔다.

my mouth, / laden with baskets full of meat, / which had
                  고기로 가득한 바구니를 메고,

been provided and sent thither / by the king's orders, /
마련되어 그곳으로 보내진   왕의 명령으로,

upon the first intelligence / he received of me. I observed
처음 알고서   나에 대한 소식을.   나는 봤지만

/ there was the flesh of several animals, / but could not
    몇 가지의 살코기가 있는 것을.

distinguish them / by the taste. There were shoulders,
식별할 수 없었다   맛으로는.   어깨 살, 다리 살, 허리 살이 있었다,

legs, and loins, / shaped like those of mutton, / and very
                  양고기와 모양이 똑같은,

well dressed, / but smaller than the wings of a lark. I ate
잘 요리되어 있었지만,   종달새의 날개보다도 작았다.   나는 그것을

them / by two or three at a mouthful, / and took three
먹었고   한 입에 두세 개씩,   빵 덩어리 세 개를 먹었다

loaves / at a time, / about the bigness of musket bullets.
          한꺼번에.   소총 탄환 크기만한.

They supplied me / as fast as they could, / showing a
그들은 내게 공급해 주면서   가능한 한 빠르게,

thousand marks of wonder and astonishment / at my bulk
수없이 놀라며 경탄을 보였다   내 큰 체격과 식욕에

and appetite. I then made another sign, / that I wanted
대해.   그리고 나서 나는 다른 신호를 보냈다,   마실 것을 원한다고.

drink. They found / by my eating / that a small quantity
그들은 알았다   내가 먹는 양을 보고   적은 양으로 충분하지 않을 것이라고;

would not suffice me; / and being a most ingenious people,
또한 매우 영리한 사람들이어서.

/ they slung up, / with great dexterity, / one of their largest
그들은 매달아 올려서,   매우 교묘하게,   제일 큰 술통 하나를,

hogsheads, / then rolled it towards my hand, / and beat
내 손을 향해 굴려 보냈고,

out the top; / I drank it off / at a draught, / which I might
뚜껑을 열었다;   나는 그것을 마셨는데   한 모금에,   그것은 당연한 일이었다.

well do, / for it did not hold half a pint, / and tasted like a
왜냐하면 반 파인트도 채 안 되었으니까,

small wine of Burgundy, / but much more delicious. They
그리고 버건디 포도주 맛이 났으나,   훨씬 더 맛있었다.

brought me a second hogshead, / which I drank / in the
그들은 술통을 하나 더 갖다 주었고,   나는 그것을 마셔 버리고는

same manner, / and made signs for more; / but they had
마찬가지로,   더 달라는 몸짓을 했다;   하지만 그들은 더 이상

none to give me.
줄 것이 없었다.

When I had performed these wonders, / they shouted for
내가 이렇게 놀라운 행위를 마치자,   그들은 기뻐서 소리지르며,

joy, / and danced upon my breast, / repeating several times
내 가슴 위에서 춤을 추었다.   몇 번이나 되풀이 해 말하면서

/ as they did at first, / HEKINAH DEGUL. They made me
그들이 처음에 했던,   '헤키나 데굴'이라고.   그들은 내게 신호를 보냈다

a sign / that I should throw down the two hogsheads, / but
그 두 개의 술통을 집어 던지라고.

first warning / the people below / to stand out of the way,
하지만 먼저 경고했다   아래에 있는 사람들에게   비키라고,

/ crying aloud, BORACH MEVOLAH; / and when they
'보라크 미보라'라고 외치면서;   그리고 술통이 공중에서

saw the vessels in the air, / there was a universal shout / of
날아오는 걸 보자.   또 다시 함성이 터졌다

HEKINAH DEGUL.
'헤키나 데굴'이라는.

I confess / I was often tempted, / while they were passing
고백하건대   나는 자주 유혹을 느꼈다,   그들이 지나다니는 동안

/ backwards and forwards / on my body, / to seize forty or
이리저리   내 몸 위에서,   4~50명을 잡아서

fifty / of the first that came in my reach, / and dash them
fifty   내 손에 가장 처음 닿는,   땅에 내던지고 싶다는.

against the ground. But the remembrance of what I had
그러나 내가 겪은 기억으로는,

felt, / which probably / might not be the worst / they could
그것은 아마도   최악의 행동은 아니었을 것이다   그들이 할 수 있었던.

do, / and the promise of honor / I made them / — for so I
그리고 명예로운 약속 때문에   내가 그들에게 했던   — 나는 그렇게

interpreted / my submissive behavior — / soon drove out
해석했으니까   내가 했던 굴욕적인 행동을 —   곧 떨쳐버렸다

/ these imaginations. Besides, / I now considered / myself
그런 생각을.   더군다나.   나는 이제 생각했다

as bound by the laws of hospitality, / to a people who had
환대에 빚을 지고 있다고,   나를 대접해 준 사람들에게

treated me / with so much expense and magnificence.
그렇게 큰 비용을 들여 훌륭하게.

---

appetite 식욕 | suffice 충분하다 | ingenious 영리한 | hogshead 술통 | draught 한 모금 | tempt 유혹을
느끼다 | seize 잡다 | submissive 굴욕적인 | magnificence 훌륭함

However, / in my thoughts / I could not sufficiently wonder
하지만, 속으로는 크게 놀라지 않을 수 없었다

/ at the intrepidity / of these diminutive mortals, / who
대담성에 이 작은 인간들의,

durst venture to mount and walk / upon my body, / while
그들은 감히 올라와서 걸어 다녔다 내 몸 위를,

one of my hands was at liberty, / without trembling / at the
내가 한 손을 마음대로 움직일 수 있는데도, 전혀 겁내지 않고

very sight of so prodigious a creature / as I must appear
엄청나게 큰 존재를 보고도 그들에게 보이기에는,

to them. After some time, / when they observed / that I
얼마 후에, 그들은 알아차리자

made no more demands for meat, / there appeared before
내가 더 이상 음식을 요구하지 않는 것을, 내 앞에 나타났다

me / a person of high rank / from his imperial majesty. His
고관의 사람이 황제 폐하로부터.

excellency, / having mounted / on the small of my right leg,
그 고관은, 올라와서 내 오른쪽 다리에,

/ advanced forwards up to my face, / with about a dozen
얼굴까지 전진해 왔다, 십여 명의 수행원을 거느리고;

of his retinue; / and producing his credentials / under the
그리고 그의 신임장을 꺼내서 옥새가 찍힌,

signet royal, / which he applied close to my eyes, / spoke
내 눈에 가까이 대고,

about ten minutes / without any signs of anger, / but with a
약 10분간 말했다 화난 기색 없이,

kind of determinate resolution, / often pointing forwards, /
그러나 단호한 어조로, 종종 전방을 가리키면서,

which, as I afterwards found, / was towards the capital city,
나중에 알게된 바로는, 수도가 있는 쪽이었다.

/ about half a mile distant; / whither / it was agreed by his
약 반 마일 거리에; 그곳으로 황제 폐하가 결정했다

majesty in council / that I must be conveyed. I answered
나를 데려가기로. 나는 몇 마디 대답했지만,

in few words, / but to no purpose, / and made a sign / with
소용없었다, 그래서 신호를 보냈다

my hand that was loose, / putting it to the other / (but
자유로운 손으로, 다른 손에 갖다 대면서

over his excellency's head / for fear of hurting him or his
(하지만 고관의 머리 위로 그와 그 수행원들을 다치게 할까 봐)

train) / and then / to my own head and body, / to signify
그리고 나서 내 머리와 몸에, 자유를 바란다는 것을

that I desired my liberty. It appeared that he understood
보여 주기 위해. 그는 내 뜻을 이해한 듯 했다

me / well enough, / for he shook his head / by way of
충분히, 그가 그의 고개를 옆으로 흔들어 안 된다는 표시를

disapprobation, / and held his hand in a posture to show /
했기 때문에, 그리고 손 모양으로 나타냈다

that I must be carried / as a prisoner. However, / he made
내가 호송되어야 한다고 포로로서. 하지만, 그는 다른 신호를

other signs / to let me understand / that I should have meat
보냈다 내가 이해하도록 충분한 음식을 받을 것이라고,

and drink enough, / and very good treatment. Whereupon
그리고 매우 좋은 대접을. 그래서

/ I once more thought of / attempting to break my bonds; /
나는 다시 생각했다 나를 묶고 있는 줄을 끊어버릴까 하고;

but again, / when I felt the smart of their arrows / upon my
그러나 또 다시, 화살의 아픔을 느끼자

face and hands, / which were all in blisters, / and many of
얼굴과 손에 박힌, 거기에는 온통 물집이 생겼고, 많은 화살이

the darts / still sticking in them, / and observing likewise /
아직도 박혀 있었기 때문에, 또한 보고

that the number of my enemies increased, / I gave tokens /
적의 수가 많아졌다는 것을, 나는 신호를 보냈다

to let them know / that they might do with me / what they
그들에게 이해시키려고 나를 마음대로 해도 된다고 원하는 대로,

pleased. Upon this, / the HURGO and his train withdrew, /
그러자, '후르고'와 그 수행원들은 물러갔다.

intrepidity 대담 | durst (고어)dare의 과거: 감히~하다 | tremble 겁내다 | imperial 황제의 | excellency
고관, 각하 | retinue 수행원들 | credential 신임장 | determinate 확실한 | convey 실어나르다, 운반하다 |
disapprobation 동의하지 않음 | blister 물집 | stick 박이다

with much civility and cheerful countenances. Soon after
매우 점잖고 밝은 표정으로.   그 후 곧 나는

I heard a general shout, / with frequent repetitions of /
사방에서 고함소리를 들었다,   자주 반복되는 것을

the words PEPLOM SELAN; / and I felt / great numbers
'펩롬 세란'이란 말이;   그리고 나는 느꼈다   많은 사람들이

of people / on my left side / relaxing the cords to such a
                내 왼쪽에서   줄을 어느 정도 느슨하게 하는 것을.

degree, / that I was able to turn / upon my right, / and to
            그래서 몸을 돌릴 수 있었고   오른쪽으로,

ease myself with making water;/ which I very plentifully
편히 소변을 볼 수 있었다;   내가 본 양이 매우 많아서,

did, / to the great astonishment of the people; / who, /
사람들이 크게 놀랐다;   그들은,

conjecturing by my motion / what I was going to do, /
내 거동으로 추측하고   내가 무엇을 하려는지,

immediately opened / to the right and left on that side, / to
즉시 흩어졌다   좌우로,

avoid the torrent, / which fell / with such noise and violence
격류를 피하려고   분출되는   요란하고 사납게

/ from me. But before this, / they had daubed my face and
나로부터.   그러나 그 전에,   그들은 내 얼굴과 양손에 발라 주었다

both my hands / with a sort of ointment, / very pleasant
               일종의 연고를,

to the smell, / which, in a few minutes, / removed all the
향기가 매우 좋은,   그러자 금방,

smart of their arrows. These circumstances, / added to the
화살의 아픔이 사라졌다.   이런 상황에서,

refreshment / I had received by their victuals and drink, /
기운을 되찾자   그들이 준 음식으로,

which were very nourishing, / disposed me to sleep. I slept
매우 편해지고,   졸음이 왔다.

about eight hours, / as I was afterwards assured; / and it
나는 8시간을 잤다.   나중에 알게 되었는데;

countenance 표정 | conjecture 알다. 추측하다 | daub 바르다 | ointment 연고 | nourishing 영양이 되는.
편해지는 | dispose ~에게~의 경향을 갖게 하다 | physician 의사

was no wonder, / for the physicians, / by the emperor's
그리고 그도 그럴 것이,   의사들이,   황제의 명령으로,

order, / had mingled a sleepy potion / in the hogsheads of
              수면제를 타 놓은 것이었다   술통에.

wine.

It seems, / that upon the first moment / I was discovered
그것은 그랬다, 발견되자마자

sleeping on the ground, / after my landing, / the emperor
내가 땅에 누워 잠들어 있는 것이, 상륙한 후,

had early notice of it / by an express; / and determined
황제는 그 소식을 받았다 속보로; 그리고 회의에서 결정했다,

in council, / that I should be tied / in the manner I have
나를 묶으라고 앞서 이야기 했던 방식으로,

related, / (which was done / in the night while I slept;) /
(그것은 실행되었다 내가 잠든 밤 사이에;)

that plenty of meat and drink / should be sent to me, / and
그리고 충분한 양의 음식을 내게 보내고,

a machine prepared / to carry me to the capital city.
기계를 준비하라고 나를 수도로 옮길 .

This resolution perhaps may appear / very bold and
이러한 결정은 아마도 보일 수 있다 매우 대담하고 위험하게,

dangerous, / and I am confident / would not be imitated /
그리고 확신하건대 그렇게 하지 않았으리라고

by any prince in Europe / on the like occasion. However,
유럽의 왕이라면 누구도 그런 경우에. 하지만,

/ in my opinion, / it was extremely prudent, / as well as
내 생각에는, 그것은 극히 너그럽기도 하고,

generous: / for, / supposing these people had endeavored
또한 신중했다: 왜냐하면, 만일 이 사람들이 나를 죽이려 했다면

to kill me / with their spears and arrows, / while I was
창과 화살로, 내가 잠들어 있는 동안,

asleep, / I should certainly have awaked / with the first
나는 분명히 깨어났을 것이기에 아픔을 느끼자마자,

sense of smart, / which might so far have roused / my rage
그리고 그것이 자극해서

and strength, / as to have enabled me to break the strings /
내 분노와 힘을, 줄을 끊을 수도 있었을 것이다

wherewith I was tied; / after which, / as they were not able
나를 묶고 있는; 그리고 그 후에는, 그들은 저항할 수 없으므로,

to make resistance, / so they could expect no mercy.
용서도 바라지 못했을 것이다.

These people are most excellent mathematicians, / and
이 사람들은 수학에 뛰어났고,

arrived to a great perfection / in mechanics, / by the
완벽한 경지에 도달해 있었다   기계공학에서,

countenance and encouragement of the emperor, / who
황제의 원조와 장려에 의해,

is a renowned patron of learning. This prince has several
학문에 이름난 후원자인.   이 왕은 여러 대의 기계를 가지고 있었다

machines / fixed on wheels, / for the carriage of trees and
바퀴가 달려 있는,   나무와 기타 무거운 물건을 운반하기 위한.

other great weights. He often builds / his largest men of
                그는 자주 만드는데   초대형 전함을,

war, / whereof some are nine feet long, / in the woods where
      그 중에는 길이가 9피트나 되는 것도 있었다.   목재가 자라는 숲에서,

the timber grows, / and has them carried / on these engines
                그리고 그것을 운반한다   이런 기계에 실어서

/ three or four hundred yards to the sea. Five hundred
  300~400야드 떨어진 해안까지.

carpenters and engineers / were immediately set at work /
500명의 목수와 기술자가   즉시 작업을 시작했다

to prepare the greatest engine / they had. It was a frame of
가장 큰 기계를 가동시키기 위해서   그들이 가진 것 중. 그것은 목재 구조물이었다

wood / raised three inches from the ground, / about seven
        땅에서 3인치 높이의.

feet long, / and four wide, / moving upon twenty-two wheels.
길이가 7피트,   폭이 4피트이며,   22개의 바퀴로 움직이는.

The shout I heard was / upon the arrival of this engine, /
내가 들었던 함성은   이 기계의 도착에 대한 것이었다.

which, it seems, / set out in four hours / after my landing.
그것은 아마도,   네 시간 후에 출발했다   내가 상륙한지.

It was brought parallel to me, / as I lay. But the principal
그 기계가 내 옆에 나란히 자리잡았고,   내가 누워있을 때. 그러나 중요한 문제는

difficulty was / to raise and place me / in this vehicle.
                나를 들어 올려서 올려 놓는 것이었다 수레에 .

plenty 충분한 | imitate 흉내내다 | prudent 신중한 | endeavor 시도하다, 노력하다 | wherewith 그것으로 |
renowned 이름난 | patron 후원자 | timber 목재 | carpenter 목수

Eighty poles, / each of one foot high, / were erected / for
80개 기둥이, 각각 1피트 높이의, 세워졌다

this purpose, / and very strong cords, / of the bigness of
그 목적을 위해, 그리고 매우 튼튼한 노끈을, 포장끈만한 굵기의,

packthread, / were fastened by hooks / to many bandages,
갈고리로 고정시켰다 수많은 붕대에,

/ which the workmen had girt round / my neck, my hands,
그것을 일꾼들이 칭칭 감았다 내 목과, 손, 몸, 그리고 발에,

my body, and my legs. Nine hundred of the strongest men
900명의 가장 힘센 일꾼이 동원되었다

were employed / to draw up these cords, / by many pulleys
이 끈들을 잡아당기기 위해, 수많은 도르래를 이용해서

/ fastened on the poles; / and thus, / in less than three
기둥에 고정된; 그리하여, 채 세 시간도 안 되어,

hours, / I was raised and slung into the engine, / and there
나를 들어 올려서 수레에 태우고, 거기에 꽁꽁 묶어

tied fast. All this I was told; / for, / while the operation
놓았다. 이 모든 것은 나중에 들었다; 왜냐하면,

was performing, / I lay in a profound sleep, / by the force
그 일이 진행되는 동안, 나는 깊은 잠에 빠졌었기 때문에,

of that soporiferous medicine / infused into my liquor.
수면제로 인해 음료에 탄.

Fifteen hundred of the emperor's largest horses, / each
황제의 가장 큰 말 1,500마리가,

about four inches and a half high, / were employed / to
각각 키가 약 4인치 반 정도인, 동원되었다 나를

draw me / towards the metropolis, / which, as I said, / was
끌고 가기 위해 수도로, 그곳은, 앞서 말했듯이,

half a mile distant.
반 마일 떨어져 있었다.

About four hours / after we began our journey, / I awaked
네 시간 후 여행이 시작된지, 나는 잠이 깼다

/ by a very ridiculous accident; / for the carriage being
아주 어이없는 사고로; 수레가 잠시 멈춰 선 동안,

stopped a while, / to adjust something / that was out of
무언가를 조정하려고 고장이 난,

order, / two or three of the young natives had the curiosity
두세 명의 젊은 원주민이 호기심이 났다

/ to see how I looked / when I was asleep;/ they climbed
내가 어떻게 생겼는지 보고 싶어서   잠자고 있을 때:

up into the engine, / and advancing very softly to my face,
그들은 수레에 기어 올라와서,   내 얼굴 쪽으로 천천히 다가와서,

/ one of them, / an officer in the guards, / put the sharp
그 중 한 명이,   호위대 장교인,   그의 짧은 창 끝을 찔렀다

end of his half-pike / a good way up into my left nostril, /
내 왼쪽 콧구멍 깊숙이,

which tickled my nose / like a straw, / and made me sneeze
그러자 그것이 내 코를 간지럽혀서   지푸라기처럼,   격렬한 재채기를 일으켰다:

violently; / whereupon they stole off unperceived, / and it
그러자 그들은 슬며시 사라졌다.

was three weeks / before I knew the cause of my waking /
그리고 3주 후였다   내가 깬 원인을 알게 된 것은

so suddenly. We made a long march / the remaining part of
그렇게 갑자기.   우리는 긴 행진을 했고   그 날 내내.

the day, / and, rested at night / with five hundred guards on
밤에는 쉬었다   500명의 경비병이 내 양쪽에서 지키는 채로,

each side of me, / half with torches, / and half with bows
반은 햇불을 들고,   반은 활과 화살을 들고,

and arrows, / ready to shoot me / if I should offer to stir.
쏠 준비를 하며,   만약 내가 움직이려고 한다면.

Key Expression ♥

while의 다양한 의미

접속사 while은 '~하는 동안, ~한 반면에, ~했지만'의 뜻으로, 명사 while은 '잠 깐, 잠시, 동안'이라는 의미로 다양하게 쓰입니다.

ex) While the operation was performing, I lay in a profound sleep. (~하는 동안)
그 작업이 수행되는 동안, 나는 깊은 잠에 빠져 있었다.

…who durst venture to mount and walk upon my body, while one of my hands was at liberty, without trembling… (~했지만)
내 한 손은 자유로웠지만, 그들은 두려워하지도 않고 내 몸 위를 걸어다니는 모험을 감행했다.

I lay all this while. (동안)   나는 이 모든 동안 누워 있었다.

I awaked by a very ridiculous accident; for the carriage being stopped a while… (잠시)
나는 아주 어이없는 사고로 잠이 깼다; 왜냐하면 수레가 잠시 멈춰 선 동안…

packthread 포장끈 | bandage 붕대 | pulley 도르래 | soporiferous 최면의 | ridiculous 어이없는 | tickle
간지럽히다 | sneeze 재채기 | torch 햇불

The next morning at sunrise / we continued our march, /
다음 날 아침 해가 뜨자   우리는 행진을 계속해서,

and arrived / within two hundred yards / of the city gates
도달했다   200야드 이내 지점까지   수도 정문의

/ about noon. The emperor, and all his court, / came out
정오 경에.   황제와 모든 궁정 신하들이,   우리를 맞으러 나왔다;

to meet us; / but his great officers / would by no means
하지만 그의 근위대장은   황제를 절대 만류했다

suffer his majesty / to endanger his person / by mounting
신변이 위험할까봐 걱정하여

on my body.
내 몸 위로 올라오는 것을.

* 고어에서 80을 뜻하는 말

esteem 여겨지다 | pollute 더럽혀지다 | ornament 장식 | edifice 건물 | smith 대장장이 | padlock 자물쇠

At the place where the carriage stopped / there stood an
수레가 멈춘 곳에는   오래된 신전이 있었다.

ancient temple, / esteemed to be the largest / in the whole
                 제일 큰 것으로 여겨지는   왕국에서;

kingdom; / which, having been polluted / some years before
         그곳은 더럽혀졌다   수 년 전에

/ by an unnatural murder, / was, according to the zeal of
한 불미스러운 살인 사건으로 인해,   신앙심 깊은 사람들에 의해,

those people, / looked upon as profane, / and therefore / had
               신성 모독으로 간주된,   따라서

been applied to common use, / and all the ornaments and
일상적인 용도로 변경되어,   모든 장식과 가구는

furniture / carried away. In this edifice / it was determined
           치워진 상태였다.   이 건물에   내가 살도록 정해진 것이었다.

I should lodge. The great gate fronting to the north / was
                북쪽을 향한 대문은

about four feet high, / and almost two feet wide, / through
높이가 4피트이고,   폭은 거의 2피트였다,   그것을 통해

which / I could easily creep. On each side of the gate / was
        나는 쉽게 기어 들어갈 수 있었다. 이 대문의 양쪽에는

a small window, / not above six inches from the ground: /
작은 창이 있었다,   지면에서 6인치가 안 되는 높이에:

into that on the left side, / the king's smith conveyed / four-
왼쪽 창 안에는,   황제의 대장장이들이 들여놓았다

score* and eleven chains, / like those that hang / to a lady's
91개의 체인을,   매달려 있는 것과 같은

watch in Europe, and almost as large, / which were locked
유럽에서의 여성용 시계줄에,   그리고 그것을 내 왼발에 고정시켰다.

to my left leg / with six-and-thirty padlocks. Over against
            36개의 자물쇠로.   이 신전의 맞은편에는,

this temple, / on the other side of the great highway, / at
             큰 길 건너편에 있는,

twenty feet distance, / there was a turret / at least five feet
20피트 되는 거리에,   탑이 있었다   적어도 5피트 높이의.

33

high. Here the emperor ascended, / with many principal
여기에 황제는 올라와서,   궁정의 주요 고관들과,

lords of his court, / to have an opportunity of viewing
                                     내 모습을 보았다,

me, / as I was told, / for I could not see them. It was
      후에 들은 바에 의하면,   나는 그들을 볼 수 없었으니까.

reckoned / that above a hundred thousand inhabitants
추정되었다   10만 명 이상의 주민들이 온 것으로

came / out of the town / upon the same errand; / and, in
             마을 밖에서   같은 목적으로;

spite of my guards, / I believe / there could not be fewer
그리고, 경비병에도 불구하고,   내가 알기로   1만 명이나 되는 주민들이

than ten thousand / at several times, / who mounted my
                              수 차례,   내 몸에 올라왔다

body / by the help of ladders. But a proclamation was
         사다리를 사용해.   그러나 곧 선언이 선포되었다,

soon issued, / to forbid it / upon pain of death. When
                    그런 일을 금지하고 위반 시 사형에 처한다는.

the workmen found / it was impossible / for me to
일꾼들은 알게 되자   불가능하다는 것을   내가 도망치는 것이,

break loose, / they cut all the strings / that bound me; /
                  모든 줄을 끊었다   나를 묶었던;

whereupon I rose up, / with as melancholy a disposition
그리하여 나는 일어섰다,   가장 우울한 기분으로

/ as ever I had in my life. But the noise and astonishment
      내 평생에 가장.   그러나 사람들이 놀라는 소리는,

of the people, / at seeing me rise and walk, / are not to be
내가 서서 걷는 것을 보면서,   표현할 수 없을 정도

expressed. The chains that held my left leg / were about
였다.   내 왼발을 묶고 있던 쇠사슬은

two yards long, / and gave me not only the liberty / of
길이가 약 2야드였고,   내게 자유를 주었을 뿐만 아니라

walking backwards and forwards / in a semicircle, / but,
앞뒤로 걸을 수 있도록   반원을 그리며,   그렇지만,

/ being fixed within four inches of the gate, / allowed me
대문 안쪽의 4인치 되는 곳에 매어져 있어서,   내가 기어 들어가서,

to creep in, / and lie at my full length / in the temple.
           몸을 쭉 뻗고 누울 수 있게 해 주었다   신전 안에서 .

Key Expression ♥

분사구문의 해석

분사구문은 부사절을 분사(현재분사, 과거분사)를 사용해 부사구로 간결하게 줄인 구문을 말합니다. 대개 접속사와 주어가 생략되며 주어가 주절의 주어와 다르거나 접속사를 강조할 필요가 있을 때에는 살려두는 경우도 있습니다.
이 글에도 분사구문이 자주 등장하는데요. 분사구문을 해석할 때에는 생략된 접속사를 추측하여 해석하는 능력이 필요합니다. 분사구문의 다양한 의미를 살펴볼까요.

▶ ~하면서(while) → 가장 많이 등장하는 분사구문의 형태입니다.

ex) I continued three years and a half, / making a voyage or two into the Levant, and some other parts.
나는 3년 반 동안 계속했다. / 동부 지중해 연안으로 한 두 번, 그리고 다른 곳으로 항해하면서.

▶ ~할 때(when, as)

ex) My father now and then sending me small sums of money, / I laid them out in learning navigation
아버지가 가끔씩 적은 돈을 보낼 때면, / 나는 그것을 항해술을 배우는 데 썼다.

▶ ~한 후에(after)

ex) Having therefore consulted with my wife, and some of my acquaintance, / I determined to go again to sea.
그래서 아내나 몇몇 아는 사람들과 상담한 후에, / 나는 다시 배를 타기로 결심했다.

▶ ~때문에(because, as)

ex) There I studied physic two years and seven months, / knowing it would be useful in long voyages.
그곳에서 나는 2년 7개월 동안 물리학을 공부했다. / 그것이 긴 항해에 유용할 것임을 알았기 때문에.

그 외에도 '~하면(if)', '~하고(and)' 등의 의미로도 사용됩니다.

ascend 오르다 | errand 목적 | proclamation 선언 | disposition 성향, 기분

mini test 1

A. 다음 문장을 해석해 보세요.

(1) But my good master Bates dying / in two years after, / and I having few friends, / my business began to fail; / for my conscience would not suffer me / to imitate the bad practice / of too many among my brethren.
→

(2) When I was ashore, / in observing the manners and dispositions of the people, / as well as learning their language; / wherein I had a great facility, / by the strength of my memory.
→

(3) These people are most excellent mathematicians, / and arrived to a great perfection / in mechanics.
→

(4) Two or three of the young natives had the curiosity / to see how I looked / when I was asleep.
→

B. 다음 주어진 문장이 되도록 빈칸에 써 넣으세요.

(1) 내가 14살 때 그는 나를 캠브리지 대학의 엠마뉴엘 컬리지에 보냈다, 그리고, 그곳에서 3년 동안 살면서, <u>학업에 전념했다</u>.

He sent me to Emanuel College in Cambridge at fourteen years old, where I resided three years, and

(2) 얼마 후에 <u>나는 살아있는 무언가가 왼쪽 다리 위에서 움직이고 있음을 느꼈다</u>.

In a little time

(3) 풀려나려고 버둥거린 후, 마침내, <u>다행스럽게도 줄을 끊을 수 있었다</u>.

At length, struggling to get loose,

(4) 나는 극도로 놀랐고, 크게 소리치자, 그들은 겁에 질려 달아났다.

I was _____, and roared so loud, that they all ran back in a fright.

C. 다음 주어진 문구가 알맞은 문장이 되도록 순서를 맞춰 보세요.

(1) 나는 제임스 베이츠 씨에게 견습생으로 보내졌고, 그의 밑에서 나는 4년 동안 계속 있었다.
(whom / continued / with / four years / I)
I was bound apprentice to Mr. James Bates, _____.

(2) 배에 있던 내 동료들이 어떻게 되었는지, 나는 알 수 없다.
(found / within / I / my depth / myself)
_____, I cannot tell.

(3) 거의 기운이 다했을 때, 나는 발이 닿는다는 것을 알게 됐다.
(could / have / not / The furniture / much / simpler / been)
But when I was almost gone, and able to struggle no longer, _____.

(4) 나는 하늘 밖에 볼 수 없었다.
(nothing / the sky / see / I / except / could)
→

D. 다음 단어에 대한 맞는 설명과 연결해 보세요.

(1) scanty ▶ ◀ ① become tired of something

(2) resolve ▶ ◀ ② enough to fulfil a need

(3) weary ▶ ◀ ③ less than you expected

(4) suffice ▶ ◀ ④ make a firm decision

잘했다; 그런 점에서 나는 뛰어난 기억력을 가지고 있었다. (3) 이 사람들은 수학에 뛰어났고, 기계공학에서 완벽한 경지에 도달해 있었다. (4) 두세 명의 젊은 원주민은 내가 잠들었을 때 어떤 모습인지 보고 싶은 호기심이 생겼다. | B. (1) applied myself close to my studies (2) I felt something alive moving on my left leg (3) I had the fortune to break the strings (4) in the utmost astonishment | C. (1) with whom I continued four years, (2) What became of my companions in the boat (3) I found myself within my depth (4) I could see nothing except the sky. | D. (1) ③ (2) ④ (3) ① (4) ②

2

The emperor of Lilliput, / attended by several of the
릴리펏의 황제가,　　　　　　　　　　귀족 몇 명의 시중을 받으며,

nobility, / comes to see the author / in his confinement.
　　　　　저자를 보러 온다　　　　　　　갇혀 있는.

The emperor's person and habit described. Learned men
황제의 용모와 의상이 묘사된다.　　　　　　　　　학자들이 임명된다

appointed / to teach the author their language. He gains
　　　　　저자에게 그들의 말을 가르치기 위해.　　　　그는 호감을 산다

favor / by his mild disposition. His pockets are searched, /
온화한 성품으로.　　　　　그의 호주머니는 수색 당하고,

and his sword and pistols taken from him.
칼과 권총은 압수당한다.

When I found myself on my feet, / I looked about me, /
내가 두 발로 서서,　　　　　　　　주위를 둘러 보았을 때,

and must confess / I never beheld / a more entertaining
고백하건대　　　　　　본 적이 없었다　　　이보다 더 아름다운 경치를.

prospect. The country around appeared / like a continued
　　　　　　나라 전체가 보였다　　　　　　계속 이어져 있는 정원처럼,

garden, / and the enclosed fields, / which were generally
　　　　그리고 울타리로 에워싸인 밭은,　　대개 40평방 피트(약 12미터)였는데,

forty feet square, / resembled so many beds of flowers.
　　　　　　　마치 수많은 화단과 같았다.

These fields were intermingled / with woods of half a
이 밭들에는 섞여 있었다　　　　　　반 스탱 넓이의 숲들이

stang* / and the tallest trees, / as I could judge, / appeared
　　　그리고 제일 큰 나무는,　　　내 짐작으로,　　높이가 7피트쯤

to be seven feet high. I viewed the town / on my left hand, /
되어 보였다.　　　　　　나는 도시를 보았고　　　왼편의,

which looked like the painted scene of a city / in a theatre.
그것은 마치 그려놓은 도시 같았다　　　　　극장 무대에서.

* 웨일스 지방에서 넓이를 재는 단위의 고어. 1 스탱은 약 0.2709 헥타르

confinement 갇힘 | intermingle 섞이다 | discharge 배설하다

I had been for some hours / extremely pressed / by the
나는 오랫동안   몹시 불편했다

necessities of nature; / which was no wonder, / it being
생리적인 욕구 때문에;   그도 그럴 것이,

almost two days / since I had last disburdened myself. I
거의 이틀이나 지났으니까   마지막으로 변을 본지.

was under great difficulties / between urgency and shame.
나는 큰 어려움에 빠져 버렸다   급하기도 하고 창피하기도 해서.

The best expedient / I could think of, / was to creep into
제일 좋은 방법은   내가 생각할 수 있는,   내 집으로 기어들어가는 것이었고,

my house, / which I accordingly did; / and shutting the gate
내 집으로   결국 그렇게 했다;   그리고 문을 닫은 후,

after me, / I went as far / as the length of my chain would
             최대한 멀리 가서   쇠사슬이 허용하는 한,

suffer, / and discharged my body / of that uneasy load. But
           몸으로부터 덜어냈다   그 불편한 짐을.

this was the only time / I was ever guilty of so uncleanly
그러나 이때가 유일했다   그토록 이렇게 지저분한 행동을 했던 것은;

an action; / for which I cannot but hope / the candid reader
             바라 마지 않는다

will give some allowance, / after he has maturely and
솔직한 독자 여러분이 참작해 주기를,   성숙하고 공정하게 고려한 후,

impartially considered / my case, / and the distress I was in.
                          내 경우와,   내가 처한 상황을.

Key Expression ✿

목적격 관계대명사의 생략

관계대명사가 이끄는 문장은 선행사인 명사를 수식하는 역할을 합니다. 관계대
명사는 두 문장에서의 역할에 따라 주격, 목적격, 소유격으로 나뉘는데 목적격 관
계대명사는 생략되는 경우가 많으므로 주의해야 합니다.
문장이 '명사 + 명사/대명사 + 동사…'의 형태로 이어지고 뒷 문장의 목적어가 없
을 경우 관계대명사가 생략된 것으로 해석하세요.

ex) The best expedient ★ I could think of, was to creep into my house.
                        └ 관계대명사 that/which 생략
  내가 생각할 수 있는 제일 좋은 방법은, 내 집으로 기어들어가는 것이었다.

From this time / my constant practice was, / as soon as
이 날 이후   내 일과는,   일어나자 마자,

I rose, / to perform that business / in open air, / at the
볼일을 보는 것이었다   밖에서,

full extent of my chain; / and due care was taken / every
쇠사슬이 허용하는 한 멀리서;   그리고 적절한 조치가 취해졌다

morning / before company came, / that the offensive
매일 아침   사람들이 오기 전에,   그 거슬리는 것을

matter / should be carried off / in wheel-barrows, / by two
실어가도록 하는   손수레에,   두 명의

servants / appointed for that purpose. I would not have
인부에 의해   그 일을 하도록 임명된.   나는 그토록 장황하게 설명하지

dwelt so long / upon a circumstance that, / perhaps, / at
않았을 것이다   상황에 대해,   아마도,

first sight, / may appear not very momentous, / if I had not
언뜻 봤을 때,   중요해 보이지 않을 수도 있는,   만약 생각하지

thought / it necessary / to justify my character, / in point
않았다면   필요하다고   내 성격을 증명하는 일이,

of cleanliness, / to the world; / which, I am told, / some
청결과 관련하여,   세상 사람들에게;   왜냐하면 들었기 때문에,

of my maligners have been pleased, / upon this and other
내게 악의를 가진 사람들이 하고 싶어 한다고,   이번 일과 다른 경우에 대해,

occasions, / to call in question.
               의문을 제기하는 것을.

When this adventure was at an end, / I came back out of
이 모험이 해결되자,   나는 다시 집 밖으로 나왔다

my house, / having occasion for fresh air. The emperor
               신선한 공기를 쐬려고.

was already descended / from the tower, / and advancing
황제는 이미 내려와 있었고   탑으로부터,

on horse-back / towards me, / which had like to have cost
말을 타고 오고 있었다   내가 있는 쪽으로,   하지만 이 말 때문에 그는 큰일날 뻔했다;

him dear; / for the beast, / although very well trained, / yet
왜냐하면 그 동물은,   잘 훈련되었지만,

wholly unused to such a sight, / which appeared / as if a
그런 광경에는 익숙하지 못해서,   ~처럼 보이는

mountain moved before him, / reared up on its hinder feet:
마치 산이 움직이는 듯이, 그래서 뒷발을 딛고 번쩍 솟구쳐 올라버렸다:

/ but that prince, / who is an excellent horseman, / kept
그러나 왕은, 훌륭한 승마가인, 안장에 계속

his seat, / till his attendants ran in, / and held the bridle, /
앉아 있었다. 그의 수행원들이 달려와서, 고삐를 잡을 때까지,

while his majesty had time to dismount.
그 동안 황제는 천천히 내릴 수 있었다.

When he alighted, / he surveyed me round / with great
그는 말에서 내리자, 내 주위를 살펴보았다 크게

admiration; / but kept beyond the length of my chain.
크게 감탄하면서: 그러나 내 쇠사슬의 길이 밖에 머물러 있었다.

He ordered his cooks and butlers, / who were already
그는 요리사와 집사에게 명령했다. 이미 대기하고 있던,

prepared, / to give me victuals and drink, / which they
나에게 먹을 것과 마실 것을 주도록,

pushed forward in / a sort of vehicles upon wheels, / till I
그리고 그들은 앞으로 밀었다 바퀴 달린 수레 같은 것을,

could reach them. I took these vehicles / and soon emptied
내가 잡을 수 있는 곳까지. 나는 그 수레들을 집어 들어 금방 다 비워버렸다:

them all; / twenty of them / were filled with meat, / and
그 중 20대는 고기로 채워져 있었고,

ten with liquor; / each of the former / afforded me / two
10대는 음료로 가득했다; 각각의 고기 수레는 내게 충분한 양이었다

or three good mouthfuls; / and I emptied the liquor of ten
두세 입에 먹기에; 그리고 10대의 음료 수레도 비워버렸다.

vessels, / which was contained in earthen vials, / into one
그것은 도자기 병에 담겨 있었는데, 한 수레에

vehicle, / drinking it off at a draught; / and so I did with
담아서, 한 모금에 마셨다; 그리고 나머지도 그렇게 마셨다.

the rest.

momentous 중요한 | descend 내려오다 | hinder feet 뒷발 | dismount 내리다 | butler 집사 | earthen 흙으로 구운 | vial 병

41

The empress, / and young princes of the blood of both
황후와, 어린 황태자 및 공주들은,

sexes, / attended by many ladies, / sate at some distance
많은 시녀들의 시중을 받으며, 약간 떨어진 곳에 앉아 있었다

/ in their chairs; / but upon the accident that happened /
의자에; 그러나 사고가 발생하자

to the emperor's horse, / they alighted, / and came near
황제의 말에, 그들은 내려와서, 황제 곁으로 다가왔다,

his person, / which I am now going to describe. He is
이제 황제에 대해 묘사하겠다. 그는 키가 컸다

taller / by almost the breadth of my nail, / than any of his
내 손톱 정도 만큼, 황실의 어느 누구보다도;

court; / which alone is enough / to strike an awe / into the
그래서 그것만으로도 충분했다 경외감을 일으키기에

beholders. His features are strong and masculine, / with an
보는 사람들에게. 그의 용모는 강하고 남성적이었으며,

Austrian lip and arched nose, / his complexion olive, / his
오스트리아 사람같은 입술과 매부리코에, 올리브색 안색과,

countenance erect, / his body and limbs well proportioned,
곧은 표정을 하고, 균형 잡힌 몸과 팔다리를 지니고 있었다,

/ all his motions graceful, / and his deportment majestic.
모든 거동은 우아했고, 태도는 위풍당당 했다.

He was then past his prime, / being twenty-eight years and
그는 당시 전성기였는데, 나이는 28세 하고도 9개월로,

three quarters old, / of which he had reigned about seven
통치한지 7년째였다

/ in great felicity, / and generally victorious. For the better
태평성대를 누리며, 대부분 승리하면서.

convenience of beholding him, / I lay on my side, / so that
그를 더 잘 관찰하기 위해서, 나는 옆으로 누웠다,

my face was parallel to his, / and he stood but three yards
그 결과 내 얼굴이 그와 나란해졌고, 그는 3야드 거리에 서 있었다:

off: / however, / I have had him since many times / in my
하지만, 그 후 여러 번 그를 올렸다 내 손 위에,

hand, / and therefore / cannot be deceived in the description.
그렇기 때문에 이 묘사는 틀림없다.

His dress was very plain and simple, / and the fashion of it
그의 복장은 매우 단순하고 소박했는데, 그 패션은

/ between the Asiatic and the European; / but he had on his
유럽과 아시아 풍의 중간쯤이었다; 그러나 머리에는 썼다

head / a light helmet of gold, / adorned with jewels, / and a
금으로 된 가벼운 투구를, 보석으로 장식되고,

plume on the crest. He held his sword drawn / in his hand
꼭대기에 깃털이 달린. 그는 칼을 빼서 손에 들고 있었다

/ to defend himself, / if I should happen to break loose; / it
자신을 방어하기 위해, 만약 내가 풀려날 경우;

was almost three inches long; / the hilt and scabbard were
그 칼은 길이가 거의 3인치였다; 칼자루와 칼집은 금이었다

gold / enriched with diamonds. His voice was shrill, / but
다이아몬드가 잔뜩 박힌. 그의 목소리는 날카로웠지만,

very clear and articulate; / and I could distinctly hear it /
매우 맑고 뚜렷했다; 그래서 분명히 들을 수 있었다

when I stood up. The ladies and courtiers / were all most
내가 서 있을 때도. 시녀와 신하들도

magnificently clad; / so that the spot they stood upon /
모두 화려한 옷을 입고 있었다; 그래서 그들이 서 있는 곳은

seemed to resemble a petticoat / spread upon the ground,
속치마처럼 보였다 땅 위에 펼쳐 놓은,

/ embroidered with figures of gold and silver. His imperial
금과 은으로 수 놓인.

majesty spoke often to me, / and I returned answers: / but
황제 폐하는 종종 내게 말을 걸었고, 나도 대답했다:

neither of us / could understand a syllable. There were
하지만 둘 다 한 마디도 알아 듣지 못했다.

several of his priests and lawyers present / (as I conjectured
그 자리에 여러 명의 성직자와 법률가들이 있었는데 (그 복장으로 짐작하건대),

by their habits), / who were commanded / to address
그들은 지시를 받았다 내게 말을 걸어 보라는:

themselves to me; / and I spoke to them /
그래서 나는 그들에게 말했다

---

awe 경외감 | complexion 안색 | deportment 거동 | victorious 승리한 | distinctly 분명히 | embroider 수
놓다

in as many languages / as I had the least smattering of,
수 많은 언어들로 / 내가 조금이라도 알고 있는,

/ which were **High and Low Dutch***, / Latin, / French, /
고지 네덜란드어, 저지 네덜란드어, / 라틴어, / 프랑스어,

Spanish, / Italian, / and **Lingua Franca****, / but all to no
스페인어, / 이탈리아어, / 그리고 링구아 프랑카(공통어) 등,

purpose.
그러나 모두 소용없었다.

After about two hours / the court retired, / and I was left
약 두 시간 후 / 궁정인들이 물러갔고, / 나는 남겨졌다

/ with a strong guard, / to prevent the impertinence, /
강력한 경비대와 함께, / 무례한 짓을 막기 위해서,

and probably the malice of the rabble, / who were very
또한 있을 수도 있는 군중들의 악의를, / 그들은 내게 안달이 나서

impatient to crowd about me / as near as they durst; / and
가능한 한 가까이 다가오려 했고;

some of them had the impudence to / shoot their arrows
그 중 몇 명은 무례하게도 / 나에게 화살을 쐈다.

at me, / as I sat on the ground / by the door of my house,
내가 땅바닥에 앉아 있을 때 / 집 문 앞,

/ whereof one very narrowly missed / my left eye. But the
그 화살 중 한 개가 가까스로 비껴갔다 / 내 왼쪽 눈을.

colonel ordered / six of the ringleaders to be seized, / and
그러나 대령은 명령했다 / 주모자 6명을 체포하도록,

thought no punishment so proper / as to deliver them bound
더 적당한 처벌은 없다고 생각하며 / 그들을 묶어서 데려다 놓는 것만큼

/ into my hands; / which some of his soldiers / accordingly
내 손 안에; / 그래서 그의 부하 중 몇 명이 / 명령에 따라서,

did, / pushing them forward / with the butt-ends of their
그들을 밀어 놓았다 / 창의 반대편 끝으로

pikes / into my reach. I took them all / in my right hand, /
내 손이 닿는 위치에. / 나는 그들 모두를 붙잡아서 / 오른손으로,

put five of them into my coat-pocket; / and as to the sixth,
5명은 코트 호주머니에 넣었다; / 그리고 여섯 번째 사람에게는,

malice 악의 | rabble 무리 | narrowly 가까스로 | clemency 너그러움 | fortnight 2주

/ I made a countenance / as if I would eat him alive. The
표정을 지었다   마치 그를 산 채로 잡아 먹으려는 듯한.

poor man squalled terribly, / and the colonel and his
그 불쌍한 녀석은 죽을 듯이 비명을 질렀고,   대령과 그의 부하들도

officers / were in much pain, / especially / when they saw
매우 괴로워했다,   특히   그들이 보았을 때

me / take out my penknife: / but I soon put them out of
주머니 칼을 꺼내는 것을: 그러나 나는 곧 그들을 안심시켰다:

fear; / for, / looking mildly, / and immediately cutting
왜냐하면, 온화한 표정을 지으며,   곧 줄을 잘랐기 때문에

the strings / he was bound with, / I set him gently on the
그가 묶여 있던,   내가 그를 살며시 땅에 내려놓자,

ground, / and away he ran. I treated the rest / in the same
그는 도망쳐 버렸다.   나머지들도 다뤘다   같은 방식으로,

manner, / taking them one by one / out of my pocket; /
그들을 한 명씩   호주머니에서 꺼내면서:

and I observed / both the soldiers and people were highly
그리고 나는 보았다   군인들과 일반 군중 모두 매우 기뻐하는 것을

delighted / at this mark of my clemency, / which was
내 너그러운 행동에,   그리고 이 일은 보고됐다

represented / very much to my advantage / at court.
내게 매우 유리하게   왕실에.

Towards night / I got with some difficulty / into my house,
밤이 되자   나는 약간 어려움을 느끼며   집에 들어가,

/ where I lay on the ground, / and continued to do so /
그곳에서 바닥에 누웠다.   그리고 그런 식으로 계속 지냈다

about a fortnight; / during which time, / the emperor gave
약 2주 동안: 그리고 그 동안,   황제는 명령했다

orders / to have a bed prepared for me. Six hundred beds
나를 위한 침대를 준비하도록.

of the common measure / were brought in carriages, / and
일반 크기 매트리스 600개가   수레에 실렸고,

---

* High Dutch=High German, (현재 독일의 표준어) / Low Dutch=Low German, (북부 독일에서 쓰는 방언)

** 링구아 프랑카 : 공통어 혹은 국제어. 특정 언어가 아닌 모국어가 서로 다른 사람들끼리 소통하기 위해 쓰는 제3의 언어를 뜻하는 말.

worked up / in my house; / a hundred and fifty of their
작업이 진행됐다   내 집 안에서;   150개의 매트리스를,

beds, / sewn together, / made up the breadth and length;
같이 꿰매어,   폭과 길이를 맞췄고;

/ and these were four double: / which, / however, / kept
이것들을 4겹으로 겹쳤다: 그것은,   그러나,

me but very indifferently / from the hardness of the floor,
내게는 여전히 별 차이가 없었다   맨바닥의 딱딱함과,

/ that was of smooth stone. By the same computation, /
바닥 자체가 부드러운 돌이었기 때문에.   같은 계산법으로,

they provided me / with sheets, blankets, and coverlets, /
그들은 내게 갖다 주었다   시트, 담요, 이불을,

tolerable enough / for one / who had been so long inured /
충분히 참을 만한   사람에게는   오랫동안 단련된

to hardships.
고생에.

As the news of my arrival spread / through the kingdom,
내가 도착한 소식이 퍼지자   왕국 전체에,

/ it brought prodigious numbers of rich, / idle, and
수많은 부자들과,   할 일 없고,

curious people / to see me; / so that the villages were
호기심 많은 사람들이   나를 보러 왔다;   그래서 마을들은 거의 텅 비어서;

almost emptied; / and great neglect of tillage and
농사와 집안일을 전혀 돌보지 않는 상황이

household affairs / must have ensued, / if his imperial
일어날 뻔 했다,

majesty had not provided, / by several proclamations and
황제 폐하가 발표하지 않았다면,   여러 가지 칙령과 명령을,

orders of state, / against this inconveniency. He directed
이런 불편한 사태에 대비해.   왕은 지시했다

/ that those who had already beheld me / should return
이미 나를 구경한 사람들은   집에 돌아가야 한다는 것과,

home, / and not presume to come / within fifty yards of
들어가지 말 것을   내 집으로부터 50야드 내에는,

inure 단련하다 | prodigious 엄청난 | proclamations 선언 | dispatch 죽이다

my house, / without license from the court; / whereby / the
궁정의 허가 없이는;   그리고 이런 식으로

secretaries of state got considerable fees.
대신들은 상당한 입장료를 벌어들였다.

In the mean time / the emperor held frequent councils, /
그러는 동안   황제는 자주 회의를 열었다.

to debate / what course should be taken with me; / and I
토의하기 위해   나를 어떻게 처리할 것인지에 대해;

was afterwards assured / by a particular friend, / a person
그리고 나중에 알게 된 바로는   각별한 친구에게,

of great quality, / who was as much in the secret as any,
높은 지위에 있던,   어떤 비밀이라도 알고 있던,

/ that the court was under many difficulties / concerning
궁정은 많은 곤란을 겪고 있었다   나 때문에.

me. They apprehended my breaking loose; / that my diet
그들은 내가 풀려날까 걱정했고;   내 식사에는

/ would be very expensive, / and might cause a famine.
비용이 매우 많이 들었으며,   그 때문에 기근을 야기할 수도 있었다.

Sometimes / they determined / to starve me; / or at least /
때로는   그들은 결정했다   나를 굶겨 죽이기로;   아니면 적어도

to shoot me in the face and hands / with poisoned arrows, /
내 얼굴과 손에 쏘아서   독화살을,

which would soon dispatch me; / but again they considered,
나를 곧 죽게 하기로;   그러나 다시 그들은 생각했다.

Key Expression

enough to : ∼하기에 충분한

enough to는 to 부정사를 사용한 관용 표현 중 하나로 '∼하기에 충분한'이라는
의미로 쓰입니다. enough to의 사용법은 아래와 같으며 여기서 to 부정사는
앞의 형용사[부사]를 수식하는 부사적 용법으로 파악할 수 있습니다.

▶ 형용사[부사] + (의미상 주어 for/of + 목적격) + enough + to 동사원형
   = so + 형용사[부사] + that + 주어 + can (∼할 만큼 충분히 …하다)

ex) They provided me with sheets, blankets, and coverlets, tolerable enough for
   one who had been so long inured to hardships.
   그들은 내게 시트와 담요, 이불을 가져다 주었고 오랫동안 고생에 단련된 사람에
   게는 충분히 참을 만 했다.

47

/ that the stench of so large a carcass / might produce a
그렇게 큰 송장의 썩는 악취가   전염병을 야기하여,

plague / in the metropolis, / and probably spread / through
        수도에   퍼질 수도 있다고

the whole kingdom.
왕국 전체에.

In the midst of these consultations, / several officers of
이런 회의를 하는 중에,   여러 명의 육군 장교들이 왔고

the army went / to the door of the great council-chamber,
            대회의장의 문 앞에,

/ and two of them being admitted, / gave an account of
그 중 두 명이 허가를 받아서,   설명했다

/ my behavior / to the six criminals above-mentioned; /
   내 행동을   앞서 말한 6명의 죄인에 대한;

which made so favorable an impression / in the breast
그리고 그것이 매우 좋은 인상을 심어 주었다

of his majesty and the whole board, / in my behalf, /
황제와 모든 대신들의 마음에,   나를 대신하여,

that an imperial commission was issued out, / obliging
황제의 칙령이 발표되었다.   모든 마을에

all the villages, / nine hundred yards round the city, /
의무를 부과하는,   도시 주변의 900야드 내에 위치한,

to deliver / in every morning / six beeves, forty sheep,
배달하도록 하는 매일 아침에   소 6마리, 양 40마리, 그리고 기타 식품을

and other victuals / for my sustenance; / together with a
                    내 식량으로;

proportionable quantity / of bread, and wine, and other
상응하는 분량의   빵과, 포도주와, 기타 음료와 함께;

liquors; / for the due payment of which, / his majesty gave
         이에 대한 비용은,   황제가 지불하도록 했다

assignments / upon his treasury: / — for this prince lives
              그의 금고에서: — 왕은 주로 살았기 때문에

chiefly / upon his own demesnes; / seldom, / except upon
         그 자신의 영지를 근거로;   거의 없었다, 급한 경우를 제외하면,

carcass 시체 | consultations 의논, 상의 | an account of 설명하다 | commission 위원회 | beef 소 |
sustenance 생계, 양식 | proportionable 비례하는, 상응하는 | treasury 금고 | subsidy 보조금

great occasions, / raising any subsidies upon his subjects,
신하에게 세금을 징수하는 경우가,

/ who are bound to attend him in his wars / at their own
신하들은 전쟁에 참석해야 했다   자신들의 비용으로.

expense.

An establishment was also made / of six hundred persons
기구가 설치되었다   600명으로 구성된

/ to be my domestics, / who had board-wages allowed /
나를 시중하기 위해,   그들에게는 수당이 주어지고

for their maintenance, / and tents built for them / very
생계를 위한,   그들을 위한 천막이 지어졌다

conveniently / on each side of my door. It was likewise
매우 편리하게   내 집 문 양쪽에.   또한 명령이 내려졌다.

ordered, / that three hundred tailors should make / me a
                300명의 재봉사가 만들어 주도록

suit of clothes, / after the fashion of the country; / that six
내게 양복 한 벌을,   그 나라 양식에 따라;

of his majesty's greatest scholars / should be employed
그리고 황제의 가장 훌륭한 학자 중 6명은   임명받았다

/ to instruct me in their language; / and lastly, / that the
내게 그들의 언어를 가르치도록;   그리고 마지막으로,

emperor's horses, / and those of the nobility and troops of
황제의 말과,   귀족과 군대의 말들을

guards, / should be frequently exercised / in my sight, / to
자주 훈련시키도록 했다   내 눈 앞에서,

accustom themselves to me.
내게 익숙해지도록.

All these orders / were duly put in execution; / and in
이 모든 명령들은   제대로 시행되었다;

about three weeks / I made a great progress / in learning
약 3주 후에   나는 큰 진척을 보였다

their language; / during which time / the emperor
그 나라 언어를 배우는데;   그 기간 동안

frequently honored me with his visits, / and was pleased
황제는 황송하게도 자주 방문했고,   기꺼이 도왔다

to assist / my masters in teaching me. We began already
내 교사들이 나를 가르치는 것을.   우리는 벌써 대화를 나누게 되었다

to converse together / in some sort; / and the first words I
어느 정도;   내가 제일 처음 배운 말은,

learnt, / were to express my desire / "that he would please
내 희망을 표현하는 것이었다   "나를 자유롭게 해 주십사 하는":

give me my liberty;" / which I every day repeated / on
나는 그것을 매일 되풀이 했다

my knees. His answer, / as I could comprehend it, / was,
무릎을 꿇고.   그의 대답은,   내가 이해한 바로는,

"that this must be a work of time, / not to be thought on /
"그것은 시간이 걸리는 일이고,   생각할 수 없는 것이며

without the advice of his council, / and that first / I must
궁정 회의의 권고 없이는,   그리고 그보다 먼저

LUMOS KELMIN PESSO DESMAR LON EMPOSO;"
내가 '루모스 켈민 페소 데스마르 론 엠포소해야 한다"는 것이었다;

/ that is, / swear a peace / with him and his kingdom.
즉,   평화를 맹세하는 것이었다 황제와 그의 왕국에 대해.

However, / that I should be used / with all kindness; / and
그러나,   나는 받게 될 것이고   친절한 환대를;

he advised me / to "acquire, / by my patience and discreet
왕은 내게 충고했다   "환대를 받으려면,   인내심과 신중한 행동을 보여서,

behavior, / the good opinion of himself and his subjects."
자신과 신하들의 환심을 얻으라고."

accustom 익숙하게 하다

He desired / "I would not take it ill, / if he gave orders
그는 바랐다　　"내가 기분 나쁘게 생각하지 않기를,　　그가 관리에게 명령하더라도

to certain proper officers / to search me; / for probably /
나를 수색하라고;　　왜냐하면 혹시나

I might carry about me / several weapons, / which must
내가 소지하고 있을지 모르기 때문에　　몇 가지 무기를,

needs be dangerous things, / if they answered / the bulk of
그러면 그것은 위험한 물건임에 틀림없으므로, 만약 그것들이 비례한다면

so prodigious a person." / I said, / "His majesty should be
엄청난 몸 크기에."　　나는 말했다, "황제는 만족하실 거라고;

satisfied; / for I was ready / to strip myself, / and turn up
나는 준비됐으니까　　옷을 벗고,　　내 호주머니를 뒤집을

my pockets / before him." / This I delivered / part in words,
내 호주머니를　　그의 앞에서."　　나는 이 뜻을 전했다　　반은 말로,

/ and part in signs. He replied, / "that, by the laws of the
그리고 반은 손짓으로.　　그는 대답했다,　　"왕국의 국법에 의해서,

kingdom, / I must be searched / by two of his officers; /
나는 수색을 받아야 한다고　　두 명의 관리들에 의해;

that he knew / this could not be done / without my consent
하지만 자신도 알고 있다고　　이는 실행될 수 없을 것임을　　내 승낙과 도움 없이는;

and assistance; / and he had so good an opinion / of my
내 승낙과 도움 없이는;　　그리고 그는 높이 평가하고 있으며

generosity and justice, / as to trust their persons / in my
내 너그러움과 정의감에 대해,　　자신의 신하들을 맡기는 것에 대해

hands; / that whatever they took from me, / should be
내 손에;　　그리고 그들이 내게서 압수한 것은 무엇이든,　　되돌려 받을 것이라고

returned / when I left the country, / or paid for at the rate /
이 나라를 떠나게 될 때,　　혹은 값을 지불할 것이라고

which I would set upon them."
내가 구입한."

I took up the two officers / in my hands, / put them first /
나는 두 명의 검사관을 들어 올려　　내 손으로,　　먼저 그들을 집어 넣었다

into my coat-pockets, / and then into every other pocket
내 외투 호주머니에,　　다음으로 다른 모든 호주머니에,

---

prodigious 엄청난 | generosity 너그러움 | inventory 목록

about me, / except my two fobs, / and another secret
두 개의 시계 주머니를 제외하고,   또 하나의 비밀 호주머니와,

pocket, / which I had no mind should be searched, /
수색 당하고 싶지 않았던,

wherein I had some little necessaries / that were of no
그 안에는 몇 가지 물건들이 있었기 때문에   중요하지 않은

consequence / to any but myself. In one of my fobs / there
나 이외에는 누구에게도.   시계 주머니 중 하나에는

was a silver watch, / and in the other / a small quantity
은시계가 있었다.   그리고 또 하나에는   약간의 금화가 든 지갑이 있었다.

of gold in a purse. These gentlemen, / having pen, ink,
이 신사들은,   펜과 잉크와 종이를 준비하여,

and paper, / about them, / made an exact inventory / of
물건들에 대해,   정확한 목록을 작성했다

everything they saw; / and when they had done, / desired
그들이 본 모든 것의: 그리고 일을 마친 후,

I would set them down, / that they might deliver it / to
그들을 내려 놓아주길 바랐다   그 목록을 전할 수 있도록

the emperor. This inventory / I afterwards translated into
황제에게.   이 목록을   나는 나중에 영어로 번역했는데,

English, / and is, / word for word, / as follows: /
그것은,   단어 그대로 말하자면,   다음과 같다: /

Key Expression ♥

of + 추상명사 = 형용사

'of + 추상명사'는 종종 형용사와 같은 역할을 합니다. 특히 문어체에서 이런 어구
를 많이 볼 수 있어요. 또한 of와 추상명사 사이에 no, much, little, great
등의 형용사를 넣어 '부사 + 형용사'의 뜻으로 사용할 수도 있습니다.

▶ of importance = important (중요한)
  of consequence = consequent (중요한)
  of use = useful (유용한)
  of interest = interesting (흥미로운)
  of value = valuable (가치 있는)

ex) ···wherein I had some little necessaries that were of no consequence to any
   but myself.
   그 안에는 나 외의 사람에게는 전혀 중요하지 않은 몇 가지 물품들이 들어 있었다.
   ···if they be real gold, must be of immense value.
   만약 그것이 진짜 금이라면 엄청나게 가치 있을 것이 분명하다.

53

"IMPRIMIS, / In the right coat-pocket / of the great man-
"우선, 외투 오른쪽 호주머니에는 거대한 인간 산의"

mountain" / (for so I interpret the words / QUINBUS
(나는 이렇게 번역했다 '퀸버스 프레스트린'이란

FLESTRIN,) / "after the strictest search, / we found /
단어를,) "샅샅이 조사한 결과, 우리는 발견했다

only one great piece of coarse-cloth, / large enough to be
큰 천조각 한 장 만을, 발 깔개로 쓰기에 충분한 크기의

a foot-cloth / for your majesty's chief room of state. In the
폐하의 의전실에.

left pocket / we saw a huge silver chest, / with a cover of
왼쪽 호주머니에서 우리는 거대한 은 상자를 보았다, 같은 금속으로 된 뚜껑이 달린,

the same metal, / which we, the searchers, / were not able
그것을 우리, 조사관들은, 들어올릴 수 없었다.

to lift. We desired it should be opened, / and one of us /
우리는 그것을 열어 달라고 했고, 우리 중 한 사람이

stepping into it, / found himself up to the mid leg / in a
그 속에 들어가 보니, 무릎까지 빠졌다 일종의

sort of dust, / some part whereof flying up to our faces /
먼지 속에, 그것의 일부가 우리 얼굴에 날아와서

set us both a sneezing / for several times together. In his
모두 재채기가 났다 얼마 동안.

right waistcoat-pocket / we found a prodigious bundle of
그의 오른쪽 조끼 주머니에서 우리는 엄청난 꾸러미를 발견했다

/ white thin substances, / folded one over another, / about
하얗고 얇은 물체의, 여러 겹으로 접혀 있었고,

the bigness of three men, / tied with a strong cable, / and
세 명을 모아놓은 크기 만한, 튼튼한 끈으로 묶여 있고,

marked with black figures; / which we humbly conceive / to
검은 무늬가 그려져 있었는데; 그것을 주제넘게 추측하자면

be writings, / every letter / almost half as large as the palm
글자인 것 같았다, 글자 하나하나는 거의 우리 손바닥의 절반 만했다.

of our hands. In the left / there was a sort of engine, / from
왼쪽 주머니에는 일종의 기구가 있었는데,

coarse-cloth 거친 천 | a bundle of 한 뭉치, 덩어리 | humbly 겸손하여, 부족하지만

the back of which / were extended / twenty long poles, /
그 뒤쪽으로부터   뻗어 나와 있었다   20개의 긴 막대기가,

resembling the Pallisado's / before your majesty's court: /
마치 철책 울타리를 닮은   폐하의 궁정 앞에 있는:

wherewith we conjecture / the man-mountain combs his
우리는 그것을 추측한다   인간산이 머리를 빗는데 쓰는 물건으로:

head; / for we did not always trouble him / with questions,
우리가 항상 그에게 부담을 주진 않았다   질문으로,

/ because we found it a great difficulty / to make him
왜냐하면 매우 어렵다는 것을 알았기에   우리 말을 그에게 이해시키는

understand us. In the large pocket, / on the right side of his
것이.   큰 주머니에는,   그의 가운데 덮개 오른쪽에 있는,

middle cover, / (so I translate the word RANFULO, / by
('란푸로'란 단어를 그렇게 번역한다.

which they meant my breeches,) / we saw a hollow pillar
그들이 내 바지를 칭하는 말이라고,)   우리는 속이 빈 철 기둥을 보았다,

of iron, / about the length of a man, / fastened to a strong
사람 키 만한,   단단한 나무조각에 고정되어 있는 /

piece of timber / larger than the pillar; / and upon one side
그 기둥보다 큰: 그리고 기둥의 한 쪽에는,

of the pillar, / were huge pieces of iron sticking out, / cut
커다란 쇳조각들이 튀어나와,

into strange figures, / which we know not what to make
이상한 모양으로 꽂혀 있었다.   무엇으로 만들어진 건지 알 수 없는.

of. In the left pocket, / another engine / of the same kind.
왼쪽 주머니에는,   또 다른 도구가 있었다   같은 종류의.

In the smaller pocket / on the right side, / were several
작은 주머니에는   오른쪽의,   여러 개의 둥글고 납작한 조

round flat pieces / of white and red metal, / of different
각들이 있었다   흰 금속과 붉은 금속의,   크기가 다른:

bulk; / some of the white, / which seemed to be silver, /
흰 금속 중 일부는,   은처럼 보였는데,

were so large and heavy, / that my comrade and I / could
너무 크고 무거워서,   동료와 나는

hardly lift them. In the left pocket / were two black pillars
거의 들 수 없었다.   왼쪽 주머니에는   두 개의 검은 기둥이 있었다

/ irregularly shaped: / we could not, / without difficulty, /
불규칙한 모양의: 우리는 할 수 없었다,   어려움 없이,

reach the top of them, / as we stood / at the bottom of his
꼭대기에 닿는 것이,   서 있을 때   그의 주머니의 밑바닥에.

pocket. One of them was covered, / and seemed all of a
그 중 하나에는 덮개가 덮여 있었고,   모든 것이 한 조각으로 보였다:

piece: / but at the upper end of the other / there appeared
그러나 다른 쪽 끝에는

a white round substance, / about twice the bigness of our
희고 둥근 물체가 보였다,   우리 머리의 두 배쯤 되는 크기의.

heads. Within each of these was enclosed / a prodigious
각 조각의 안에는 들어있었다   엄청난 강철판이:

plate of steel; / which, / by our orders, / we obliged him
그것을,   우리의 요구로,   보여 달라고 명령했다.

to show us, / because we apprehended / they might be
왜냐하면 알았기 때문에   그것들이 위험한 기구가

dangerous engines. He took them / out of their cases, / and
될 수도 있음을.   그는 그것들을 꺼내어   통으로부터,

told us, / that in his own country / his practice was / to
우리에게 설명했다, 그의 나라에서   관행이라고

shave his beard with one of these, / and cut his meat with
그 중 하나로 수염을 깎고,   다른 하나로는 고기를 자르는 것이.

the other. There were two pockets / which we could not
주머니 두 개가 있었다   우리가 들어갈 수 없었던:

enter: / these he called his fobs; / they were two large slits
이것들을 그는 시계 주머니라고 불렀는데: 두 개의 큰 구멍이었다

/ cut into the top of his middle cover, / but squeezed close
가운데 덮개의 위로 길게 벤 것 같은,   하지만 딱 붙어 있는 상태였다

/ by the pressure of his belly. Out of the right fob / hung a
그의 배 압력으로 인해.   오른쪽 시계 주머니 밖으로는   거대한

great silver chain, / with a wonderful kind of engine / at
은 사슬이 매달려 있었는데,   놀라운 도구가 달려 있었다

the bottom. We directed him to draw out / whatever was
아래쪽 끝에는.   우리는 그에게 꺼내라고 지시했다

at the end of that chain; / which appeared to be a globe, /
그 사슬 끝에 달린 모든 것을;   그것은 공처럼 보였는데,

half silver, / and half of some transparent metal; / for, on the
반은 은이고. 반은 일종의 투명한 금속이었다:

transparent side, / we saw certain strange figures / circularly
투명한 쪽에서, 우리는 어떤 이상한 글자를 보았다 원형으로 그려진,

drawn, / and though we could touch them, / till we found
그리고 그것을 만져보려 했지만,

our fingers stopped / by the lucid substance. He put this
손가락은 막혀 버렸다 그 투명한 물질에 의해.

engine into our ears, / which made an incessant noise, /
그는 그 기구를 우리 귀에 댔는데, 그것은 끊임없는 소리를 냈다.

like that of a water-mill: / and we conjecture / it is either
물레방아 소리같은: 그래서 우리는 추측한다

some unknown animal, / or the god / that he worships; / but
그것이 미지의 동물이거나, 신일 거라고 그가 숭배하는;

we are more inclined / to the latter opinion, / because he
그러나 우리는 의견이 기울었다 후자 쪽으로, 왜냐하면 그가 우리에게

assured us, / (if we understood him right, / for he expressed
확실히 말했기 때문에, (우리가 제대로 알아 들었는지 모르지만, 그의 표현은

himself / very imperfectly) / that he seldom did anything
매우 불완전해서) 그가 뭔가 행하는 일은 거의 없다고

/ without consulting it. He called it his oracle, / and said, /
그것의 도움을 받지 않고. 그는 그것을 신탁이라 불렀고, 말했다.

it pointed out the time / for every action of his life. From
그것이 시간을 가리킨다고 인생의 모든 행동에 대해. 왼쪽 시계

the left fob / he took out a net / almost large enough for a
주머니로부터 그는 그물 하나를 꺼냈다 어부에게 충분히 큰,

fisherman, / but contrived to open and shut / like a purse,
그러나 일부러 열고 닫았다 지갑처럼,

/ and served him for the same use: / we found therein /
같은 용도로 쓰이는 것이었다: 우리는 그 안에서 발견했다

several massy pieces of yellow metal, / which, if they be
몇 개의 거대한 노란 금속을, 그리고, 만약 그것이 진짜 금이라면,

real gold, / must be of immense value.
틀림없이 어마어마한 가치일 것이다

irregularly 불규칙하게 | enclose 동봉된, 들어 있는 | fob 작은 주머니 | squeeze 압박하다 | belly 배 |
transparent 투명한 | incessant 끊임없는 | conjecture 추측하다 | imperfectly 불완전한 | immense 엄청난

"Having thus, / in obedience to your majesty's commands,
"이렇게 하고서, 황제 폐하의 명령에 따라서,

/ diligently searched all his pockets, / we observed a girdle
철저히 그의 모든 주머니를 조사한 후, 우리는 허리띠를 관찰했다

/ about his waist / made of the hide of some prodigious
그의 허리에 매어진 어떤 거대한 동물의 가죽으로 만들어졌고,

animal, / from which, on the left side, / hung a sword / of
그 왼쪽 편에는, 칼이 매달려 있었다

the length of five men; / and on the right, / a bag or pouch
사람 다섯 명의 키 만한: 그리고 오른쪽에는, 자루나 주머니가 있었다

/ divided into two cells, / each cell capable of holding /
두 개의 방으로 나뉘어진, 각각의 방은 수용할 수 있었다.

three of your majesty's subjects. In one of these cells /
황제의 하인 세 명을 그 방 중 한 곳에는

were several globes, or balls, / of a most ponderous metal,
몇 개의 구형, 혹은 공 모양의 물건이 있었다, 아주 굉장한 금속으로 된,

/ about the bigness of our heads, / and requiring a strong
크기는 우리 머리 만 했으며, 들기 위해서는 강한 힘이 필요했다:

hand to lift them: / the other cell contained / a heap of
또 다른 방에는 들어 있었는데

certain black grains, / but of no great bulk or weight, / for
검은 곡식 알갱이 더미가, 크지도 무겁지도 않았다,

we could hold above fifty of them / in the palms of our
우리도 50개 이상을 들 수 있었으니까 손바닥 안에.'

hands."

"This is an exact inventory / of what we found / about
"이것이 정확한 목록이다 우리가 발견한 것들의

the body of the man-mountain, / who used us / with great
인간산의 몸 수색에서. 그는 우리를 대했다 매우 정중하게,

civility, / and due respect / to your majesty's commission.
그리고 존경을 표하면서 폐하의 명령에 대해.

Signed and sealed / on the fourth day of the eighty-ninth
서명하고 봉인함 89월 4일에

moon / of your majesty's auspicious reign.
황제 폐하의 상서로운 치세의.

CLEFRIN FRELOCK, / MARSI FRELOCK."
'클레프린 프레록', '마르시 프레록.'"

When this inventory was read / over to the emperor, / he
이 목록을 낭독되자 황제 앞에서,

directed me, / although in very gentle terms, / to deliver
황제는 내게 명령했다. 매우 온화한 어조였으나,

up the several particulars. He first called for my scimitar, /
그 물건들을 내놓으라고. 그는 제일 먼저 내 언월도(칼)를 요구했으며,

which I took out, / scabbard and all. In the mean time / he
나는 그것을 내놓았다. 칼집째로 모두. 그 동안에

ordered three thousand of his choicest troops / (who then
그는 3,000명의 최정예 기병대에게 명령했다

attended him) / to surround me / at a distance, / with their
(그때 그를 지키고 있던) 나를 포위하라고 조금 떨어진 곳에서,

bows and arrows / just ready to discharge; / but I did not
활과 화살을 들고 쏠 태세를 하고; 그러나 나는

observe it, / for mine eyes were wholly fixed / upon his
그것을 보지 못했다. 왜냐하면 내 시선은 오로지 고정되어 있었으므로 황제에게만.

majesty. He then / desired me to draw my scimitar, / which,
그는 그리고 나서 내 칼을 빼 보라고 했다. 그 칼은,

Key Expression

관계대명사 what의 용법

관계대명사 what은 선행사를 포함한 관계대명사로, 즉 'the thing
which[that]'의 뜻이며 '~한 것'이라고 해석합니다.
관계대명사 what이 이끄는 명사절은 문장에서 주어, 보어, 목적어로 사용됩
니다. what이 주어나 목적어가 부족한 불완전한 문장을 이끌 경우 관계대명사
what을 의심해 보세요.

ex) This is an exact inventory of what we found.
   이것은 우리가 발견한 것에 대한 정확한 목록이다.

in obedience to ~따라서, 복종하여 | diligently 부지런히, 열심히 | ponderous 무거운 | auspicious 상서로운 |
scimitar 언월도 | scabbard 칼집 | troop 군대

/ although it had got some rust / by the sea water, / was, in
약간 녹이 슬었지만   바닷물 때문에,   전체적으로는,

most parts, / exceeding bright. I did so, / and immediately
매우 반짝였다.   나는 그렇게 했고, 그러자 순간

/ all the troops gave a shout / between terror and surprise;
전 부대가 함성을 질렀다   공포와 경악 사이의:

/ for the sun shone clear, / and the reflection dazzled their
왜냐하면 햇빛이 찬란하여,   반사하는 빛이 눈을 부시게 했기 때문이었다.

eyes, / as I waved the scimitar to and fro / in my hand. His
눈을,   내가 칼을 이리 저리 흔들자   손에 들고.

majesty, / who is a most magnanimous prince, / was less
황제는,   매우 대담한 왕이어서,

daunted / than I could expect: / he ordered me / to return it
덜 무서워했다   내가 예상했던 것보다: 그는 내게 명령했다

into the scabbard, / and cast it on the ground / as gently as
그것을 칼집에 도로 넣고,   땅에 던지라고   가능한 한 살며시,

I could, / about six feet from the end of my chain. The next
나를 묶은 사슬 끝에서 약 6피트 되는 곳에.   그 다음에

thing / he demanded / was one of the hollow iron pillars; /
그가 요구한 것은   속이 빈 철 기둥 중 하나였다:

by which he meant my pocket pistols. I drew it out, / and
즉 내 소형 권총을 뜻하는 것이었다.   나는 그것을 꺼내서,

at his desire, / as well as I could, / expressed to him / the
그의 바람대로,   내가 할 수 있는 한,   그에게 설명했다

use of it; / and charging it only with powder, / which, / by
그 용도를;   그리고 화약을 장전했다.   화약은,

the closeness of my pouch, / happened to escape wetting
화약 쌈지가 꼭 닫혀 있어서,   바닷물에 젖는 것을 피할 수 있었다

in the sea / (an inconvenience / against which all prudent
(귀찮은 일이다   모든 신중한 선원들이

mariners / take special care to provide,) / I first cautioned
각별히 주의하여 예방해야 하는 사항이다.)   나는 먼저 황제에게 경고하고

the emperor / not to be afraid, / and then I let it off / in the
놀라지 말라고,   그것을 발사했다   공중에.

air. The astonishment here / was much greater / than at
이때 보인 놀라움은 / 훨씬 더 컸다

the sight of my scimitar. Hundreds fell down / as if they
언월도를 봤을 때보다. / 수백 명이 쓰러졌고 / 마치 맞아 죽은 것

had been struck dead; / and even the emperor, / although
처럼; / 그리고 황제조차도,

he stood his ground, / could not recover himself / for
땅에 서 있긴 했지만, / 정신을 차리지 못했다

some time. I delivered up both my pistols / in the same
한동안. / 나는 두 자루의 권총을 건넸다 / 같은 방식으로

manner / as I had done my scimitar, / and then / my
언월도를 건넸던 것과, / 그리고 나서 /

pouch of powder and bullets; / begging him / that the
화약 쌈지와 탄환도; / 그에게 당부하면서

former might / be kept from fire, / for it would kindle
앞의 것(화약 쌈지)은 / 불에 가까이 놓지 말라고, / 왜냐하면 그것은 인화되어,

/ with the smallest spark, / and blow up / his imperial
작은 불꽃에도 / 폭발하여 / 궁궐을 날려 버릴 수

palace / into the air. I likewise delivered up my watch,
있으므로 / 공중에. / 나는 마찬가지로 내 시계도 건넸다,

/ which the emperor was / very curious to see, / and
황제는 그것을 / 매우 보고 싶어 하며,

commanded / two of his tallest yeomen of the guards /
명령했다 / 가장 큰 근위병 두 명에게

to bear it / on a pole upon their shoulders, / as draymen
그것을 가져오라고 / 어깨에 맨 장대 위에 올려서,

in England do a barrel of ale. He was amazed / at the
마치 영국에서 짐꾼이 맥주통을 운반하듯. / 그는 놀라워 했다

continual noise it made, / and the motion of the minute-
시계가 내는 계속되는 소리와, / 그리고 분침의 움직임을,

hand, / which he could easily discern; / for their sight is
그는 쉽게 알아보았다;

much more acute than ours: / he asked the opinions / of
그들의 눈은 우리보다 훨씬 예민하기 때문에; / 그는 의견을 물었고

shone 빛나다(shine의 과거, 과거분사) | dazzle 눈이 부시게 하다 | continual 거듭되는, 끊임없는

his learned men about it, / which were various and remote,
학자들에게 그것에 관해,　　　　의견들은 다양하고 제각각이었다,

/ as the reader may well imagine / without my repeating;
독자 여러분도 짐작하겠지만　　　　내가 반복해서 말하지 않아도;

/ although indeed / I could not very perfectly understand
비록 정말로　　　　내가 그들을 완전히 이해한 것은 아니었지만,

them. I then gave up / my silver and copper money, / my
나는 다음으로 내놓았다　은화와 동전,

purse, / with nine large pieces of gold, / and some smaller
지갑을,　　9개의 큰 금화와,　　　　작은 금화들이 들어 있던:

ones; / my knife and razor, / my comb and silver snuff-box,
그리고 주머니 칼과 면도칼,　　빗과 은으로 만든 코담배 갑,

/ my handkerchief and journal-book. My scimitar, / pistols,
손수건과 수첩도.　　　　내 언월도와　　　　권총과

/ and pouch, / were conveyed / in carriages / to his majesty's
화약 쌈지는,　　운반되었다　　마차에 실어　　황제의 창고로:

stores; / but the rest of my goods / were returned me.
그러나 나머지 물건들은　　　　내게 돌려 주었다.

I had as I before observed, / one private pocket, / which
앞에서 말했듯이,　　　　비밀 호주머니 하나가 있었다.

escaped their search, / wherein there was a pair of
그들의 수색을 피한,　　그 속에는 안경이 있었다

spectacles / (which I sometimes use / for the weakness
(이따금 쓰는　　　　시력이 약해서)

of mine eyes,) / a pocket perspective, / and some other
또 소형 망원경과,　　　　기타 자질구레한 물건들이:

little conveniences; / which, being of no consequence /
그것들은 중요하지 않았으니

to the emperor, / I did not think myself bound in honor to
황제에게,　　　신의에 어긋나지 않는다고 생각했다.

discover, / and I apprehended / they might be lost or spoiled
그리고 알고 있었다　　그것들이 분실되거나 망가질 수도 있음을

/ if I ventured them out of my possession.
만약 굳이 그것들을 내놓는다면.

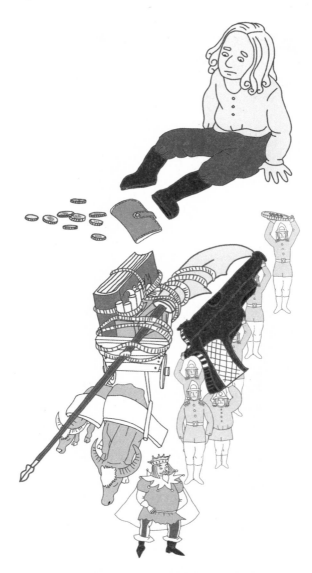

snuff-box 코담배 갑 | spectacles 안경 | perspective 망원경 | possession 소유물

mini test 2

A. 다음 문장을 해석해 보세요.

(1) I had been for some hours extremely pressed / by the necessities of nature; / which was no wonder, / it being almost two days / since I had last disburdened myself.
    →

(2) I made a countenance / as if I would eat him alive.
    →

(3) I treated the rest in the same manner, / taking them one by one / out of my pocket.
    →

(4) Whatever they took from me, / should be returned / when I left the country, / or paid for at the rate / which I would set upon them.
    →

B. 다음 주어진 문구가 알맞은 문장이 되도록 순서를 맞춰보세요.

(1) 내가 생각할 수 있는 제일 좋은 방법은 집으로 기어들어 가는 것이었다.
    (I / expedient / best / The / think of / could)
    ＿＿＿＿＿＿＿＿＿＿＿＿ of was to creep into my house.

(2) 나는 쇠사슬이 허용하는 한 가장 멀리까지 갔다.
    (as / the length / would / as / of / far / suffer / my chain)
    I went ＿＿＿＿＿＿＿＿＿＿＿＿ .

(3) 그는 황실의 어느 누구보다도 내 손톱 정도 만큼 키가 컸다.
    (my nail / of / the breadth / almost / by)
    He is taller ＿＿＿＿＿＿＿＿＿＿ , than any of his court.

A. (1) 나는 오랫동안 생리적인 욕구 때문에 몹시 불편했다; 그도 그럴 것이, 마지막으로 변을 본지 거의 이 틀이나 지났으니까. (2) 나는 마치 그를 산 채로 잡아 먹으려는 듯한 표정을 지었다. (3) 나는 그 나머지들 도 한 명씩 호주머니에서 꺼내면서 같은 방식으로 다뤘다. (4) 그들이 내게서 압수한 것은 무엇이든, 내가

64   Gulliver's Travels

(4) 그들 중 몇 명은 <u>무례하게도 나에게 화살을 쐈다.</u>
(me / the impudence / to / shoot / had / their arrows / at)
Some of them

C. 다음 주어진 문장이 본문의 내용과 맞으면 T, 틀리면 F에 동그라미 하세요.

(1) His majesty was so timid that he was afraid of Gulliver.
(T / F)

(2) The author was provided with a house and enough food.
(T / F)

(3) The author was searched by some officers from his majesty.
(T / F)

(4) The author could protect his pistol and sword.
(T / F)

D. 의미가 서로 비슷한 것끼리 연결해 보세요.

(1) intermingle   ▶   ◀ ① appearance

(2) clemency   ▶   ◀ ② guess

(3) complexion   ▶   ◀ ③ generosity

(4) conjecture   ▶   ◀ ④ mix

3

The author diverts the emperor, / and his nobility of both
저자가 황제를 즐겁게 해 준다.   그리고 남녀 귀족들을,

sexes, / in a very uncommon manner. The diversions of the
매우 기묘한 방법으로.   릴리펏의 궁중 오락이

court of Lilliput / described. The author has his liberty /
묘사된다.   저자가 자유를 갖게 된다

granted him / upon certain conditions.
그에게 허락된   일정한 조건들 하에서.

My gentleness and good behavior / had gained so far / on
나의 유순함과 착한 행동으로   지금까지 환심을 얻었다

the emperor and his court, / and indeed / upon the army
황제와 그의 신하들에게,   그리고 특히

and people in general, / that I began to conceive / hopes
군대와 일반 사람들에게.   그래서 나는 품게 되었다

of getting my liberty / in a short time. I took all possible
자유를 얻으리라는 희망을   곧.   나는 가능한 모든 방법을 썼다

methods / to cultivate this favorable disposition. The natives
이 호감을 증진시키기 위해.   주민들은,

came, / by degrees, / to be less apprehensive / of any danger
점점,   덜 느끼게 되었다   나에 대한 두려움을.

from me. I would sometimes lie down, / and let five or six
나는 때때로 드러누워서,   대여섯 명을 춤추게 했다

of them dance / on my hand; / and at last / the boys and girls
내 손 위에서;   그리고 마침내   소년 소녀들이

/ would venture to come / and play at hide-and-seek / in my
겁 없이 와서   숨바꼭질을 하곤 했다   내 머리

hair. I had now made a good progress / in understanding
속에서. 나는 이제 큰 진척을 보였다

and speaking the language. The emperor had a mind one
그들의 언어를 이해하고 말하는데.   황제는 어느 날 마음 먹었다

day / to entertain me / with several of the country shows,
나를 즐겁게 해 주겠다고   그 나라의 오락거리로,

/ wherein they exceed / all nations I have known, / both
그것들은 뛰어 넘는 수준이었다   내가 아는 모든 나라를,

for dexterity and magnificence. I was diverted / with none
재주나 화려함 두 가지 측면 모두.   나는 즐거워 했다

so much as / that of the rope-dancers, / performed upon
무엇보다도   줄타기 곡예사들의 춤에,   가느다란 흰 실 위에서 공연되는,

a slender white thread, / extended about two feet, / and
약 2피트 길이의,

twelve inches from the ground. Upon which / I shall desire
지상으로부터 12인치 높이에서.   이것에 관해   나는 하려 한다,

liberty, / with the reader's patience, / to enlarge a little.
독자 여러분이 양해한다면,   좀 더 자세한 묘사를.

This diversion is only practised / by those persons / who
이 곡예는 오직 공연된다   사람들에 의해서만

are candidates for great employments, / and high favor at
높은 고위 공직자 후보들이나,   궁정의 총애를 얻고자 하는.

court. They are trained / in this art / from their youth, /
그들은 훈련을 받았다   이 기술을   어릴 때부터,

and are not always of noble birth, / or liberal education.
그리고 반드시 귀족 출신이거나,   일반 교양 교육을 받은 사람은 아니었다.

When a great office is vacant, / either by death or disgrace
어떤 높은 관직이 공석일 때,   사망이나 수치스러운 일로 인해

/ (which often happens,) / five or six of those candidates
(이것은 자주 있다.)   대여섯 명의 지원자들이

/ petition the emperor / to entertain his majesty and the
황제에게 청원을 낸다   황제와 궁정에 즐거움을 주겠다고

court / with a dance on the rope; / and whoever jumps the
줄타기 춤으로;   그리고 제일 높이 뛰는 사람이,

highest, / without falling, / succeeds in the office. Very
떨어지지 않고,   그 자리를 계승한다.

often / the chief ministers themselves are commanded /
빈번하게   주요 대신들 자신이 명령 받기도 했다

divert 즐겁게 하다 | diversion 오락 | hide-and-seek 숨박꼭질 | dexterity 재주, 기술 | liberal education
일반 (교양) 교육 | petition 청원하다

to show their skill, / and to convince the emperor / that
재주를 보여 주고, 황제에게 확신시키라고

they have not lost their faculty. Flimnap, / the treasurer, /
그들이 재주를 잃지 않았음을. 플림냅은, 재무 대신인,

is allowed to cut a caper / on the straight rope, / at least an
인정받았다 가느다란 실에서 뛰는 것을.

inch higher / than any other lord / in the whole empire. I
1인치 이상 더 높게 어떤 귀족보다도 그 나라의

have seen him do the summerset / several times together, /
나는 그가 재주 넘는 것을 보았다. 연거푸 몇 번이나.

upon a trencher fixed on a rope / which is no thicker than a
줄 위에 고정된 나무 쟁반 위에서 보통 노끈보다도 얇은

common pack-thread / in England. My friend Reldresal, /
영국의. 내 친구 렐드레살은,

principal secretary for private affairs, is, / in my opinion, /
국무 대신인, 내 생각으로는,

if I am not partial, / the second after the treasurer; / the rest
편견을 가진 게 아니라면, 재무 대신 다음가는 2인자였지;

of the great officers / are much upon a par.
나머지 고위 관료들은 실력들이 서로 비슷하다.

These diversions are often attended / with fatal accidents,
이런 여흥에는 자주 수반되었다 치명적인 사고가.

/ whereof great numbers are on record. I myself have seen
그에 관한 많은 사건이 기록되어 있다. 나 자신도 보았다

/ two or three candidates break a limb. But the danger
두세 명의 지원자의 팔다리가 부러지는 것을. 그러나 위험은 훨씬 더하다,

is much greater, / when the ministers themselves are
대신들 자신이 황제의 명령을 받아

commanded / to show their dexterity; / for, / by contending
재주를 보여 줄 때; 왜냐하면, 능가하려고 애쓴 나머지

to excel / themselves and their fellows, / they strain so far
자신과 동료들을, 너무나 긴장해서,

/ that there is hardly one of them / who has not received a
거의 없기 때문이다 떨어지지 않는 사람이.

fall, / and some of them two or three. I was assured that, /
어떤 이는 두세 번 떨어지기도 한다.　　　　　　나는 전해 들었다,

a year or two before my arrival, / Flimnap would infallibly
내가 오기 1~2년 전에,　　　　　　플림냅은 목이 부러질 뻔했다고.

have broke his neck, / if one of the king's cushions, / that
　　　　　　만약 왕의 방석 하나가,

accidentally lay / on the ground, / had not weakened / the
우연히 놓여 있어서　　　땅에,　　　약화시키지 않았다면

force of his fall.
떨어지는 충격을.

Key Expression ♥

문장부호 콜론, 세미콜론, 대시의 쓰임

이 글에는 콜론, 세미콜론 등의 문장부호가 자주 등장합니다. 이들 문장부호의 쓰임을 알고 해석에 응용해 보세요.

▶ ; (세미콜론)

가장 자주 등장하는 문장부호인 ; (세미콜론)은 ,(콤마) + 접속사의 축약형으로 and, but, or, for 등을 대신하여 쓰입니다. 문장에 따라서 '그리고(그래서), 그러나(반면에), 왜냐하면' 등으로 해석합니다.

ex) Twelve of our crew were dead by immoderate labor and ill food; the rest were in a very weak condition. (=and)

선원들 중 12명이 과로와 영양실조로 숨을 거뒀다. 그리고 나머지도 매우 허약한 상태였다.

I could only look upwards; the sun began to grow hot, and the light offended my eyes. (=but)

나는 위쪽 밖에 볼 수 없었다. 그러나 태양이 뜨거워지기 시작했고 햇빛이 시야를 방해했다.

▶ : (콜론)

: (콜론)은 무언가를 열거할 때 사용하며, 또한 '말하자면(동격), 예를 들면(예시), ~라고(인용)' 등의 뜻으로도 쓰입니다.

ex) When I left Mr. Bates, I went down to my father: where, I got forty pounds, and a promise of thirty pounds a year to maintain me at Leyden: There I studied physic…

내가 베이츠 씨를 떠났을 때, 나는 아버지에게 갔다. 그리고 그곳에서 나는 40파운드와 1년에 30파운드씩 주겠다는 약속을 받았다. 그리고 거기서 나는 의학을 공부했다…

그 외에도 ——(대시)가 있는데 이는 보충설명에 쓰이는 문장부호로 괄호와 같은 역할을 합니다. 여는 대시와 닫는 대시가 함께 쓰이기도 하고 하나만 쓰이기도 합니다.

faculty 재주 | summerset 재주넘기, 공중제비 | fatal 죽음을 초래하는, 치명적인 | infallibly 틀림없는 | accidentally 우연히

There is likewise another diversion, / which is only shown
마찬가지로 또 하나의 여흥이 있다.   오직 펼쳐지는

/ before the emperor and empress, and first minister, /
황제와 황후, 그리고 총리 대신 앞에서만

upon particular occasions. The emperor lays on the table /
어떤 특별한 경우에.   황제는 탁자 위에 놓는다

three fine silken threads / of six inches long; / one is blue,
가느다란 비단실 세 가닥을   6인치 길이의;   하나는 푸른색,

/ the other red, / and the third green. These threads are
또 하나는 붉은색,   그리고 세 번째는 녹색이다.   이 실들은 상으로 하사하기

proposed as prizes / for those persons / whom the emperor
위한 것이다   사람들에게   황제가 구별하기를 원하는

has a mind to distinguish / by a peculiar mark of his
                          특별한 총애의 표시로.

favor. The ceremony is performed / in his majesty's great
        이 의식은 거행되는데   황제의 의전실에서,

chamber of state, / where the candidates are to undergo /
                여기에서 지원자는 받는다

a trial of dexterity / very different from the former, / and
재주의 시험을   전임자와는 전혀 다른,   그리고

such as / I have not observed / the least resemblance of / in
그런 것을   나는 본 일이 전혀 없었다   비슷한 것도

any other country / of the new or old world. The emperor
어느 나라에서도   현재나 과거의 세계에서건.   황제가 막대기 하나를

holds a stick / in his hands, / both ends parallel to the
들고 있으면   양 손에,   양 끝이 바닥과 평행이 되도록,

horizon, / while the candidates advancing, / one by one, /
            지원자가 나와서,   차례차례로,

sometimes leap over the stick, / sometimes creep under it,
때로는 뛰어 넘거나,   때로는 그 아래를 기어다닌다,

/ backward and forward, / several times, / according as the
앞뒤로,   여러 번,

stick is advanced or depressed. Sometimes / the emperor
막대기가 앞뒤로 움직임에 따라.   때로는

holds one end of the stick, / and his first minister the
황제가 막대기의 한 끝을 잡고,   또 한 끝은 총리 대신이 잡는다;

other; / sometimes / the minister has it entirely to himself.
때로는   총리가 혼자서 다 잡기도 한다.

peculiar 특별한 | resemblance 비슷함 | parallel 평행한 | horizon 수평선

Whoever performs his part / with most agility, / and holds
재주를 선보인 사람이나　　　　　　　　가장 민첩하게,　　　　　　가장 오랫동안

out the longest / in leaping and creeping, / is rewarded with
계속하는 사람이　　　뛰어넘고 기는 것을,　　　　　　　푸른색 비단실을 상으로

the blue-colored silk; / the red is given to the next, / and the
받는다:　　　　　　　　붉은 실은 두 번째 사람에게,　　　　그리고 녹색

green to the third, / which they all wear girt / twice round
은 세 번째 사람에게 수여된다,　그리고 그들은 모두 착용한다　허리에 두 번 감아서:

about the middle; / and you see few great persons / about
고위 관리는 거의 없다

this court / who are not adorned / with one of these girdles.
이 궁정에서　장식하지 않은 사람은　　　이 비단실 허리띠를 하나라도.

The horses of the army, / and those of the royal stables,
기병 부대의 말과,　　　　　　황실 축사의 말들은,

/ having been daily led before me, / were no longer shy,
매일 내 앞으로 데려와서,　　　　　이제는 더 이상 겁도 안 내고,

/ but would come up to / my very feet / without starting.
오히려 바짝 다가왔다　나의 발 아래　놀라지도 않고.

The riders would leap them / over my hand, / as I held it on
기수들은 뛰어 넘곤 했다　　　내 손 위를,　　내가 손을 땅에 대고

the ground; / and one of the emperor's huntsmen, / upon
있으면;　　　황제의 수렵관 중 한 사람은,

a large courser, / took my foot, / shoe and all; / which was
큰 준마를 타고,　　　내 발을 뛰어 넘었는데,　구두를 신고 있는:

indeed a prodigious leap. I had the good fortune / to divert
그것은 실로 엄청난 도약이었다.　　나는 운 좋게도　　　황제를 즐겁게

the emperor / one day / after a very extraordinary manner.
해 줄 기회를 가졌다　어느 날　매우 진기한 방법으로.

I desired / he would order / several sticks / of two feet high,
나는 부탁했다　황제에게 명령해 달라고　막대기를 몇 개 가져오도록　높이가 2피트인,

/ and the thickness of an ordinary cane, / to be brought
굵기는 보통 지팡이만한,　　　　　　　　　내게 갖다 달라고;

me; / whereupon his majesty commanded / the master of
그러자 폐하는 명령했다　　　　　　목재 관리인에게

his woods / to give directions accordingly; / and the next
그러한 지시를 내리라고;
다음 날 아침

morning / six woodmen arrived / with as many carriages,
여섯 명의 목재 관리인이 왔다   수레 여러 대를 끌고,

/ drawn by eight horses to each. I took nine of these sticks,
각각 여러 마리의 말이 끄는.   나는 가져온 막대 중 아홉 개를 골라서,

/ and fixing them firmly in the ground / in a quadrangular
땅에 단단히 박았다.   정사각형 모양으로,

figure, / two feet and a half square, / I took four other
가로 세로 2피트 반 크기의,   나는 네 개의 막대를 더 골라,

sticks, / and tied them parallel / at each corner, / about two
나란히 고정시켰다   각각 네 모서리에,

feet from the ground; / then I fastened my handkerchief
지상으로부터 약 2피트 높이에;   그런 다음 내 손수건을 매고

/ to the nine sticks / that stood erect; / and extended it on
9개의 막대기에   똑바로 서 있는;   사방에서 잡아 당겨,

all sides, / till it was tight / as the top of a drum; / and the
팽팽하게 했다   북의 표면처럼;

four parallel sticks, / rising about five inches higher / than
그래서 4개의 나란한 막대기는,   약 5인치 정도 높아져서

the handkerchief, / served as ledges / on each side. When
손수건의 면보다,   울타리 구실을 하게 되었다   사방에서.

I had finished my work, / I desired the emperor / to let a
작업을 다 마치고 나서,   나는 황제에게 부탁했다

troop of his best horses / twenty-four in number, / come
최정예 기병대를   24명으로 구성된,

and exercise / upon this plain. His majesty approved of the
데려와 훈련하도록   이 (손수건) 평원에서.   폐하는 이 제안을 받아들였고,

proposal, / and I took them up, / one by one, / in my hands,
나는 그들을 올려놓았다,   한 명씩,   손으로,

/ ready mounted and armed, / with the proper officers
말을 타고 무장한 기병과,   그들을 훈련시킬 담당 장교를.

to exercise them. As soon as they got into order / they
그들은 대열을 가다듬자마자

divided into two parties, / performed mock skirmishes, /
두 편으로 갈라져서,   모의 전투를 벌였다.

discharged blunt arrows, / drew their swords, / fled and
끝이 무딘 화살을 쏘고,   칼을 빼 들었고,   도망치고 추격했고,

pursued, / attacked and retired, / and in short / discovered
공격하고 물러섰다,   요컨대

the best military discipline / I ever beheld. The parallel
가장 훌륭한 군사 훈련을 보인 것이다   내가 이제까지 본.   수평 막대가 막아 주었다

sticks secured / them and their horses / from falling over
기병들과 말들이   무대에서 떨어지지 않게;

the stage; / and the emperor was so much delighted, / that
그러자 황제는 너무나 기뻐하며,

he ordered / this entertainment to be repeated / several
명령했다   이 여흥을 되풀이 하도록   여러 날 동안,

days, / and once was pleased to be lifted up / and give the
그리고 한 번은 기꺼이 올라와서   명령을 내리기도 했다;

word of command; / and with great difficulty / persuaded
그리고 매우 어렵게

even the empress herself / to let me hold her / in her
황후마저 설득해서   내게 붙잡게 하여

close chair / within two yards of the stage, / when she
가마에 태운 채로   무대로부터 2야드 내에,

was able to take a full view / of the whole performance.
그녀가 한눈에 볼 수 있었다   모든 활동을.

It was my good fortune, / that no ill accident happened /
내게는 다행스러운 일이었다,   치명적인 사고가 일어나지 않았다는 것이

in these entertainments; / only once / a fiery horse, / that
이 여흥에서;   다만 한 번   성미 급한 말이,

belonged to one of the captains, / pawing with his hoof, /
어느 대장의 소유였던,   앞발을 내딛다가,

struck a hole in my handkerchief, / and his foot slipping,
손수건에 구멍을 내고,   발이 미끄러지면서,

/ he overthrew his rider and himself; / but I immediately
기수와 더불어 넘어져 버렸다;   하지만 내가 즉각 그들을 구했고,

relieved them both, / and covering the hole with one hand,
한쪽 손으로 구멍을 막으면서,

delighted 아주 기뻐(즐거워) 하는 | persuade 설득하다 | paw 긁다 | hoof (말 등의) 발굽 | overthow
뒤집어지다, 전복시키다 | substance 물건 | oddly 기묘하게, 이상하게 | bedchamber 침실

/ I set down the troop with the other, / in the same manner
기병대원들을 내려놓았다.   같은 방식으로

/ as I took them up. The horse that fell / was strained in the
들어 올렸던 때와.   넘어진 말은   왼쪽 어깨를 삐었지만.

left shoulder, / but the rider got no hurt; / and I repaired my
                기수는 아무 부상이 없었고;   나는 손수건을 수선했다

handkerchief / as well as I could: / however, / I would not
              가능한 한 잘: 그러나,

trust to the strength of it / any more, / in such dangerous
나는 (손수건의) 힘을 믿을 수 없었다   더 이상,   그런 위험한 여흥을 감당할 거라고.

enterprises.

About two or three days before / I was set at liberty, / as I
약 2~3일 전   내가 자유의 몸이 되기.

was entertaining the court / with this kind of feat, / there
내가 궁정을 즐겁게 해 주고 있을 때   이런 종류의 묘기로.

arrived an express / to inform his majesty, / that some of his
급사가 도착해서   황제에게 보고했다.   몇 명의 신하가.

subjects, / riding near the place / where I was first taken up,
            말을 타고 지나가다가   내가 처음 붙잡혔던 곳 근처를.

/ had seen a great black substance / lying on the around, /
    검은색의 거대한 물체를 봤다고   땅 위에 놓여 있는.

very oddly shaped, / extending its edges round, / as wide as
매우 기묘하게 생기고,   그 둘레가 뻗어 있으며.

his majesty's bedchamber, / and rising up in the middle / as
폐하의 침실만한 넓이로.   그 가운데가 솟아 올라있는

high as a man; / that it was no living creature, / as they at
사람의 키만큼;   그것은 살아있는 생명체는 아니었다.

first apprehended, / if or it lay on the grass / without motion;
그들이 처음에 염려했던 것처럼.   풀밭에 놓여 있었기 때문에   아무 움직임 없이;

/ and some of them had walked round it / several times; /
    그들 중 몇 사람이 그 주위를 걸어보았다   몇 번이나;

that, / by mounting upon each other's shoulders, / they had
그래서, 그들이 서로의 어깨를 딛고 올라가,

got to the top, / which was flat and even, / and, / stamping
꼭대기에 도달해 보니, 평평하고 납작했다. 또한, 쿵쿵 발을

upon it, / they found that it was hollow within; / that they
굴러보고, 그 속이 비어 있음을 알았다:

humbly conceived / it might be something / belonging to the
그들은 추측했으며 그것이 혹시 물건이 아닌지 인간산의 소유인:

man-mountain; / and if his majesty pleased, / they would
폐하가 원하신다면,

undertake to bring it / with only five horses. I presently
그것을 운반해 오겠다고 했다 말 다섯 필만 있으면. 나는 금새 알았고

knew / what they meant, / and was glad at heart / to receive
그들이 무엇을 말하는지, 마음속으로 매우 기뻐했다

this intelligence. It seems, / upon my first reaching the shore
그 소식을 듣고. 그것은 ~같았다, 내가 처음 해안에 닿았을 때

/ after our shipwreck, / I was in such confusion, / that before
우리 배가 난파당한 후, 정신이 하나도 없어서,

I came to the place / where I went to sleep, / my hat, / which
도착하기 전까지 내가 잠들었던 곳에, 내 모자가,

I had fastened / with a string to my head / while I was
묶어 두었던 끈으로 머리에 보트를 젓고 있는 동안,

rowing, / and had stuck on all the time / I was swimming, /
그래서 내내 붙어 있었던 헤엄치는 동안에,

fell off / after I came to land; / the string, / as I conjecture,
떨어진 것이었다 육지에 도착한 후; 그 끈이, 짐작하건데,

/ breaking by some accident, / which I never observed, /
우연히 끊어져서, 내가 그것을 알지 못했고,

but thought / my hat had been lost at sea. I entreated his
다만 생각했다 바다에서 모자를 잃어버렸다고.

imperial majesty / to give orders / it might be brought to
나는 황제 폐하께 간청했다 명령을 내려 달라고 그것을 내게 가져다 달라고

me / as soon as possible, / describing to him / the use and
가능한 한 빨리, 그에게 설명하면서

the nature of it: / and the next day / the waggoners arrived
그 물건의 용도와 특징을; 그리고 다음 날 마부들이 그것을 가지고 도착했지만,

with it, / but not in a very good condition; / they had bored
상태가 썩 좋지 않았다:　　　　　　　　　　그들은 챙에 두 개의 구멍

two holes in the brim, / within an inch and half of the edge,
을 뚫었고,　　　　　　　가장자리에서 1인치 반만큼 안쪽에,

/ and fastened two hooks in the holes; / these hooks were
그 구멍에 두 개의 갈고리를 걸어서;　　　　　그 갈고리를 연결했다

tied / by a long cord / to the harness, / and thus my hat was
긴 줄로　　　　마구에,　　　　그래서 내 모자는 땅에 끌려왔다

dragged along / for above half an English mile; / but, / the
　　　　영국 단위로 반 마일 이상의 거리를;　　　그러나,

ground in that country / being extremely smooth and level, /
그 나라 땅은　　　　　극히 매끄럽고 평평해서,

it received less damage / than I expected.
손상이 덜했다　　　　　　예상보다는.

Two days after this adventure, / the emperor, / having
이런 사건이 있은 지 이틀 후,　　　　황제는,　　　명령을 내리고

ordered / that part of his army which quarters / in and
주둔하고 있는 군대에

about his metropolis, / to be in readiness, / took a fancy of /
수도와 그 근방에,　　　　출동 준비를,　　　생각해 냈다

diverting himself / in a very singular manner. He desired /
심심풀이 오락을　　　매우 기묘한 방법으로.　　　그는 내게 부탁했다

I would stand like a Colossus, / with my legs as far asunder
거인상처럼 서 있어 달라고,　　　　양다리를 되도록 넓게 벌린 채

/ as I conveniently could. He then commanded / his general
편하게 할 수 있는 한.　　　그는 그리고 나서 명령했다　　장군에게

/ (who was an old experienced leader, / and a great patron
(그는 나이 든 경험 많은 지휘관이고,　　　나의 좋은 후견인이기도 했다)

of mine) / to draw up the troops in close order, / and march
군대를 밀집 대형으로 정렬시키고,　　　　행진시키라고

them / under me; / the foot by twenty-four abreast, / and
내 양 다리 아래로;　24명의 보병과,

the horse by sixteen, / with drums beating, / colors flying,
16명의 기병이,　　　　북을 치고,　　　　군기를 날리며,

waggoner 마차 | drag 끌다 | quarter (병사의) 막사 | readiness 준비 | abreast 나란히

/ and pikes advanced. This body consisted of / three
창을 받들어 행진했다.　　　　　　이 부대는 구성되었다

thousand foot, / and a thousand horse. His majesty gave
3,000의 보병과,　　　1,000의 기병으로.　　　　폐하는 명령을 내렸다.

orders, / upon pain of death, / that every soldier in his
위반 시에 사형에 처한다면서,　　행진하는 모든 군인은

march / should observe the strictest decency / with regard
　　　엄격하게 예의를 지켜야만 한다고

to my person; / which however / could not prevent / some
나에 대해서;　　그럼에도 불구하고　　막을 수 없었다

of the younger officers / from turning up their eyes / as
몇몇 젊은 장교들이　　　올려다 보는 것을

they passed under me: / and, / to confess the truth, / my
내 밑을 지날 때마다:　　그리고,　사실 고백하자면,

breeches were at that time / in so ill a condition, / that they
나의 바지는 그때　　　　　이미 다 해져서,

afforded some opportunities / for laughter and admiration.
그들에게 기회들을 제공하는 상태였다　　　웃음과 놀라움의.

I had sent so many memorials and petitions / for my
나는 청원서와 탄원서를 수없이 올렸다　　　내 자유를 청하는,

liberty, / that his majesty at length / mentioned the matter,
때문에 폐하는 드디어　　　　이 안건을 내놓았다.

/ first in the cabinet, / and then in a full council; / where it
우선 각료 회의에,　　다음으로 총회의에:

was opposed by none, / except Skyresh Bolgolam, / who
여기에서 아무도 반대하지 않았다,　　스키레쉬 볼고람을 제외하고는,　　　그는 기꺼이,

was pleased, / without any provocation, / to be my mortal
　　　그럴 만한 이유도 없이,　　내 철천지원수가 된 사람이었다.

enemy. But / it was carried against him / by the whole
그러나　그의 뜻과는 반대로　　　전체 회의에서 통과되고,

board, / and confirmed by the emperor. That minister
황제의 인준도 받았다.　　　　그 대신은 갈베트,

was GALBET, / or admiral of the realm, / very much in
　　즉 그 나라의 해군 대신으로,

his master's confidence, / and a person well versed in
황제의 신임이 두텁고,　　　일의 처리에 능란한 사람이지만,

affairs, / but of a morose and sour complexion. However,
무뚝뚝하고 까다로운 성격이었다. 그러나,

/ he was at length / persuaded to comply; / but prevailed
그도 마침내 동의하도록 설득 당했다; 하지만 주장했다

/ that the articles and conditions / upon which I should be
조항과 조건들을 나를 석방시키는데 있어서,

set free, / and to which I must swear, / should be drawn up
내가 서약해야 하는, 그 자신이 작성해야 한다고.

by himself. These articles were brought to me / by Skyresh
이 조항들은 내게 가져왔다 스키레쉬 볼고람과

Bolgolam in person / attended by two under-secretaries, /
두 명의 차관이 직접,

and several persons of distinction. After they were read, /
여러 고관을 대동하고. 조항들을 읽은 후,

I was demanded / to swear to the performance of them; /
내게 요구했다 그것을 지키겠다고 맹세하라고;

first in the manner of my own country, / and afterwards in
우선 내 나라에서 하는 방식으로,

the method prescribed by their laws; / which was, / to hold
그리고 나서 그들이 법이 규정하는 방식으로; 그 방식은,

my right foot in my left hand, / and to place the middle
왼손으로 오른발을 잡은 후, 오른손의 가운데 손가락을 놓고

finger of my right hand / on the crown of my head, / and
머리 꼭대기에,

my thumb on the tip of my right ear. But because the reader
엄지 손가락을 오른쪽 귀에 대는 것이었다. 그러나 독자 여러분은 궁금할 것이기

may be curious / to have some idea of the style and manner
때문에 문체와 표현 방식이

of expression / peculiar to that people, / as well as to know
그들 특유의, 알고 싶을 뿐만 아니라

/ the article upon which I recovered my liberty, / I have
내 자유를 되찾게 된 조건을,

made a translation of the whole instrument, / word for
전문을 번역하여,   글자 그대로,

word, / as near as I was able, / which I here offer to the
       가능한 한 충실하게,   여기에 공개하는 바이다.

public.

Golbasto Momarem Evlame Gurdilo Shefin Mully
골바스토 모마렘 에브라메 구르딜로 셰핀 물리 울리 구에 넘은,

Ully Gue, / most mighty Emperor of Lilliput, / delight
            가장 강대한 릴리펏인 황제이신,

and terror of the universe, / whose dominions extend
전 우주의 기쁨과 공포이시며,   그 분의 영토는 이른다

/ five thousand BLUSTRUGS / (about twelve miles in
  5,000블러스트럭에   (지름 약 12마일)

circumference) / to the extremities of the globe; / monarch
                  지구의 끝까지;   그 분은 왕 중

of all monarchs, / taller than the sons of men; / whose feet
의 왕이시며,   모든 사람보다 키가 크시고,

press down to the centre, / and whose head strikes against
두 발은 땅의 중심까지 누르며,   머리는 태양과 맞닿아 있다;

the sun; / at whose nod / the princes of the earth shake
              그 분의 고갯짓에   이 땅의 모든 왕이 무릎을 벌벌 떤다;

their knees; / pleasant as the spring, / comfortable as the
                그 분은 봄처럼 상쾌하고,   여름처럼 편안하며,

summer, / fruitful as autumn, / dreadful as winter: / his
가을처럼 풍성하고,   겨울처럼 무서우시다:

most sublime majesty proposes / to the man-mountain, /
가장 숭고하신 황제는 제안한다   인간산에게,

lately arrived at our celestial dominions, / the following
최근 우리 천국 같은 나라에 온,   다음의 조항을,

articles, / which, by a solemn oath, / he shall be obliged to
            이것을, 엄숙한 서약으로,   반드시 실천해야 할 것이다: —

perform: — /

1st, / The man-mountain shall not depart from our
첫째.   인간산은 이 나라를 떠나서는 안 된다.

dominions, / without our license under our great seal.
옥새가 날인된 허가서 없이는.

2d, / He shall not presume to come into our metropolis, /
둘째.   그는 수도에 들어와서는 안 된다.

without our express order; / at which time, / the inhabitants
특별한 명령 없이;   그런 경우에는,

shall have two hours warning / to keep within doors.
주민에게 두 시간 전에 경고해야 한다   집 안에 머물러 있도록.

3d, / The said man-mountain shall confine his walks / to
셋째.   앞서 말한 인간산은 보행이 허용되며

our principal high roads, / and not offer to walk, / or lie
주요 대로에서만,   걷거나,   드러누워서는

down, / in a meadow or field of corn.
안 된다.   들판이나 보리밭에.

4th, / As he walks the said roads, / he shall take the utmost
넷째.   앞서 말한 대로를 걸을 때,   그는 세심한 주의를 기울여야 한다

care / not to trample / upon the bodies of any of our loving
밟지 않도록   우리의 사랑하는 백성들의 몸이나,

subjects, / their horses, / or carriages, / nor take any of our
그들의 말,   또는 마차를,   또한 백성들을 손으로 잡아서는

subjects into his hands / without their own consent.
안 된다   그들의 동의 없이는.

Key Expression ♟

with regard to~ : ~에 대하여

regard는 동사로 '~로 여기다', 명사로 '관심, 고려' 등의 뜻으로 주로 쓰이는 단어
지만 with regard to는 '~에 대하여'라는 의미가 숨어있습니다. 같은 의미의 전
치사로 regarding, concerning, about이 있으며 반대로 regardless of
는 '~와 관계없이'라는 뜻입니다.

ex) Every soldier in his march should observe the strictest decency with regard
to my person;
행진하는 모든 군인은 나에 대해 엄격한 예의를 지켜야 한다.

---

instrument (법률)문서 | word for word 글자 그대로 | dominion 통치력 | circumference 둘레 | extremity
끝 | monarch 군주, 왕 | dreadful 준엄한, 무시무시한 | celestial 천상의, 하늘의 | oath 서약 | presume 감히 ~
하다. 대담하게 ~하다 | meadow 목초지 | utmost 최대의, 최고의 | consent 동의

5th, / If an express requires extraordinary dispatch, / the
다섯째, 긴급한 속보를 전달할 필요가 있을 경우,

man-mountain shall be obliged to carry, / in his pocket,
인간산은 운반해야 한다. 그의 호주머니에 넣어,

/ the messenger and horse / a six days journey, / once in
전달자와 그의 말을 6일 간의 여정만큼,

every moon, / and return the said messenger back / (if so
매달 한 번씩, 그리고 앞서 말한 전달자를 다시 (그렇게

required) / safe to our imperial presence.
할 필요가 있다면) 안전하게 폐하 앞으로 데려와야 한다.

6th, / He shall be our ally / against our enemies / in the
여섯째, 인간산은 우리 편이 되어야 한다 우리의 적에 대항하여

island of Blefuscu, / and do his utmost / to destroy their
블레프스큐 섬의, 그리고 그 온 힘을 다하여 그들의 함대를 격멸해야 한다.

fleet, / which is now preparing to invade us.
지금 우리를 침공하려고 준비 중인.

7th, / That the said man-mountain shall, / at his times
일곱째, 앞서 말한 인간산은, 한가한 때,

of leisure, / be aiding and assisting to our workmen, / in
우리의 일꾼을 돕고 협조해야 한다.

helping to raise certain great stones, / towards covering
큰 바윗돌을 들어올리는 것을 도우며, 벽을 구축하기 위하여

the wall / of the principal park, / and other our royal
주요 공원과, 기타 왕실 건물의 벽도.

buildings.

8th, / That the said man-mountain shall, / in two moons
여덟째, 앞서 말한 인간산은, 2개월 이내에,

time, / deliver in an exact survey / of the circumference
정확한 측량을 제출해야 한다 우리 영토의 둘레를,

of our dominions, / by a computation of his own paces /
발걸음의 수를 계산하여

round the coast.
해안 주위을 걸어서.

Lastly, / That, upon his solemn oath / to observe all the
마지막으로.   엄숙한 서약을 하고 나서야   위의 모든 조항을 모두 준수하겠

above articles, / the said man-mountain shall have / a
다는,   앞서 말한 인간산은

daily allowance of meat and drink / sufficient for the
매일 하루 분량의 고기와 음료를   먹이기에 충분한

support / of 1724 of our subjects, / with free access to our
support   우리 백성 1,724명을,   황제에게 접근할 수 있는 자유와 함께,

royal person, / and other marks of our favor. Given at our
                    또한 다른 호의의 표시를.

palace at Belfaborac, / the twelfth day of the ninety-first
벨포락 궁정에서 수여함,   통치 91월 12째 날.

moon of our reign.

Key Expression ♀

once in every moon : 매달 한 번씩

'모든'이란 의미를 가진 every가 hour, day, week, month, year 등 때를 나
타내는 명사와 함께 쓰이면 '매 ~마다'라는 의미의 빈도를 나타내는 말로 쓰입
니다. 이 때 명사 앞에 수사를 삽입할 때에는 다음의 규칙을 따르며 every 앞에
once, twice, three times 등을 삽입해 횟수를 나타내기도 합니다.

▶ every + 기수 + 복수명사 : every three months
▶ every + 서수 + 단수명사 : every third month

ex) If an express requires extraordinary dispatch, the man-mountain shall be
obliged to carry, in his pocket, the messenger and horse a six days journey,
once in every moon.
만약 긴급한 급보를 전달할 필요가 있을 경우, 인간산은 매달 한 번씩, 6일 간의
여정 동안, 전달자와 그의 말을 호주머니에 넣어 운반해야 한다.

fleet 함대 | invade 침입하다

I swore and subscribed to these articles / with great
나는 그 조항들을 서약하고 서명했다

cheerfulness and content, / although some of them /
기쁘고 만족스럽게,　　　비록 이중 몇 개는

were not so honorable / as I could have wished; / which
그다지 명예롭지 않았지만　　　내가 예상했던 만큼;

proceeded wholly / from the malice of Skyresh Bolgolam,
그것은 전부 나온 것일 터였다　전부 스키레쉬 볼고람의 악의로부터,

/ the high-admiral: / whereupon my chains were /
해군 제독인:　　　그러자 나를 묶고 있던 사슬이

immediately unlocked, / and I was at full liberty. The
즉시 풀렸고,　　　나는 완전히 자유를 얻었다.

emperor himself, / in person, / did me the honor / to be
황제 자신이,　　　몸소,　　　영광스럽게도

by at the whole ceremony. I made my acknowledgements
예식 내내 참석하셨다.　　　나는 감사를 표했다

/ by prostrating myself at his majesty's feet: / but he
황제 발 밑에 엎드려:

commanded me to rise; / and after many gracious
그러나 그는 내게 일어나라고 했다;　　　그리고 여러 가지 은혜로운 축하 표현을 한 뒤,

expressions, / which, / to avoid the censure of vanity, /
그것은,　　　잘난 체 한다는 비난을 피하기 위해,

I shall not repeat, / he added, / "that he hoped / I should
되풀이 하지 않겠다,　　그는 덧붙였다.　　"그는 바란다고

prove a useful servant, / and well deserve all the favors /
내가 유능한 신하가 되어 주기를,　　호의에 보답하도록

he had already conferred upon me, / or might do for the
그가 이미 내게 베풀었고,　　　또는 앞으로 베풀어 줄."

future."

The reader may please to observe, / that, / in the last article
독자 여러분은 보았을 것이다,　　　그것을,　마지막 조항에서

of the recovery of my liberty, / the emperor stipulates
나를 자유롭게 해 주는 포고문의,　　　황제가 내게 주겠다고 명기한 것을

cheerfulness 기분 좋음 | high-admiral 해군 제독 | prostrate 엎드리다 | gracious 은혜로운 | censure 비난
| vanity 자만, 잘난척 | stipulates 약정하다 | determinate 명확한, 구체적인 | quadrant 사분의(옛날의 천체고도
측정기) | proportion 비율 | ingenuity 총명함

to allow me / a quantity of meat and drink / sufficient
고기와 음료를

for the support of 1724 Lilliputians. Sometime after, /
1,724명을 먹이기에 충분한 분량의.   얼마 후에,

asking a friend at court / how they came to fix on / that
궁정에 있는 한 친구에게 물어보니   어떻게 그렇게 정하게 되었는지

determinate number, / he told me / that his majesty's
구체적인 수치를.   그는 내게 말했다   폐하의 수학자들이,

mathematicians, / having taken the height of my body / by
내 키를 쟀고

the help of a quadrant, / and finding it / to exceed theirs /
사분의를 이용하여,   알아냈다   그들보다 크다는 것을

in the proportion of twelve to one, / they concluded / from
내가 12대 1의 비율로,   따라서 그들은 결론 내렸다

the similarity of their bodies, / that mine must contain at
그들의 몸과 비슷하다는 점으로부터,   내 몸이 적어도 그들의 1,724배는 되며,

least 1724 of theirs, / and consequently would require / as
따라서 음식이 필요할 것이라고

much food as was necessary / to support that number of
충분한 양만큼   그만한 수의 릴리펏인을 먹이기에.

Lilliputians. By which the reader may conceive / an idea
이것으로 독자 여러분은 짐작할 수 있을 것이다

of the ingenuity of that people, / as well as the prudent and
그 사람들의 재주를.   뿐만 아니라 알뜰하고 정확한 경제 관념을

exact economy / of so great a prince.
위대한 왕의.

mini test 3

A. 다음 문장을 해석해 보세요.

(1) I began to conceive / hopes of getting my liberty / in a short time.
→

(2) Very often / the chief ministers themselves are commanded / to show their skill, / and to convince the emperor / that they have not lost their faculty.
→

(3) The horses of the army, / and those of the royal stables, / having been daily led before me, / were no longer shy, / but would come up to my very feet / without starting.
→

(4) The emperor himself, / in person, / did me the honor / to be by at the whole ceremony.
→

B. 다음 주어진 문장이 되도록 빈칸에 써 넣으세요.

(1) 나는 때때로 드러누워서, 대여섯 명을 내 손 위에서 춤추게 했다.

I would sometimes lie down, and [   ]

(2) 누구든 떨어지지 않고 제일 높이 뛰는 사람이 그 자리를 계승한다.

[   ] succeeds in the office.

(3) 내 친구 렐드레살은 재무 대신 다음가는 2인자였다.

My friend Reldresal is [   ] the treasurer.

(4) 행진하는 모든 군인은 나에 대해서 엄격하게 예의를 지켜야만 한다.

Every soldier in his march should observe the strictest decency [   ].

A. (1) 나는 곧 자유를 얻을 것이라는 희망을 품게 되었다. (2) 빈번하게 주요 대신들은 직접 자신의 재주를 보여 주고, 그들이 재주를 잃지 않았음을 황제에게 확신시키도록 명령받았다. (3) 기병부대의 말과, 황실 축사의 말들은, 매일 내 앞으로 데려와서, 이제는 더 이상 겁도 안 내고, 오히려 놀라지도 않으며 나의 발

86   Gulliver's Travels

C. 다음 주어진 문구가 알맞은 문장이 되도록 순서를 맞춰 보세요.

(1) 나머지 고위 관료들은 실력들이 서로 비슷하다.
(par / much / a / upon)
→ The rest of the great officers are _____.

(2) 그는 나에게 양다리를 편하게 가능한 한 넓게 벌린 채 거인상처럼 서 있어
달라고 부탁했다.
(I / my legs / conveniently / far / asunder / with / as / could / as)
→ He desired I would stand like a Colossus, _____.

(3) 나는 매우 기쁘고 만족스럽게 그 조항들에 서약하고 서명했다.
(cheerfulness / content / great / and / with)
→ I swore and subscribed to these articles _____.

(4) 나는 완전히 자유로웠다.
(full / I / liberty / at / was)
→

D. 다음 단어에대한맞는 설명과 연결해 보세요.

(1) determinate ▶   ◀ ① very large or impressive

(2) peculiar ▶   ◀ ② fixed and definite

(3) prodigious ▶   ◀ ③ strange or unusual

(4) abreast ▶   ◀ ④ facing in the same direction

4

Mildendo, / the metropolis of Lilliput, / described, /
밀덴도가,   릴리펏의 수도인,   묘사된다,

together with the emperor's palace. A conversation
황제의 궁궐과 함께.   저자와 국무 대신 간의 대화,

between the author and a principal secretary, / concerning

the affairs of that empire. The author's offers / to serve the
제국의 여러 문제에 관한.   저자의 제안   황제를 돕겠다는

emperor / in his wars.
      전쟁 시.

The first request I made, / after I had obtained my liberty,
내가 제일 먼저 요청한 것은,   자유를 얻은 후,

/ was, that I might have license / to see Mildendo, / the
   허가증을 갖게 해 달라는 것이었다   밀덴도를 볼 수 있게,

metropolis; / which the emperor easily granted me, /
수도인;   황제는 쉽게 나를 허락했지만,

but with a special charge / to do no hurt / either to the
특별히 경고했다   해를 입히지 말라고

inhabitants or their houses. The people had notice, / by
주민들이나 그들의 집에.   주민들은 알게 됐다,

proclamation, / of my design to visit the town. The wall
포고에 의해,   내 수도 방문 계획을.

which encompassed it / is two feet and a half high, / and
도시를 둘러싼 성벽은   높이가 2피트 반이었고,

at least eleven inches broad, / so that a coach and horses
폭은 적어도 11인치였다,   그래서 마차와 말들이

/ may be driven very safely / round it; / and it is flanked
매우 안전하게 다닐 수 있을 듯 했다   그 주변을;   그리고 견고한 탑이 측면에

with strong towers / at ten feet distance. I stepped over
있었다   10피트 간격으로.   나는 서쪽 큰 문을 넘어,

the great western gate, / and passed very gently, / and
      매우 살며시 걸었다,

sidling, / through the two principal streets, / only in my
미끄러지듯,   두 개의 주 도로를 통과하여,

short waistcoat, / for fear of damaging / the roofs and
짧은 조끼만 입은 채,   손상을 입힐까봐   지붕과 처마에

eaves of the houses / with the skirts of my coat. I walked
내 코트 자락으로.

with the utmost circumspection, / to avoid treading on any
나는 아주 조심해서 걸었다.   주민들을 밟지 않도록

stragglers / who might remain in the streets, / although
혹시 길에 남아서 돌아다닐 수 있는,

the orders were very strict, / that all people should keep /
비록 엄명이 있었음에도 불구하고,   모든 사람은 있어야만 한다는

in their houses, / at their own peril. The garret windows
그들의 집에,   자신들의 위험을 각오하고.   집들의 다락방 창문과 옥상은

and tops of houses / were so crowded with spectators, /
구경꾼으로 가득 차 있어서,

that I thought / in all my travels / I had not seen / a more
나는 생각했다   내 모든 여행 중에서   본 적이 없다고   이렇게 사람이

populous place. The city is an exact square, / each side
모여 있는 것은.   그 도시는 정확한 정사각형이고,   사방의 성벽 길이는

of the wall / being five hundred feet long. The two great
각각 500피트였다.   두 개의 큰 길은,

streets, / which run across and divide it / into four quarters,
도시를 나누고 있었는데   네 구역으로,

Key Expression 🎯

for fear of~ : ~할까 봐, ~하지 않도록

for fear of~는 '~할까 봐, ~하지 않도록'이라는 의미를 가진 숙어입니다. of
뒤에는 명사나 동명사가 오며 절을 동반할경우 of 대신 that을 사용하고,
that절에는 대개 should(때에 따라 may, would 등도 사용)를 동반합니다.
또한 for fear that~은 lest~should 구문으로 바꾸어 쓸 수 있습니다.

ex) I stepped over the great western gate, only in my short waistcoat, / for fear of
damaging the roofs and eaves of the houses with the skirts of my coat.
나는 짧은 조끼만 입은 채 서쪽 문을 넘었다. / 내 코트 자락으로 지붕과 처마에
손상을 입힐까 봐.

proclamation 포고 | encompassed 둘러싸다 | flank ~이 측면에 있다 | circumspection 신중한 행동 | tread
밟다 | straggler 주민 | populous 인구가 많은

/ are five feet wide. The lanes and alleys, / which I could
그 폭은 5피트였다.   좁은 도로와 골목길은,   내가 들어 갈 수 없어서,

not enter, / but only view them as I passed, / are from
지나면서 보기만 했던,

twelve to eighteen inches. The town is capable of holding
12에서 18인치 정도였다.   도시는 수용할 수 있었다

/ five hundred thousand souls: / the houses are from three
50만 명의 인구를: 집들은 3~5층 사이의 높이였고:

to five stories: / the shops and markets well provided.
상점과 시장은 잘 갖춰져 있었다.

The emperor's palace is / in the centre of the city / where
황제의 궁궐은 있었다   시내의 한복판에

the two great streets meet. It is enclosed by a wall / of two
두 개의 대로가 만나는.   그것은 성벽으로 둘러싸여 있었다   높이가

feet high, / and twenty feet distance / from the buildings. I
2피트이며,   20피트의 거리를 둔   건물로부터.

had his majesty's permission / to step over this wall; / and,
나는 폐하의 허가를 받아   이 성벽을 넘었다;   그리고,

/ the space being so wide / between that and the palace, /
공간이 매우 넓어서   성벽과 궁궐 사이의,

I could easily view it / on every side. The outward court
나는 그것을 잘 볼 수 있었다   사방에서.   바깥쪽 정원은

is / a square of forty feet, / and includes two other courts:
한 면이 40피트인 정사각형이었고,   그 속에 두 개의 다른 궁궐이 있었다:

/ in the inmost / are the royal apartments, / which I was
그 제일 안쪽에   황제의 거처가 있었기에,   나는 매우 보고 싶었다.

very desirous to see, / but found it extremely difficult; /
하지만 그것은 극히 힘들었다;

for the great gates, / from one square into another, / were
왜냐하면 대문의 높이가   한쪽 정원에서 다른 쪽으로 통하는,

but eighteen inches high, / and seven inches wide. Now
겨우 높이가 18인치에,   폭이 7인치 밖에 안 되었기 때문에.

the buildings of the outer court were / at least five feet
바깥쪽 정원의 건물들은   높이가 적어도 5피트는 되어,

high, / and it was impossible / for me to stride over them /
불가능했다   내가 그것들을 넘어가는 것이

without infinite damage to the pile, / though the walls were
건물에 큰 손상을 주지 않고,   비록 벽은 튼튼히 지어졌지만

strongly built / of hewn stone, / and four inches thick.
                     잘라낸 돌들로,   4인치 두께로.

At the same time / the emperor had a great desire / that I
동시에   황제는 무척 열망했다

should see / the magnificence of his palace; / but this / I
내가 봐야 한다고   그의 화려한 궁궐을;   그러나 이것을

was not able to do / till three days after, / which I spent in
나는 할 수 없었다   사흘 동안은,   그 동안 나는 베는 데 시간을

cutting down / with my knife / some of the largest trees
보냈다   내 칼로   가장 큰 나무 몇 그루를

/ in the royal park, / about a hundred yards distant from
황실 산림원에서,   도시에서 100야드 떨어진.

the city. Of these trees / I made two stools, / each about
        이 나무들로   나는 두 개의 의자를 만들었다.   각각 높이가 3피트이고,

three feet high, / and strong enough / to bear my weight.
                 충분히 튼튼했다   내 몸무게를 견딜 만큼.

Key Expression

spend in ~ing : ~하는데 시간을 보내다

동사 spend는 '(시간을) 보내다, (돈을) 쓰다, (노력을) 들이다'라는 의미로 쓰이며, 그 대상을 표현할 경우에는 in~ing, 혹은 on+명사의 형태가 뒤에 따라 옵니다. 또한 '낭비하다'라는 의미의 waste도 같은 형식으로 사용합니다. 다음과 같이 정리해서 기억해 볼까요.

▶ spend/waste + (in)~ing : ~하는 데 시간을 보내다/낭비하다
▶ spend/waste + (돈/시간) + (in)~ing : ~하는 데 (시간/돈)을 쓰다/낭비하다
    (*이때, in은 자주 생략됨)
▶ spend/waste + (돈/시간) + on 명사 : ~에 (시간/돈)을 쓰다/낭비하다
▶ spend/waste + (돈/시간) + to 동사 : ~하기 위해 시간/돈을 쓰다/낭비하다

ex) I spent in cutting down with my knife some of the largest trees in the royal park.
    나는 내 칼로 황실 산림원에서 가장 큰 나무 몇 그루를 베는 데 시간을 보냈다.

permission 허가 | inmost 가장 안쪽 | desirous 바라는 | stride ~ 를 건너뛰다 | hewn 잘라낸

The people having received notice / a second time, / I
주민들은 통보를 받았다   두 번째로,

went again / through the city / to the palace / with my
나는 다시   시내를 통과해   궁전으로 갔다

two stools in my hands. When I came / to the side of the
두 개의 의자를 손에 들고.   도착하자   궁궐 바깥쪽 측면에.

outer court, / I stood upon one stool, / and took the other
                나는 의자 위에 올라섰다,   또 하나는 손에 든 채;

in my hand; / this / I lifted over the roof, / and gently
                이것을   지붕 너머로 들어 올려서,   살며시 내려 놓았다

set it down / on the space / between the first and second
            공간에   첫 번째와 두 번째 궁궐 사이의.

court, / which was eight feet wide. I then / stept over the
          넓이가 8피트 되는.   그 다음 나는

building very conveniently / from one stool to the other,
매우 편리하게 건물들을 넘어갔다   의자를 교대로 밟으며,

/ and drew up the first after me / with a hooked stick. By
    그리고 첫 번째 의자를 끌어올렸다   갈고리 모양의 막대로.

this contrivance / I got into the inmost court; / and, / lying
이런 장치로   나는 가장 안쪽에 있는 궁궐에 들어갔다;   그리고,

down upon my side, / I applied my face / to the windows
옆으로 드러누워서,   얼굴을 갖다 대었다   중간층의 창에.

of the middle stories, / which were left open / on purpose, /
                        그것은 열려 있었고   일부러,

and discovered the most splendid apartments / that can be
정말 화려한 방이 보였다   상상을 초월할 만큼.

imagined. There / I saw the empress and the young princes,
                거기에서   나는 황후와 황태자들을 보았다,

/ in their several lodgings, / with their chief attendants
    각자의 방에 있던,   시종장들과 함께,

about them. Her imperial majesty was pleased / to smile
              황후 마마는 기뻐하며

very graciously upon me, / and gave me out of the window
내게 아주 부드럽게 미소를 지었고,   창 밖으로 손을 내밀어 주었다

her hand / to kiss.
          입맞출 수 있도록.

But / I shall not anticipate / the reader / with further
그러나   나는 더 이상 하지 않겠다   독자 여러분에게

descriptions of this kind, / because I reserve them / for
더 이상 이런 종류의 이야기는,   왜냐하면 그것들을 남겨 두었기 때문에

a greater work, / which is now / almost ready for the
더 큰 책을 위해,   이제 막   인쇄를 앞두고 있는;

press; / containing a general description of this empire, /
이 제국에 대한 전반적인 설명이 포함되어 있고,

from its first erection, / through a long series of princes;
건국으로부터,   여러 왕들을 거치는 동안;

/ with a particular account / of their wars and politics, /
특히 설명과 함께   그들의 전쟁과 정치,

laws, learning, and religion; / their plants and animals; /
법률, 학문, 그리고 종교에 관한;   또한 그들의 동식물과;

their peculiar manners and customs, / with other matters
그들의 독특한 풍습과 습관,

very curious and useful; / my chief design at present /
기타 매우 기묘하고 유용한 사항들도;   지금 내 주된 계획은

being only to relate / such events and transactions / as
관한 것 뿐이다   그런 사건과 그 처리에

happened to the public or to myself / during a residence /
그 나라와 내게 일어났던   사는 동안

of about nine months / in that empire.
9개월 간   그 제국에.

Key Expression

for / during / while : ~동안

for, during, while은 모두 '~동안'이라는 의미를 가지고 있지만 각각의 쓰임이 다릅니다. 여기에서 for와 during은 전치사로 명사나 명사구를, while은 접속사로서 절을 동반합니다.

▶ for + (숫자로 표현하는) 구체적 시간/날짜

▶ during + 기간/사건/행사

▶ while + 주어 + 동사

ex) ···during a residence of about nine months in that empire
    그 제국에서 9개월 간 사는 동안
    ···for six-and-thirty moons past 지난 36개월 동안
    ···while he was a boy 그가 소년이었던 동안

conveniently 편리하게 | stool 발판 | contrivance 장치 | splendid 찬란한 | lodging 방, 하숙 | graciously 영예롭게 | anticipate 기대하다 | reserve 따로 남겨 두다 | erection 건립, 건국 | residence 체류

One morning, / about a fortnight / after I had obtained my
어느 날 아침, 약 2주가 지난 내가 자유를 얻은 후,

liberty, / Reldresal, / principal secretary / (as they style
렐드레살이, 국무 대신인 (그들이 그를 부르는 것에

him) / for private affairs, / came to my house / attended
따르면) 개인적인 일로, 내 집에 왔다

only by one servant. He ordered his coach to wait / at
하인 하나만 데리고, 그는 마차를 대기시키고

a distance, / and desired / I would give him an hour's
조금 떨어진 곳에, 부탁했다 내게 한 시간만 접견 시간을 내 달라고:

audience; / which I readily consented to, / on account of
나는 그것을 흔쾌히 승낙했다,

his quality and personal merits, / as well as of the many
그의 높은 신분과 인격 때문에, 뿐만 아니라 많은 도움도

good offices / he had done me / during my solicitations
그가 내게 해 준 내가 조정에서 간청했을 때,

at court. I offered to lie down / that he might the more
나는 눕겠다고 제안했다 그의 말이 더 쉽게 내 귀에 들리도록,

conveniently reach my ear, / but he chose / rather to let
그러나 그는 선택했다 차라리 그를 올려 달라고

me hold him / in my hand / during our conversation. He
내 손에 우리가 대화하는 동안.

began with compliments / on my liberty; / said / "he might
그는 말을 시작했다 내 자유를 축하하며; 말하기를

pretend to some merit in it;" / but, however, / added, /
"자신도 그 일에 도움이 됐을지 모른다고" 그러나, 덧붙여 말하기를,

"that if it had not been for / the present situation of things
"만약 없었다면 궁궐이 처한 현재의 상황이,

at court, / perhaps / I might not have obtained it / so soon.
아마도 나는 자유를 얻지 못했을 것이라고 그렇게 빨리.

For," / said he, / "as flourishing a condition / as we may
왜냐하면," 그의 말은 이랬다, "매우 풍요로운 상황처럼 우리가 보일지 모르지만

appear to be in / to foreigners, / we labor under two mighty
외국인에게는, 우리는 두 가지 커다란 재앙을 겪고 있습니다:

audience 접견, 알현 | solicitation 청원 | conveniently 편리하게, 쉽게 | compliment 칭찬, 찬사 | agreeable
적합한, 알맞은 | administration 행정기관 | animosities 적개심 | compute 추정하다

94   Gulliver's Travels

evils: / a violent faction at home, / and the danger of an
국내의 격렬한 당파 싸움과, 침략의 위험입니다.

invasion, / by a most potent enemy, / from abroad. As to
매우 강력한 적국의, 바다 건너. 전자의 경우,

the first, / you are to understand, / that for about seventy
당신은 이해해야 합니다. 지난 70개월 동안

moons past / there have been two struggling parties /
두 개의 당파가 싸우고 있다는 것을

in this empire, / under the names of TRAMECKSAN
이 제국에서. 트라멕산 당과 슬라멕산 당이라 불리우는,

and SLAMECKSAN, / from the high and low heels of
이 이름은 그들의 신발 굽이 높고 낮은 것에서

their shoes, / by which they distinguish themselves. It is
유래했습니다. 서로를 식별하기 위하여. 주장되고

alleged, / indeed, / that the high heels are most agreeable
있습니다. 사실은, 높은 굽이 가장 적합하다고

/ to our ancient constitution; / but, / however this be, / his
우리의 고대 헌법에서는: 하지만, 그것이 어떻든,

majesty has determined / to make use only of low heels /
황제께서 결정하셨습니다 낮은 굽만을 사용하기로

in the administration of the government, / and all offices /
정부의 행정기관에서는. 모든 공식석상에서

in the gift of the crown, / as you cannot but observe; / and
황제가 부여하는. 당신도 보았듯이;

particularly that his majesty's imperial heels are / lower
특히 폐하의 굽은

at least by a DRURR / than any of his court / (DRURR
적어도 1드러는 낮습니다 궁정의 그 누구보다도

is a measure about the fourteenth part of an inch). The
(1드러는 1인치의 14분의 1 길이이다).

animosities between these two parties / run so high, / that
이 두 당파 간의 적개심은 매우 높아서,

they will neither eat, / nor drink, nor talk with each other.
그들은 절대 같이 먹지도 않고, 같이 마시지도, 이야기 하지도 않습니다.

We compute / the TRAMECKSAN, or high heels, / to
우리가 계산하기에 트라멕산, 또는 높은 굽 당이,

exceed us / in number; / but the power is / wholly on our
우리를 능가합니다 수 적으로는; 하지만 권력은 전적으로 우리 편에 있습니다.

side. We apprehend / his imperial highness, / the heir to the
우리는 알고 있습니다 황태자가, 왕위 계승자인,

crown, / to have some tendency / towards the high heels; /
기울어지고 있다고 높은 굽 당으로;

at least / we can plainly discover / that one of his heels is
적어도 우리는 분명히 볼 수 있습니다 그의 한쪽 발 굽이 다른 쪽보다 높아서,

higher than the other, / which gives him a hobble / in his
절룩거리는 것을 걸을 때.

gait. Now, / in the midst of these intestine disquiets, / we are
이제, 이러한 불안정한 소용돌이 속에서,

threatened with an invasion / from the island of Blefuscu, /
우리는 침공에 대한 위협을 받고 있습니다 블레프스큐 섬으로부터,

which is the other great empire of the universe, / almost as
그 나라는 세상에서 또 하나의 거대한 제국으로,

large and powerful / as this of his majesty. For as to what
크기와 국력에 있어 거의 맞먹습니다 우리와. 우리가 들은 바에 대해

we have heard / you affirm, / that there are other kingdoms
당신이 주장하는 것을, 이 세상에는 다른 왕국과 나라가 있다고

and states in the world / inhabited by human creatures as
당신의 크기와 같은 인간이 살고 있는,

large as yourself, / our philosophers are in much doubt, /
우리 학자들은 매우 회의적이며,

and would rather conjecture / that you dropped from the
그보다 추측하고 있습니다 당신이 달로부터 내려왔다고,

moon, / or one of the stars; / because it is certain, / that
혹은 별의 세계로부터; 왜냐하면 확실히,

a hundred mortals of your bulk / would in a short time
당신과 같은 큰 체격의 인간이 100명 있으면 순식간에 없애버릴 것이기에

destroy / all the fruits and cattle of his majesty's dominions:
이 제국에 있는 모든 과일과 가축을:

/ besides, / our histories of six thousand moons / make no
게다가, 6,000개월의 우리 역사에 아무 언급도 없습니다

plainly 분명히 | hobble 절뚝거리다 | gait 걸음걸이 | intestine 내부의 | disquiet 불안 | threaten 위협하다

mention / of any other regions / than the two great empires
다른 지역들에 대해   릴리펏과 블레스큐라는 양대 제국 외에는.

of Lilliput and Blefuscu.

Which two mighty powers have, / as I was going to tell
이 양대 강국은,   제가 말하고자 하는 것처럼,

you, / been engaged in a most obstinate war / for six-
매우 끈질긴 전쟁을 해 오고 있습니다

and-thirty moons past. It began / upon the following
지난 36개월 동안.   이것은 시작되었습니다   다음 사건 때문에.

occasion. It is allowed on all hands, / that the primitive
어디에서나 인정되고 있습니다.   달걀을 깨는 원래의 방법이,

way of breaking eggs, / before we eat them, / was upon
그것을 먹기 전에,   큰 쪽의 끝을 먼저

the larger end; / but his present majesty's grandfather, /
깬다는 것이;   그러나 현 황제의 할아버지께서,

while he was a boy, / going to eat an egg, / and breaking
어렸을 때,   달걀을 먹으려고,

it according to the ancient practice, / happened to cut
옛날 방식대로 깨다가,   손가락을 베이게 되었습니다.

one of his fingers. Whereupon / the emperor his father
그러자   부친인 황제께서

/ published an edict, / commanding all his subjects, /
포고령을 발표했습니다.   모든 신하에게 명령하는,

upon great penalties, / to break the smaller end of their
위반 시 엄벌에 처하며,   달걀의 작은 쪽 끝을 깨야 한다고.

eggs. The people so highly resented this law, / that our
사람들은 이 법에 매우 분노해서,

histories tell us, / there have been six rebellions raised /
우리의 역사책에 따르면,   여섯 번의 반란이 일어났습니다

on that account; / wherein / one emperor lost his life, /
그 일 때문에;   그 과정에서   한 황제는 목숨을 잃고,

and another his crown. These civil commotions / were
또 다른 황제는 제위를 상실했습니다.   이러한 국민들의 소요 사태는

constantly fomented / by the monarchs of Blefuscu; /
끊임없이 조장되었습니다   블레프스큐의 역대 황제들에 의해;

and when they were quelled, / the exiles always fled /
그래서 반란이 진압되면,   탈주자들은 언제나 도망쳤습니다

for refuge / to that empire. It is computed / that eleven
망명을 위해   블레프스큐로.   추정됩니다

thousand persons / have at several times / suffered
총 1만1천 명의 사람들이   여러 차례에 걸쳐   죽음을 감수했습니다.

death, / rather than submit / to break their eggs at the
굴복하는 대신   달걀의 작은 쪽을 깨는 파에.

smaller end. Many hundred large volumes / have been
수백 권의 책이   출판되었습니다

published / upon this controversy: / but the books of
이 논쟁에 관해서: 그러나 큰 쪽 깨기 파의 책은

the Big-endians / have been long forbidden, / and the
오랫동안 금지 되었고,

whole party rendered incapable / by law / of holding
이들은 모두 불가능 했습니다   법률에 의해   공직을 갖는 것이.

employments. During the course of these troubles, / the
이런 소동을 겪는 동안,

emperors of Blefuscu did frequently expostulate / by
블레프스큐의 황제들을 자주 충고했고

their ambassadors, / accusing us / of making a schism in
대사를 보내서,   우리를 비난했습니다 종교의 분열을 일으킨다고.

religion, / by offending against a fundamental doctrine /
우리의 근본 교리를 어김으로써

of our great prophet Lustrog, / in the fifty-fourth chapter
위대한 예언자 러스트록의,   블런데크랄의 54장에 있는

of the Blundecral / (which is their Alcoran). This, /
(그들의 성경을 말한다).   이것은,

however, / is thought to be a mere strain / upon the text;
그러나,   약간 왜곡했다고 생각됩니다   구절에 대해;

/ for the words are these: / 'that all true believers / break
왜냐하면 구절은 이렇습니다: '진실한 신자는   그들의

their eggs / at the convenient end.'
달걀을 깬다   편리한 쪽으로.'

---

obstinate 고집 센 | edict 포고 | rebellions 반란 | commotions 소요사태 | foment 조장하다 | quell 진압하다
| controversy 논란 | forbidden 금지된 | expostulate 충고하다 | fundamental 근본의 | doctrine 교리 |
prophet 예언자

And which is the convenient end, / seems, / in my
그리고 어디가 편리한 끝인지는,   ~인 것 같습니다,

humble opinion / to be left to every man's conscience,
내 얕은 생각으로는   각자의 양심에 있거나,

/ or at least in the power / of the chief magistrate to
적어도 결정권에 있다고   최고 위정자의,

determine. Now, / the Big-endian exiles / have found so
현재,   큰 쪽 깨기 파의 망명객들은   큰 신임을 받고 있고

much credit / in the emperor of Blefuscu's court, / and so
블레프스큐 황제의 궁궐에서,

much private assistance and encouragement / from their
수많은 사적인 원조와 격려를   국내에 있는 그들

party here at home, / that a bloody war has been carried
당파로부터 받고 있어서,   피비린내 나는 싸움이 계속되어 왔습니다

on / between the two empires / for six-and-thirty moons,
두 제국 간에   지난 36개월 동안,

/ with various success; / during which time / we have
승패를 거듭하며;   그 동안

lost forty capital ships, / and a much a greater number
우리는 40척의 대함정을 잃었고,   그보다 훨씬 더 많은 작은 선박과,

of smaller vessels, / together with thirty thousand of our
3만 명의 최정예 선원과 병사들을 잃었습니다;

best seamen and soldiers; / and the damage received by
그리고 적군이 입은 피해는

the enemy / is reckoned to be somewhat greater than
우리보다 약간 더 큰 것으로 추정됩니다.

ours. However, / they have now equipped a numerous
그러나,   그들은 지금 방대한 함대를 구축하고,

fleet, / and are just preparing / to make a descent upon
막 준비 중입니다   우리를 침공하려고;

us; / and his imperial majesty, / placing great confidence
그래서 황제는,   크게 신임하여

/ in your valor and strength, / has commanded me / to lay
당신의 용기와 힘을,   내게 명령하셨습니다

this account of his affairs before you.
이 문제를 당신에게 설명하라고.

I desired the secretary / to present my humble duty /
나는 대신에게 부탁했다   내 겸손한 충성을 전해 달라고

to the emperor; / and to let him know, / "that I thought
황제에게;   그리고 그에게 말해 달라고.   "나는 생각합니다

/ it would not become me, / who was a foreigner, / to
내게는 적합하지 않다고.   외국인으로서.

interfere with parties; / but I was ready, / with the hazard
당파 간의 문제에 개입하는 것은;   하지만 나는 준비됐습니다.

of my life, / to defend his person and state / against all
목숨을 바쳐서.   폐하의 신변과 나라를 지킬   모든 침략자로부터."

invaders."

Key Expression ♥

as의 다양한 쓰임

as는 전치사, 부사, 접속사 등 다양한 의미로 쓰이는 단어입니다. 자주 쓰이는 as
의 의미를 정리해 볼까요.

▶ 전치사 as
   ① ~처럼
   ② (자격·기능) ~로
▶ 부사 as
   ① ~만큼(as~as의 형태로 ~만큼 ~한)
   ② ~듯이
▶ 접속사 as
   ① ~하는 동안, ~할 때
   ② ~하는 대로
   ③ ~때문에
   ④ ~하듯이
   ⑤ ~이긴 하지만

ex) ···almost as large and powerful as this of his majesty. (~만큼)
    거의 왕국만큼 크고 강력한
    I could not enter, but only view them as I passed. (~하는 동안)
    나는 들어갈 수 없었고, 다만 지나가는 동안 그들을 볼 수 있었다.
    Reldresal, principal secretary (as they style him) (~하는 대로)
    궁내 대신(그들이 그를 부르는 바로는)인 렐드레살은
    ···as flourishing a condition as we may appear to be in to foreigners.
    (~이긴 하지만)
    우리가 외국인에게는 풍요로워 보일지 모르지만,
    ···as you cannot but observe; (~하듯이)
    당신이 볼 수밖에 없듯이;

magistrate 치안 판사 | equip 장비를 갖추다 | valor 용기 | interfere 개입하다 | with the hazard of ~을 걸고

mini test 4

A. 다음 문장을 해석해 보세요.

(1) The first request I made, / after I had obtained my liberty, / was, / that I might have license to see Mildendo, / the metropolis.
→

(2) I stepped over the great western gate, / and passed very gently, / only in my short waistcoat, / for fear of damaging / the roofs and eaves of the houses / with the skirts of my coat.
→

(3) I then / stept over the building very conveniently / from one stool to the other, / and drew up the first after me / with a hooked stick.
→

(4) It is computed / that eleven thousand persons / have at several times / suffered death, / rather than submit to break their eggs at the smaller end.
→

B. 다음 주어진 문구가 알맞은 문장이 되도록 순서를 맞춰 보세요.

(1) 내가 건물에 큰 손상을 주지 않고 <u>그것들을 넘어가는 것은 불가능</u> 했다.
(It was / impossible / for / me / to / stride / over / them)

_____ them without

infinite damage to the pile.

(2) 만약 궁궐이 처한 현재의 상황이 없었다면, 나는 그렇게 빨리 자유를 얻지 못했을지도 몰랐다.
(the present situation / had not been / if / of things / it / at court / for)

_____ , perhaps

I might not have obtained it so soon.

(3) <u>외국인에게는 매우 풍요로워 보일지 모르지만</u>, 우리는 두 가지 큰 재앙을 겪고 있습니다.

(to foreigners / we / a condition / be in / flourishing / as / may appear to / As)

_____, we

labor under two mighty evils.

(4) <u>그는 차라리</u> 우리가 대화하는 동안 <u>그를 내 손 위에 올려 달라고 선택했다</u>.

(rather / chose / He / me / him / to let / in my hand / hold)

_____ during

our conversation.

C. 다음 주어진 문장이 본문의 내용과 맞으면 T, 틀리면 F에 동그라미 하세요.

(1) The author was allowed to see the palace.
(T / F)

(2) The author described the metropolis in detail.
(T / F)

(3) The author is going to press a book about Liliput.
(T / F)

(4) The author rejected to participate the war between Lilliput and Blefuscu.
(T / F)

D. 의미가 비슷한 것끼리 서로 연결해 보세요.

(1) encompass   ▶   ◀ ① announcement

(2) anticipate   ▶   ◀ ② expect

(3) reserve   ▶   ◀ ③ surround

(4) edict   ▶   ◀ ④ save

5

The author, / by an extraordinary stratagem, / prevents
저자가,　　　　기상천외한 전략으로,

an invasion. A high title of honor is conferred / upon him.
침공을 막아낸다.　명예로운 호칭이 수여된다　　　　그에게.

Ambassadors arrive / from the emperor of Blefuscu, /
대사가 도착하여　　　　블레프스큐 황제로부터,

and sue for peace. The empress's apartment on fire / by
화친을 청한다.　　　황후의 거처에 화재가 발생한다

an accident; / the author instrumental / in saving the rest
사고로;　　　저자가 중요한 역할을 한다　　　궁궐의 나머지를 구하는데.

of the palace.

The empire of Blefuscu is an island / situated to the
블레프스큐 제국은 섬으로　　　　　　　릴리펏의 북동쪽에 위치한,

north-east of Lilliput, / from which it is parted / only by
분리되어 있다　　　　해협에 의해

a channel / of eight hundred yards wide. I had not yet
폭이 겨우 800야드 밖에 안 되는.　　　나는 아직 그것을 보지

seen it, / and upon this notice / of an intended invasion, /
못했고,　　통보를 받은 후　　침략 계획에 대한,

I avoided appearing / on that side of the coast, / for fear
나타나는 것을 삼갔다　　해변가에,　　　발견될까봐

of being discovered, / by some of the enemy's ships, /
걱정하여,　　　적의 함정에 의해,

who had received no intelligence of me; / all intercourse
나에 관한 정보가 전혀 없는:　　　모든 교류는

between the two empires / having been strictly forbidden
두 나라 간의　　엄격히 금지되었고

/ during the war, / upon pain of death, / and an embargo
전쟁 동안,　　위반자는 사형에 처해졌으며,　금지령이 내려졌다

laid / by our emperor / upon all vessels whatsoever. I
황제에 의해   모든 종류의 선박들에.

communicated to his majesty / a project I had formed
나는 황제에게 전했다   내가 생각해 낸 계획을

/ of seizing the enemy's whole fleet; / which, / as our
적의 함대를 송두리째 포획할;   한대는,   우리 정찰병이

scouts assured us, / lay at anchor in the harbor, / ready
확인한 바에 따르면,   항구에 정박 중이었다.   출항하려고

to sail / with the first fair wind. I consulted / the most
첫 순풍이 불면.   나는 조언을 구했다

experienced seamen / upon the depth of the channel, /
가장 경험 많은 선원들에게   해협의 깊이에 관해서,

which they had often plumbed; / who told me, / that in the
자주 측정해 본 적 있는;   그들은 말했다,   한복판의 깊이는,

middle, / at high-water, / it was seventy GLUMGLUFFS
만조 때,   70 글럼글러프라고.

deep, / which is about six feet / of European measure; /
이는 약 6피트이다   유럽의 척도로는;

and the rest of it fifty GLUMGLUFFS / at most. I walked
그리고 그 나머지는 50글럼글러프라고   기껏해야.

towards the north-east coast, / over against Blefuscu,
나는 북동쪽 해안으로 걸어가서,   블레프스큐가 내려다 보이는,

Key Expression

at most : 기껏해야

at most는 '많아 보았자', 즉 '기껏해야'라는 의미를 가진 숙어로, not more than과 같은 의미입니다. 비슷한 형태의 숙어들을 함께 알아봅니다.

▶ not more than : 기껏해야, 많아야 (=at most)
▶ no more than : 단지, ~일 뿐 (= only)
▶ not less than : 적어도 (=at least)
▶ no less than : ~만큼이나, 자그마치 (=as much as)

ex) …and the rest of it fifty GLUMGLUFFS at most.
그리고 그 나머지는 기껏해야 50글럼글러프이다.

/ where, lying down behind a hillock, / I took out my
작은 언덕에 누워서,　　　　　　　　　　내 소형 망원경을 꺼내어,

small perspective glass, / and viewed the enemy's fleet at
정박 중인 적의 함대를 관찰했다.

anchor, / consisting of about fifty men of war, / and a great
50척의 군함과,

number of transports: / I then came back to my house, /
수많은 수송선으로 구성된:　　　그리고 나서 집으로 돌아와서,

and gave orders / (for which I had a warrant) / for a great
요청했다　　　　（왜냐하면 나는 권한을 받았기 때문에)　　많은 양의

quantity / of the strongest cable and bars of iron. The
튼튼한 밧줄과 쇠막대기를.

cable was about as thick as packthread / and the bars of /
밧줄의 굵기는 짐 꾸리는 노끈 정도였고　　　　막대기는

the length and size of a knitting-needle. I trebled the cable
뜨개질 바늘만한 길이와 크기였다.　　　　나는 밧줄을 꼬았고

/ to make it stronger, / and for the same reason / I twisted
강도를 높이려고,　　　　　같은 이유로

three of the iron bars together, / bending the extremities /
세 개의 쇠막대기도 겹쳐서,　　　　　　그 끝을 구부렸다

into a hook. Having thus / fixed fifty hooks / to as many
갈고리 모양으로.　이렇게 해서　　50개의 갈고리를 고정시키고　같은 수의 밧줄에,

cables, / I went back to the north-east coast, / and putting
북동쪽 해안으로 다시 가서,

off my coat, shoes, and stockings, / walked into the sea,
코트, 신발, 양말을 벗고,　　　　　　바다 속으로 걸어 들어갔다,

/ in my leathern jerkin, / about half an hour before / high
가죽 조끼를 입은 채,　　　　30분쯤 전

water. I waded with / what haste I could, / and swam /
만조가 되기.　나는 물 속을 걸었다　가능한 한 빨리,　　　그리고 헤엄쳤다

in the middle / about thirty yards, / till I felt ground. I
한복판에서는　　　약 30야드를,　　　　발이 땅에 닿을 때까지.

arrived at the fleet / in less than half an hour. The enemy
나는 함대에 도달했다　　30분도 안 되어.

hillock 작은 언덕 | knitting-needle 뜨개질 바늘 | treble 3배로 만들다 | extremity 끝, 말단 | tackling 밧줄
| prow 뱃머리

was so frightened / when they saw me, / that they leaped
적군은 너무 놀라서　　　　　　나를 보자,　　　　　　배에서 뛰어내려,

out of their ships, / and swam to shore, / where there could
　　　　　　　　해안으로 헤엄쳤다,

not be fewer than thirty thousand souls. I then / took my
그곳에는 3만 명 이상 있는 것 같았다.　　　　　　나는 다음으로　준비한 밧줄을

tackling, / and, / fastening a hook to the hole / at the prow
꺼냈다.　　그리고,　구멍에 갈고리를 걸고　　　　　　각 배의 뱃머리에,

of each, / I tyed all the cords together / at the end.
　　모든 밧줄을 합쳐서 묶었다　　　그 한쪽 끝을.

While I was thus employed, / the enemy discharged
내가 이 작업을 하는 동안,　　　　　　　　　　적군은 수천 개의 화살을 발사했고,

several thousand arrows, / many of which stuck / in my
　　　　　　　　　　　그 중 많은 수가 박혔다

hands and face, / and, / beside the excessive smart, /
내 손과 얼굴에,　　　　그래서,　　　몹시 아팠을 뿐만 아니라,

gave me much disturbance / in my work. My greatest
꽤 방해가 됐다　　　　　　　　내 작업에.

apprehension was for mine eyes, / which I should have
내가 제일 염려한 것은 눈으로,　　　　　　나는 분명히 실명했을 것이다.

infallibly lost, / if I had not suddenly thought of an
　　　　　　　　만약 갑자기 좋은 생각이 나지 않았다면.

expedient. I kept, / among other little necessaries, / a
　　　　나는 지녔었다.　　다른 사소한 일용품 중에,

pair of spectacles / in a private pocket, / which, / as I
안경을　　　　　　　비밀 주머니 속에,　　　　그리고 그것은,

observed before, / had escaped the emperor's searchers.
앞서 말했듯이,　　　　황제의 검사관들을 피했었다.

These I took out and fastened / as strongly as I could /
나는 이것을 꺼내어 고정시켰다　　　　　가능한 한 단단하게

upon my nose, / and thus armed, / went on boldly with
내 코에,　　　　이렇게 방어를 갖춘 후,　　대담하게 일을 계속했다.

my work, / in spite of the enemy's arrows, / many of
　　　　　　　　　적의 화살에도 불구하고,

which struck / against the glasses of my spectacles, /
화살을 많이 맞았으나　　내 안경알에,

but without any other effect, / further than a little to
별 다른 영향은 없었다　　　　　　　약간 불편했던 것 외에는.

discompose them. I had now fastened all the hooks, /
　　　　　　　　　드디어 갈고리를 다 걸었고,

and, / taking the knot in my hand, / began to pull; / but
그리고 나서,　묶은 매듭을 한 손에 쥐고,　　　잡아당기기 시작했다;　　그러나

not a ship would stir, / for they were all too fast held /
단 한 척의 배도 움직이지 않았다,　　모두 너무 단단하게 고정되어 있었기 때문에

---

disturbance 방해 | infallibly 확실히, 분명히 | boldly 용감하게 | discompose 안정을 잃게 하다, 뒤흔들다 |
knot 매듭 | resolutely 단호하게, 대담하게

their anchors, / so that the boldest part / of my enterprise
닻에 의해,　　그 때문에 가장 대담한 부분이　　내 작업의

/ remained. I therefore let go the cord, / and leaving the
남았다.　　그래서 나는 밧줄을 놓고,　　갈고리를 배에 건 채,

looks fixed to the ships, / I resolutely cut with my knife /
칼로 단호하게 잘라버렸다

the cables that fastened the anchors, / receiving about two
닻에 매여 있는 줄을.　　200발 이상의 화살을 맞으며

hundred shots / in my face and hands; / then I took up the
손과 얼굴에;

knotted end of the cables, / to which my hooks were tied, /
그리고 나서 밧줄의 매듭을 잡고서,　　갈고리가 매여 있는.

and with great ease / drew fifty of the enemy's largest men
매우 손쉽게　　가장 큰 적의 군함 50척을 끌었다.

of war after me.

Key Expression ♥

as strongly as I could : 가능한 한 단단하게
'as + 형용사/부사 + as + 주어 + can'은 '가능한 한 ~한(하게)'라는 의미를 가진
구문입니다. 여기에서 '주어 + can'은 possible로 바꾸어 쓸 수 있습니다.

ex) These I took out and fastened as strongly as I could upon my nose.
　　나는 이것을 꺼내어 가능한 한 단단하게 내 코에 고정시켰다.

The Blefuscudians, / who had not the least imagination
블레프스큐 인들은,   전혀 상상도 못해서

/ of what I intended, / were at first / confounded with
내가 무엇을 하려는지,   처음에는   놀라서 우왕좌왕 했었다.

astonishment. They had seen me cut the cables, / and
그들은 내가 밧줄 자르는 것을 보고,

thought / my design was / only to let the ships run adrift /
생각했다   나의 계획은   다만 군함들을 바다에 떠내려 보내거나

or fall foul on each other: / but when they perceived / the
서로 부딪치게 하려는 것이라고: 그러나 알았을 때

whole fleet moving in order, / and saw / me pulling at the
함대 전체가 질서 있게 움직이는 걸,   그리고 봤을 때 내가 그 앞에서 끌고 가는 걸,

end, / they set up such a scream / of grief and despair / as
그들은 비명을 질렀다   큰 슬픔과 절망의

it is almost impossible to describe or conceive. When I
형언할 수 없을 정도로.

had got out of danger, / I stopped awhile / to pick out the
위험에서 벗어나자,   나는 잠시 멈춰 서서   화살을 뽑아내고

arrows / that stuck in my hands and face; / and rubbed on
얼굴과 손에 박힌;

some of the same ointment / that was given me / at my first
연고를 약간 문질러 발랐다   받았던   처음 이곳에

arrival, / as I have formerly mentioned. I then took off my
왔을 때,   앞서 말했듯이.   그리고 나서 안경을 벗고,

spectacles, / and waiting about an hour, / till the tide was a
약 한 시간 동안 기다리다가,   밀물이 약간 빠질 때까지,

little fallen, / I waded through the middle / with my cargo,
해협의 중심부를 건너서   그 짐들을 끌며,

/ and arrived safe / at the royal port of Lilliput.
무사히 도착했다   릴리펏의 항구에.

---

adrift 표류하다 | hostile 적의, 적군의 | puissant 권력 있는, 강세한

The emperor and his whole court stood / on the shore, /
황제와 그의 모든 신하들은 서 있었다   해안가에,

expecting the issue of this great adventure. They saw the
이 대 모험의 결과를 기대하면서.   그들은 배들이 전진하

ships move forward / in a large half-moon, / but could not
는 것을 보았으나   커다란 반달형 대열로,

discern me, / who was up to my breast in water. When
나를 발견하지 못했다, 가슴까지 물 속에 있었기 때문에.

I advanced to the middle of the channel, / they were yet
내가 해협의 한복판에 도착했을 때,   그들은 더욱 괴로워 했다.

more in pain, / because I was under water to my neck.
            왜냐하면 내가 목까지 물에 잠겼기 때문에.

The emperor concluded / me to be drowned, / and that
황제는 결론 지었다   내가 물에 빠져 죽었고,

the enemy's fleet was approaching / in a hostile manner:
적 함대가 다가 오고 있으니   공격하려고:

/ but he was soon eased of his fears; / for the channel
    그러나 그는 곧 두려움에서 벗어났다: 해협이 얕아졌기 때문에

growing shallower / every step I made, / I came in a
내가 발걸음을 옮길 때마다,

short time within hearing, / and holding up the end of the
나는 곧 소리가 들리는 곳까지 왔고,   밧줄의 끝을 쳐들며,

cable, / by which the fleet was fastened, / I cried in a loud
        함대가 묶여 있는,   큰 소리로 외쳤다,

voice, / "Long live the most puissant king of Lilliput!"
        "가장 강력하신 릴리펏 황제 만세!"

This great prince received me / at my landing / with all
황제는 나를 맞이했다   내가 상륙하자

possible encomiums, / and created me a NARDAC / upon
온갖 찬사로,   그리고 내게 나르닥 작위를 수여했다

the spot, / which is the highest title of honor among them.
즉석에서,   그것은 그 나라에서 최고의 명예 호칭이다.

His majesty desired / I would take some other opportunity
황제는 바랐다   내가 또 한 번 시도하기를

/ of bringing all the rest of his enemy's ships / into his
남아 있는 적의 함대를 모두 끌고 오도록   그의 항구로.

ports. And so unmeasureable is the ambition of princes,
그리고 황제의 야망은 끝이 없어서,

/ that he seemed to think of / nothing less than reducing
그는 생각하는 것 같았다   다름 아닌 정복만을

/ the whole empire of Blefuscu into a province, / and
블레프스큐 제국 전체를 자신의 영토로 하고,

governing it, / by a viceroy; / of destroying the Big-endian
통치하는 것을,   총독으로 하여금;   그리고 큰 쪽 깨기 파의 망명자들을 죽이고,

exiles, / and compelling that people / to break the smaller
사람들에게 강요하는 것을   작은 쪽 끝으로 달걀을 깨도록,

end of their eggs, / by which he would remain the sole
유일한 군주가 되어서

monarch / of the whole world. But I endeavoured to divert
전 세계의.   그러나 나는 그를 설득했다

him / from this design, / by many arguments drawn /
그 야망을 버리도록,   많은 이유를 들어

from the topics of policy as well as justice; / and I plainly
정의 뿐 아니라 정책적인 면에서;   그리고 나는 분명히

protested, / "that I would never be an instrument / of
선언했다,   "나는 결코 협력하지 않겠다

bringing a free and brave people into slavery." And, / when
자유롭고 용감한 국민을 노예로 삼는 것에"라고.   그리고,

the matter was debated in council, / the wisest part of the
이 문제가 궁정 회의에서 논의되었을 때,   현명한 대신들은

ministry / were of my opinion.
나와 같은 생각이었다.

This open bold declaration of mine was / so opposite / to
이렇게 공개적이고 대담한 나의 선언은   정반대였다

the schemes and politics / of his imperial majesty, / that
계획과 정책에   황제 폐하의,

he could never forgive me. He mentioned it / in a very
그래서 그는 나를 결코 용서할 수 없었다.   그는 이것을 언급했다   매우 교묘하게

artful manner / at council, / where I was told that / some
궁정 회의에서,   그곳에서 내가 들은 바에 의하면

of the wisest appeared, / at least by their silence, / to be of
일부 현명한 대신들은 표현했다.   최소한 침묵을 지킴으로써,   내 의견에

my opinion; / but others, / who were my secret enemies,
동조하는 것을;   하지만 다른 사람들은, 비밀스런 나의 적들인,

/ could not forbear some expressions / which, / by a side-
발언을 참지 못했고   그것은,   넌지시,

wind, / reflected on me. And from this time / began an
나를 비난했다.   그리고 이때부터   음모가 시작되었다

intrigue / between his majesty and a junto of ministers,
황제와 대신들 간에,

/ maliciously bent against me, / which broke out / in less
내게 악의를 품은,   그것은 표면화 되었고

than two months, / and had like to have ended / in my utter
두 달이 채 지나지 않아,   끝날 뻔 했다   내게 완전한 파멸

destruction. Of so little weight / are the greatest services
을 주며.   그렇게 너무나 가벼워졌다   황제에 대한 엄청난 공헌은,

to princes, / when put into the balance / with a refusal / to
저울질 하면   거절함과

gratify their passions.
그들의 열정을 충족시키기에.

Key Expression ❢

nothing less than : 다름 아닌 바로
nothing less than은 '다름 아닌 바로, 그야말로'라는 의미를 가진 숙어입니다.
less than과 의미를 구별하여 기억하세요.

ex) He seemed to think of nothing less than reducing the whole empire of Blefuscu
into a province.
그는 다름 아닌 블레프스큐 제국의 모든 영토를 자신의 영토로 정복하는 것만을
생각하는 것 같았다.
And from this time began an intrigue between his majesty and a junto of
ministers, maliciously bent against me, which broke out in less than two months.
그리고 이때부터 황제와 내게 악의를 품은 대신들 간의 음모가 시작되었고, 그것은
두 달이 채 지나지 않아 표면화 되었다.

unmeasureable 극도의, 과도의 | viceroy 총독 | endeavour 설득하다 | bold 대담한 | declaration 선언 |
scheme 계략 | intrigue 음모 | side-wind 간접적인 공격 | junto 당파 | maliciously 악의적인

About three weeks after this exploit, / there arrived a
이런 공적을 세운 뒤 약 3주 후에, 격식을 차린 사절단이 도착했다

solemn embassy / from Blefuscu, / with humble offers of
블레프스큐로부터, 공손히 평화를 청하면서,

a peace, / which was soon concluded, / upon conditions /
그것은 곧 체결되었다. 조건으로

very advantageous to our emperor, / wherewith / I shall
우리 황제에게 매우 유리한, 이것으로 독자 여러분을

not trouble the reader. There were six ambassadors, / with
번거롭게 하지는 않겠다. 여섯 명의 대사가,

a train of about five hundred persons, / and their entry was
약 500명의 수행원과 함께 왔는데, 그들의 등장은 매우 화려해서,

very magnificent, / suitable to / the grandeur of their master,
어울렸다 그들의 군주의 위엄과,

/ and the importance of their business. When their treaty
그들의 임무의 중요성에. 조약의 체결될 때,

was finished, / wherein I did them several good offices /
그것에 나는 여러 가지 도움이 되었다

by the credit I now had, / or at least appeared to have, / at
내가 그때 갖게 된 신임으로, 혹은 적어도 갖게 된 것처럼 보였던.

court, / their excellencies, / who were privately told / how
궁정에서, 그 대사들은, 은밀히 듣고서

much I had been their friend, / made me a visit in form.
내가 그들에게 얼마나 우호적인지를, 공식적으로 나를 방문했다.

They began with many compliments / upon my valour and
그들은 많은 찬사의 말로 대화를 시작했고 내 용기와 너그러움에 대해,

generosity, / invited me to that kingdom / in the emperor
나를 그들의 나라에 초대했다 자신들의 황제 폐하의

their master's name, / and desired me to show them / some
이름으로, 그리고 내게 보여 달라고 부탁했다

proofs of my prodigious strength, / of which they had heard
나의 굉장한 능력에 대한 몇 가지 증거를, 그들이 전해 들은

/ so many wonders; / wherein I readily obliged them, / but
수많은 놀라운 사실들 중에서; 나는 흔쾌히 그 요구를 승낙했다,

shall not trouble the reader / with the particulars.
하지만 독자 여러분을 지루하게 하지 않겠다 그 자세한 내용으로.

When I had for some time / entertained their excellencies,
내가 얼마 동안 그 사절단을 즐겁게 해 주자,

/ to their infinite satisfaction and surprise, / I desired / they
그들은 매우 만족하고 놀라워 했다. 나는 부탁했다

would do me the honor / to present my most humble respects
영광을 베풀어 달라고 내 겸허한 경의를 전하는

/ to the emperor their master, / the renown of whose virtues
그들의 황제에게, 그 군주의 덕망에 관한 명성은

/ had so justly filled the whole world / with admiration, / and
당연히 전 세계를 벅차게 했으며 경탄으로,

whose royal person / I resolved to attend, / before I returned
그런 폐하를 뵙기로 결심했다. 고국으로 돌아가기 전에.

to my own country. Accordingly, / the next time / I had the
따라서, 다음 번

honor to see our emperor, / I desired his general license / to
우리 폐하를 보게 되었을 때, 나는 그에게 허가를 부탁했다

wait on the Blefuscudian monarch, / which he was pleased
블레프스큐의 군주를 만나기 위한, 그는 흔쾌히 승낙했으나,

to grant me, / as I could perceive, / in a very cold manner;
내가 느끼기에, 매우 냉정한 태도였다:

/ but could not guess the reason, / till I had a whisper /
하지만 그 이유를 짐작할 수 없었다, 귓속말로 들을 때까지는

from a certain person, / "that Flimnap and Bolgolam had
누군가에게, "플림냅과 볼고람이 말했다고

represented / my intercourse with those ambassadors / as a
나의 그 대사들과의 교류가

mark of disaffection;" / from which I am sure / my heart was
반역을 의도하는 증거라고;" 하지만 그 점에 대해 확신하건대 나는 절대 그럴 마음이

wholly free. And this was the first time / I began to conceive
없었다. 그리고 이때 처음으로 나는 품기 시작했다

/ some imperfect idea / of courts and ministers.
좋지 않은 생각을 궁정 사람들과 대신들에 대해.

---

wherewith 그것으로 | entry 등장 | treaty 조약 | privately 남몰래, 은밀히 | infinite 무한한 | intercourse
교제 | imperfect 불완전한, 결함이 있는

It is to be observed, / that these ambassadors spoke to
언급해야 할 것이다.   대사들이 내게 말했다는 것을,

me, / by an interpreter, / the languages of both empires /
통역을 통해서.   두 나라의 언어는

differing as much from each other / as any two in Europe,
서로 많이 달랐다   유럽의 어떤 두 나라의 언어만큼이나,

/ and each nation priding itself / upon the antiquity,
그리고 양국은 자부심을 갖고 있어서   전통, 아름다움, 에너지에 대해

beauty, and energy / of their own tongue, / with an avowed
자신들의 언어의.   노골적으로 멸시했다

contempt / for that of their neighbor; / yet our emperor, /
상대방의 언어에 대해;   그러나 우리 황제는,

standing upon the advantage / he had got by the seizure
유리한 입장에 서게 된   자신이 그들의 함대를 점령했다는,

of their fleet, / obliged them / to deliver their credentials,
그들에게 강요했다   신임장을 제출할 것과,

/ and make their speech, / in the Lilliputian tongue. And
대화할 것을,   릴리펏 말로.

it must be confessed, / that from the great intercourse /
그리고 고백하자면,   교류가 많았고

of trade and commerce / between both realms, / from the
무역과 상업상   양국 간에,

continual reception of exiles / which is mutual among
끊임없이 망명자를 받아들였기 때문에   서로 상대방의 나라에서,

them, / and from the custom, / in each empire, / to send
그리고 관행이 있었기 때문에,   양국 간에,

their young nobility and richer gentry to the other, / in
젊은 귀족들과 부유층 자제들을 보내는,

order to polish themselves / by seeing the world, / and
교양을 쌓기 위해서   세계를 보고

understanding men and manners; / there are few persons
사람들과 풍습을 이해함으로써;   그래서 사람은 거의 없었다,

/ of distinction, or merchants, or seamen, / who dwell in
상류층, 상인, 또는 선원들,

the maritime parts, / but what can hold conversation / in
또는 해안 지역 주민들 중에는,   대화할 수 없는 사람이;

both tongues; / as I found some weeks after, / when I went
두 나라의 언어를 모두; 수 주 후에 내가 발견한 것에 따르면, 알현하러 갔을 때

to pay my respects / to the emperor of Blefuscu, / which, /
블레프스큐 황제를, 그러나 그 사건은,

in the midst of great misfortunes, / through the malice of
엄청난 불행에 놓이게 되었다. 내 정적들의 악의에 의해,

my enemies, / proved a very happy adventure to me, / as I
내게는 매우 즐거운 모험이었지만,

shall relate / in its proper place.
이는 다시 이야기 하겠다. 적당한 곳에서.

antiquity 전통 | maritime 해안 가까이 사는

The reader may remember, / that when I signed those
독자 여러분은 기억할 것이다,   내가 조항에 서명했을 때

articles / upon which I recovered my liberty, / there were
          내 자유 회복에 대한,

some which I disliked, / upon account of their being too
내가 싫어했던 것이 있었다,   너무 굴욕적이었기 때문에;

servile; / neither could anything / but an extreme necessity
아무것도 할 수 없었다   절대적인 필요성 때문에 순응하는 것 밖에.

have forced me to submit. But being now a NARDAC of
                    그러나 이제는 가장 높은 계급인 나르닥이 되었으니

the highest rank / in that empire, / such offices were looked
                    그 나라에서,   그러한 일은 내 품위에 어긋나는 것으로

upon as below my dignity, / and the emperor / (to do him
보였고,   폐하도   (공정하게 하기 위해),

justice), / never once mentioned them to me. However, / it
              한 번도 그것을 언급하지 않았다.   그러나,

was not long before / I had an opportunity / of doing his
얼마 안 되어서   기회가 생겼다   황제를 위해 일할,

majesty, / at least as I then thought, / a most signal service.
              적어도 그때 내가 생각하기로는,   아주 귀중한 봉사를.

I was alarmed at midnight / with the cries of many hundred
나는 한밤중에 놀랐다   수백 명의 사람들의 고함에

people / at my door; / by which, / being suddenly awaked, /
내 집 문 앞에서;   그 소리에,   갑자기 깨어나서,

I was in some kind of terror. I heard the word BURGLUM
일종의 공포에 빠졌다.   나는 '버글럼'이란 단어가 되풀이되는 것을 들었다:

repeated incessantly: / several of the emperor's court, /
                    황제의 궁전에서 온 사람들이,

making their way through the crowd, / entreated me /
군중을 뚫고 나와서,   내게 간청했다

to come immediately to the palace, / where her imperial
즉시 궁전으로 와 달라고,

majesty's apartment was on fire, / by the carelessness of a
황후 마마의 거처에 불이 났다는 것이다,   한 시녀의 부주의로 인해,

incessantly 끊임없는 | carelessness 부주의한 | fall asleep 잠들다 | trample 밟다 | bucket 물통 | thimble
골무 | stifle 끄다 | deplorable 한탄스러운 | infallibly 틀림없이 | plentifully 많이

maid of honor, / who fell asleep / while she was reading a
잠이 들어버린   연애소설을 읽다가.

romance. I got up in an instant; / and orders being given
나는 즉시 일어섰다: 명령이 내려졌고

/ to clear the way before me, / and it being likewise a
내 앞길을 가로 막지 말라는.   달빛이 비추이는 밤이어서.

moonshine night, / I made a shift to get to the palace /
나는 궁정으로 향했다

without trampling on any of the people. I found they had
아무도 밟지 않고.   나는 그들이 이미 사다리를

already applied ladders / to the walls of the apartment, /
설치한 것을 발견했다   거처의 벽에.

and were well provided with buckets, / but the water was at
그리고 물이 채워진 물통이 마련되었다.   하지만 물까지는 상당한 거리였다.

some distance. These buckets were about the size of large
이 물통들은 큰 골무 정도의 크기였는데.

thimbles, / and the poor people supplied me with them / as
불쌍한 사람들은 내게 그것을 갖다 주었다

fast as they could: / but the flame was so violent / that they
가능한 한 빨리: 그러나 불꽃이 너무 강해서

did little good. I might easily have stifled it with my coat, /
그것은 별로 소용 없었다. 내 코트로 쉽게 불을 끌 수 있었겠지만.

which I unfortunately left behind me for haste, / and came
불행히도 서두르느라 그걸 놓아둔 채.

away only in my leathern jerkin. The case seemed wholly
가죽 조끼만 입고 왔다.

desperate and deplorable; / and this magnificent palace
사태는 아주 절망적이고 한탄스러웠다:

would have infallibly been burnt down to the ground, / if, /
그리고 이 화려한 궁전은 틀림없이 잿더미가 될 터였다.   만약,

by a presence of mind unusual to me, / I had not suddenly
내가 보통 때와 달리 서두르지 않고 침착하게.

thought of an expedient. I had, / the evening before, / drunk
갑자기 묘안을 떠올리지 않았더라면.   나는,   그 전 날 밤,

plentifully of a most delicious wine / called GLIMIGRIM,
매우 맛 좋은 포도주를 많이 마셨다   글리미그림이라 불리우는.

/ (the Blefuscudians call it FLUNEC, / but ours is
(블레프스큐 사람들은 이것을 플루넥이라 불렀는데,   우리 것이 인정되어 있었다

esteemed / the better sort,) / which is very diuretic. By
더 좋은 종류로,)   그리고 그것은 이뇨 작용이 매우 강했다.

the luckiest chance in theworld, / I had not discharged
매우 다행스럽게도   나는 아직 배출하지 않았다

myself / of any part of it. The heat I had contracted / by
그것을 조금도.   내가 받은 열과

coming very near the flames, / and by laboring to quench
불꽃에 바짝 다가선 영향으로,   그것을 끄려는 노력으로,

them, / made the wine begin to operate / by urine; /
포도주가 나오기 시작했다   소변으로;

which I voided in such a quantity, / and applied so well
나는 엄청난 양을 방출했고,   그것이 작용하여

/ to the proper places, / that in three minutes / the fire
적절한 장소에,   3분 만에   불은 완전히 꺼졌고,

was wholly extinguished, / and the rest of that noble pile,
        귀중한 건축물의 나머지도,

/ which had cost so many ages in erecting, / preserved
여러 세대 걸쳐서 건축된,   파괴로부터 지켜냈다.

from destruction.

Key Expression♟

it is not long before : 머지 않아

it is not long before~는 '~머지 않아, 곧'이라는 의미의 구문으로 before
long이나 soon과 같은 뜻을 가지고 있습니다. 여기에서 before는 시간의 접속
사로 쓰였으며 주로 시제에 따라 다음과 같이 사용합니다.

▶ it won't be long before S + 현재V ~ : 머지않아 ~할 것이다
  (시간의 부사절이므로 현재 시제가 미래를 대신)

▶ it was not long before S + 과거V ~ : 오래지 않아 ~했다

ex) It was not long before I had an opportunity of doing his majesty.
  오래지 않아 황제에게 도움이 될 기회가 생겼다.

It was now day-light, / and I returned to my house /
이제 날이 밝았고,　　　　　　나는 집으로 돌아왔다

without waiting / to congratulate with the emperor: /
기다리지도 않고　　　황제에게 축하하기 위해:

because, / although I had done / a very eminent piece
왜냐하면,　　비록 내가 했으나　　　매우 훌륭한 일을,

of service, / yet I could not tell / how his majesty might
알 수 없었기 때문에　　황제가 얼마나 분개할지

resent / the manner by which I had performed it: / for,
내가 일을 처리한 방법으로 인해:　　　　　　왜냐하면,

/ by the fundamental laws of the realm, / it is capital /
이 나라 기본법에 의하면,　　　　　　중형이기 때문에

in any person, / of what quality soever, / to make water
누구라도,　　어떠한 신분이든,　　　소변을 보면,

/ within the precincts of the palace. But I was a little
궁정 경내에서　　　　　　　그러나 나는 조금 안심했다

comforted / by a message from his majesty, / "that he
황제의 전갈에 의하면,

would give orders / to the grand justiciary / for passing
"황제는 명령했다　　대법관에게

my pardon in form:" / which, however, / I could not
내게 사면장을 내리라"고:　　그러나 그것을,　　나는 받지 못했고:

obtain; / and I was privately assured, / "that the empress,
은밀히 들었다,　　　　　　"황후가,

/ conceiving the greatest abhorrence / of what I had done,
극도의 혐오감을 느껴서　　　　　　내가 한 일에 대해서,

/ removed to the most distant side of the court, / firmly
궁궐의 제일 먼 쪽으로 이사했고,　　　　　단호하게

resolved / that those buildings should never be repaired /
결심했다고　　그 건물들을 수리하지 않겠다고

for her use: / and, / in the presence of her chief confidents
다시 사용하기 위해: 그리고, 그녀의 심복들이 있는 데에서

/ could not forbear vowing revenge."
복수를 맹세하는 것을 삼가지 않았다"라고.

esteem 인정하다 | flame 불꽃 | quench (타는 불을) 끄다 | void 비워내다 | extinguish 불을 끄다 | eminent
훌륭한 | justiciary 대법관 | vow 맹세하다 | revenge 복수

mini test 5

A. 다음 문장을 해석해 보세요.

(1) I communicated to his majesty / a project I had formed / of seizing the enemy's whole fleet.

→

(2) The enemy was so frightened / when they saw me, / that they leaped out of their ships, / and swam to shore.

→

(3) While I was thus employed, / the enemy discharged several thousand arrows, / many of which stuck / in my hands and face, / and, / beside the excessive smart, / gave me much disturbance / in my work.

→

(4) So unmeasureable is the ambition of princes, / that he seemed to think of / nothing less than reducing / the whole empire of Blefuscu into a province.

→

B. 다음 주어진 문장이 되도록 빈칸에 써 넣으세요.

(1) 나는 <u>적의 함정에 의해 발견될까봐 걱정하여</u> 해변가에 등장하는 것을 삼갔다.

I avoided appearing on that side of the coast, ⬚

⬚.

(2) <u>만약 갑자기 좋은 생각이 나지 않았다면</u>, 나는 분명히 실명했을 것이다.

Which I should have infallibly lost, ⬚

⬚.

(3) 블레프스큐 인들은, 내가 뭘 하려는지 전혀 상상도 못 해서, 처음에는 놀라서 우왕좌왕 했었다.

The Blefuscudians, ⬚

⬚, were at first confounded with astonishment.

`Answer`

A. (1) 적의 함대를 송두리째 포획한다는 내가 생각해 낸 계획을 황제에게 전했다. (2) 적군은 나를 보자 너무 놀라서, 배에서 뛰어내려, 해안으로 헤엄쳤다. (3) 내가 이 작업을 하는 동안, 적군은 수천 개의 화살을 발사했고, 그중 많은 수가 내 손과 얼굴에 박혔다. 그래서, 몹시 아팠을 뿐만 아니라, 작업에 꽤 방해가 됐다. (4) 황제의 야망은 끝이 없어서,

(4) 그러나, 얼마 안 되어서 황제를 위해 일할 기회가 생겼다, 적어도 그때 내가 생각하기로는, 가장 중요한 일이었다.

However, ＿＿＿＿＿＿＿＿＿＿＿＿＿＿＿＿＿＿＿＿＿＿, at least as I then thought, a most signal service.

C. 다음 주어진 문구가 알맞은 문장이 되도록 순서를 맞춰 보세요.

(1) 나는 이것을 꺼내서 가능한 한 단단하게 내 코에 고정시켰다.
(could / strongly / as / my nose / as / I / upon)
→ These I took out and ＿＿＿＿＿＿＿＿＿＿＿＿＿＿.

(2) 그들은 내가 밧줄 자르는 것을 보고 내 계획이 다만 군함들을 바다로 떠내려 보내는 것이라고 생각했다.
(let / to / adrift / only / run / the ships)
→ They had seen me cut the cables, and thought my design was ＿＿＿＿＿＿＿＿＿＿＿＿.

(3) 황제는 내가 물에 빠져 죽었다고 결론 내렸다.
(me / be / concluded / The emperor / drowned / to)
→ ＿＿＿＿＿＿＿＿＿＿＿＿＿＿＿＿＿＿＿

(4) 절대적인 필요성 때문에 순응하는 것밖에 아무것도 할 수 없었다.
(anything / Neither / but / could)
→ ＿＿＿＿＿＿＿＿＿＿＿＿＿＿＿＿ an extreme necessity have forced me to submit.

D. 다음 단어에 대한 맞는 설명과 연결해 보세요.

(1) embargo ▶ ◀ ① try very hard
(2) endeavour ▶ ◀ ② official announcement
(3) declaration ▶ ◀ ③ forbid trade
(4) intrigue ▶ ◀ ④ making of secret plans

6

Of the inhabitants of Lilliput; / their learning, laws, and
릴리펏 주민에 대해 묘사;   그들의 학문, 법률, 관습에 관해;

customs; / the manner of educating their children. The
그들의 자녀 교육 방법에 대해.

author's way of living / in that country. His vindication of
저자의 생활 방식   그 나라에서의.   한 귀부인에 대한 그의 변호.

a great lady.

Although I intend to leave / the description of this empire
비록 남겨둘 생각이지만   이 제국에 대한 자세한 설명은

/ to a particular treatise, / yet, / in the mean time, / I am
별도의 논문을 위해.   그러나,   그 사이에,

content to gratify / the curious reader / with some general
기쁘게 해 주고 싶다   호기심 많은 독자 여러분을   몇 가지 대략적인 설명으로.

ideas. As the common size of the natives / is somewhat
주민들의 평균 키는

under six inches high, / so there is an exact proportion
6인치보다 약간 작으며,   그래서 정확히 비례한다

/ in all other animals, / as well as plants and trees: / for
기타 모든 동물의 크기도,   식물과 나무뿐 아니라:

instance, / the tallest horses and oxen are / between
예를 들어,   가장 큰 말과 소는

four and five inches in height, / the sheep an inch and
키가 4와 5인치 사이이고,   양은 약 1인치 반 정도이며,

half, / more or less: / their geese about the bigness of a
거의: 그곳 거위는 우리의 참새 크기만 했다.

sparrow, / and so the several gradations downwards /
그렇게 점점 작아져서

till you come to the smallest, / which to my sight, / were
가장 작은 것에 이르면,   내 눈에는,

almost invisible; / but nature has adapted / the eyes of
거의 안 보이게 된다;   그러나 자연은 조절해 주었다   릴리펏인들의 눈을

the Lilliputians / to all objects proper for their view: / they
모든 것을 볼 수 있도록:

see with great exactness, / but at no great distance. And, /
그들은 아주 정확하게 볼 수 있으나,   먼 거리는 잘 볼 수 없다.   그래서,

to show the sharpness of their sight / towards objects that
그들 시력의 예민함을 보여 주면   가까운데 있는 물체에 대해,

are near, / I have been much pleased / with observing / a
나는 매우 감탄했었다   보면서

cook pulling a lark, / which was not so large as a common
요리사가 종달새의 깃털을 뽑거나,   일반 파리 크기보다도 작은:

fly; / and a young girl threading / an invisible needle / with
또는 어린 소녀가 바느질을 할 때   보이지 않는 바늘과

invisible silk. Their tallest trees are / about seven feet high:
보이지 않는 비단실로. 제일 큰 나무는   높이가 약 7피트 정도이다:

/ I mean some of those in the great royal park, / the tops
황실대공원에 있는 나무들 말인데.

whereof / I could but just reach / with my fist clenched. The
그 꼭대기는   내가 겨우 닿을 수 있었다   손을 쭉 뻗어야.

other vegetables are in the same proportion; / but this / I
다른 식물들도 같은 비율이지만: 이것은

leave to the reader's imagination.
독자의 상상에 맡기겠다.

Key Expression

not so[as] ~ as… : …만큼 ~하지 않다
동등한 두 개의 대상을 비교할 때 쓰는 원급비교(동등비교)에는 as ~ as가 사용
됩니다. 하지만 여기에 not이 삽입되면 비교의 의미를 가지게 됩니다.

▶A is as ~ as B : A = B
▶A is not as/so ~ as B : A < B

ex) I have been much pleased with observing a cook pulling a lark, which was
   not so large as a common fly.
   └ (=smaller than)
   나는 요리사가 일반 파리보다도 작은 종달새의 깃털을 뽑는 것을 보고 감탄했었다.

---

vindication 변호 | gratify 만족하다 | sparrow 참새 | gradation 단계적 차이 | exactness 정확함 | invisible
보이지 않는 | whereof ~에 대해

I shall say but little / at present / of their learning, / which,
조금만 얘기하겠다   지금은   그들의 학문에 대해서는,

for many ages, / has flourished in all its branches among
오랜 시대 동안,   모든 분야에서 번성해 온:

them: / but their manner of writing is very peculiar, / being
그러나 그들의 글쓰기 방식은 매우 독특한 것으로,

neither from the left to the right, / like the Europeans, / nor
왼쪽에서 오른쪽으로도 아니고,   유럽인처럼,

from the right to the left, / like the Arabians, / nor from up
오른쪽에서 왼쪽으로도 아니고,   아랍인처럼,   위에서 아래로도

to down, / like the Chinese, / but aslant, / from one corner
아니었다,   중국인처럼,   사선 방향이었다,

of the paper to the other, / like ladies in England.
종이의 한쪽 구석에서 다른 쪽 구석으로,   영국의 숙녀들처럼.

They bury their dead / with their heads directly
그들은 죽은 사람을 묻는다   머리를 아래 쪽으로 똑바로 향하게 하여,

downward, / because they hold an opinion, / that in eleven
왜냐하면 그들은 믿었다,   11,000개월이 지나면

thousand moons / they are all to rise again; / in which
그들이 모두 부활한다고;   그 기간 동안

period / the earth / (which they conceive to be flat) / will
지구는   (그들이 평평하다고 생각한)

turn upside down, / and by this means / they shall, / at
뒤집어 질 것이고,   이런 방식으로   그들이,

their resurrection, / be found ready standing / on their feet.
부활했을 때,   설 준비가 된다는 것이다   두 발로 똑바로.

The learned among them / confess the absurdity / of this
학자들 중에는   어리석음을 시인하기도 하지만   이 믿음의;

doctrine; / but the practice still continues, / in compliance
그 관습은 여전히 계속되고 있다,   서민들의 관행에 따라서.

to the vulgar.

flourish 번성하다 | peculiar 톡특한, | upside down 뒤집혀, 거꾸로 | compliance 관행 | vulgar 서민 |
justification 타당한 이유, 변명 | be tempted to ~하고 싶어지다 | execute 수행히다, 이행하다 | severity 엄격,
엄중 | innocence무죄 | ignominious 불명예스러운 | quadruply 네 배가 되다 | recompensed 보상하다 |
underwent 겪다(undergo의 과거형) | proclamation 선포, 공포

There are some laws and customs / in this empire / very
법률과 관습이 있는데   이 제국에는

peculiar; / and if they were not so directly contrary / to
매우 독특한;   만약 그것들이 그렇게 정반대되는 것이 아니라면

those of my own dear country, / I should be tempted to say
사랑하는 내 조국의 것들과,   약간 말하고 싶어졌을 것이다

a little / in their justification. It is only to be wished / they
그들에 대한 해명을.   오직 바랄 뿐이다

were as well executed. The first I shall mention, / relates to
그것들이 잘 실행되어 가기를.   첫 번째로 내가 말하고자 하는 것은,   밀고자에 대한

informers. All crimes against the state, / are punished here
법이다.   국가에 반대하는 모든 범죄는,   여기에서는 처벌된다

/ with the utmost severity; / but, / if the person accused /
가장 엄중하게;   그러나,   만약 고발당한 사람이

makes his innocence plainly to appear / upon his trial, /
자신의 무죄를 명백히 입증하면   재판에서,

the accuser is immediately / put to an ignominious death;
고발한 사람은 즉시   불명예스런 사형에 처해지고;

/ and out of his goods or lands / the innocent person
그의 재산이나 토지를 가지고   무죄인 사람은 네 배로 보상 받는다

is quadruply recompensed / for the loss of his time, /
이를 충분히 보충해 준다   그가 입은 시간적 손실과,

for the danger he underwent, / for the hardship of his
겪은 위험에 대해,   투옥으로 인한 고초에 대해,

imprisonment, / and for all the charges / he has been at in
그리고 모든 경비에 대해   그가 변호를 위해 지불해 온;

making his defence; / or, / if that fund be deficient, / it is
혹은,   만약 자금이 부족할 경우,

largely supplied / by the crown. The emperor also confers
이를 충분히 보충해 준다   황실에서.   황제는 또한 그에게 부여하고

on him / some public mark of his favor, / and proclamation
공식적인 총애의 표시를,   그의 결백이 공포된다

is made of his innocence / through the whole city.
온 도시에.

They look upon / fraud as a greater crime than theft, / and
그들은 여겨서 사기를 절도보다 더 큰 범죄로,

therefore / seldom fail to punish it with death; / for they
그러므로 사형으로 처벌하지 않은 적이 없다; 그들이 주장하기를,

allege, / that care and vigilance, / with a very common
조심하고 경계하면, 보통의 이해력을 가진 사람이라면,

understanding, / may preserve a man's goods from thieves,
자기 재산을 도적으로부터 지킬 수 있으나,

/ but honesty hath no fence / against superior cunning;
정직한 사람은 당해낼 방어 수단이 없다는 것이었다 극도로 교활한 자에게는:

/ and, / since it is necessary / that there should be a
또한, 필요하기 때문에

perpetual intercourse / of buying and selling, / and dealing
지속적인 교류가 이뤄지는 것이 상거래에 있어서, 신용에 기초한

upon credit, / where fraud is permitted and connived at,
사기 행위가 허용되거나 묵인되는 곳에서는,

/ or has no law to punish it, / the honest dealer is always
혹은 그것을 처벌할 법이 없다면, 정직한 상인은 언제나 망하고,

undone, / and the knave gets the advantage. I remember,
악당만 이득을 본다는 것이다. 기억난다,

/ when I was once interceding / with the emperor / for
한 번 중재했던 때가 왕에게

a criminal / who had wronged his master / of a great
한 범죄자에 대해서 주인을 속여서 큰 돈을 빼앗고,

sum of money, / which he had received by order / and
그는 어음으로 받아서

ran away with; / and happening to tell his majesty, / by
도망쳤던; 그래서 황제에게 말하게 되었고,

way of extenuation, / that it was only a breach of trust, /
정상참작의 방법을, 그것은 단지 신용을 깨뜨린 것뿐이므로,

the emperor thought / it monstrous in me / to offer as a
그러자 황제는 생각했다 내 행동이 이상하다고 변호하는 것이

defence / the greatest aggravation of the crime; / and truly
극악무도한 중죄에 대해;

I had little to say in return, / farther than the common
정말 나는 대답할 말이 없었다, 일반적인 대답 밖에는,

answer, / that different nations had different customs; / for,
나라마다 관습이 다르다는:

I confess, / I was heartily ashamed.
고백하자면,   마음 깊이 창피함을 느꼈다.

Although we usually call / reward and punishment the two
우리는 흔히 말하지만   상과 벌이 두 중심축이라고

hinges / upon which all government turns, / yet I could
        모든 행정을 움직이는,   그러나 난 본 적 없었다

never observe / this maxim to be put in practice / by any
        이 말이 그렇게 철저히 실천되는 것을

nation except that of Lilliput. Whoever can there bring
릴리펏 외의 어떤 나라에서도.   증거를 충분히 제시할 수 있는 사람은 누구나,

sufficient proof, / that he has strictly observed / the laws
                엄격히 준수했다는

of his country / for seventy-three moons, / has a claim to
그 나라 법을   73개월 동안,

certain privileges, / according to his quality or condition
일정한 특권을 요구할 수 있다.   그의 신분과 생활 사정에 따라,

of life, / with a proportionable sum of money / out of a
              상응하는 액수의 돈과 함께

fund appropriated for that use: / he likewise acquires /
그 용도를 위해 배정된 기금에서 나오는: 그는 또한 호칭을 받는다

the title of SNILPALL, or legal, / which is added to his
스닐팔, 또는 법률가라는,   그의 이름 앞에 붙여지는

Key Expression 🔑

look upon A as B : A를 B로 여기다

look upon(on(on) A as B는 'A를 B로 여기다'라는 의미를 가진 숙어입니다.
이때 look upon 대신 'regard, consider, think of'를 쓸 수 있습니다.

refer to/look upon/think of/regard +목(A) + as +보어(B) A를 B로 여기다
= take A for B

ex) They look upon fraud as a greater crime than theft.
    그들은 사기를 절도보다 큰 범죄로 여겼다.

---

allege 단언하다, 주장하다 | vigilance 경계 | hath have의 3인칭 단수·현재·직설법으로 쓰이는 고어 | intercede
중재하다 | extenuation 죄의 완화, 정상 참작 | aggravation 악화 | sufficient 충분한 | proportionable
상응하는

name, / but does not descend to his posterity. And these
그러나 자손들이 물려 받지 않는다.   그리고 이 사람들은

people thought / it a prodigious defect of policy among
생각했다   그것이 우리 나라 정책의 엄청난 결함이라고.

us, / when I told them / that our laws were enforced / only
내가 그들에게 말했을 때   우리의 법은 집행되고 있다고

by penalties, / without any mention of reward. It is upon
오직 벌에 의해,   보상에 대한 규정 없이.   이런 이유들에 의해

this account / that the image of Justice, / in their courts
정의의 여신상이,   그들의 재판소에는,

of judicature, / is formed with six eyes, / two before,
눈이 여섯 개 달린 채 있다,   앞에 둘,

/ as many behind, / and on each side one, / to signify
뒤에 둘,   그리고 양 옆에 하나씩,   신중함을 상징하기 위해;

circumspection; / with a bag of gold open in her right
그 여신상은 오른손에 열려진 황금 주머니를,

hand, / and a sword sheathed in her left, / to show / she is
왼손에 칼집에 든 칼을 들고,   보여 준다   정의의 여신

more disposed to / reward than to punish.
이 더 선호한다는 것을   징벌보다 보상을 .

Key Expression ♀

far from ~ing : 결코 ~가 아닌

동명사를 이용한 관용표현 중 하나인 far from ~ing는 '결코 ~가 아닌, ~이기
는 커녕'이라는 강한 부정의 의미를 가지고 있습니다. 같은 뜻으로 쓰이는 표현으
로 never, anything but, by no means 등이 있어요.

ex) They thought the want of moral virtues was so far from being supplied by
    superior endowments of the mind
    그들은 도덕적인 덕목이 부족한 사람은 결코 우수한 자질로 보충될 수 없다고
    생각한다.

posterity 자손 | courts of judicature 재판소 | circumspection 조심성 | sublime 숭고한 | temperance
절제 | ignorance 무시

In chusing persons for all employments, / they have more
모든 직업에서 사람을 선택하는 것은, 그들의 훌륭한 도덕성에

regard to good morals / than to great abilities; / for, / since
더 중점을 둔다 뛰어난 능력보다,; 왜냐하면,

government is necessary to mankind, / they believe, / that
정부란 인류에게 필요한 것이기에, 그들은 믿는다,

the common size of human understanding / is fitted to
일반적인 이해력을 가진 사람은 어떤 자리라도 맞는다고;

some station or other; / and that Providence never intended
그리고 신의 섭리는 결코 의도하지 않는다고

/ to make the management of public affairs a mystery /
공무 수행을 비밀로 만드는 것을

to be comprehended / only by a few persons of sublime
이해될 수 있는 몇 명의 천재들에 의해서만,

genius, / of which there seldom are three born / in an age: /
세 명도 채 안 나오는 한 시대에 :

but they suppose / truth, justice, temperance, and the like, /
그러나 그들은 생각한다 진실, 정의, 절제 등의 덕목이,

to be in every man's power; / the practice of which virtues,
모든 사람의 힘이라고; 따라서 덕을 수행하며,

/ assisted by experience and a good intention, / would
경험과 선의가 뒷받침 된다면,

qualify any man / for the service of his country, / except
누구라도 자격이 있다고 국가를 위해 봉사할,

where a course / of study is required. But they thought /
분야를 제외하고 전문 연수 과정이 필요한, 그러나 그들은 생각했다

the want of moral virtues / was so far from being supplied
도덕적인 덕목이 부족한 사람은 좀처럼 보충될 수 없다고

/ by superior endowments of the mind, / that employments
우수한 정신적인 능력에 의해서도, 그래서 공직을 맡길 수 없다고

could never be put / into such dangerous hands / as those
그런 위험한 사람의 손에는

of persons so qualified; / and, at least, / that the mistakes
그들이 자질을 갖췄다고 해도; 그리고, 적어도, 몰라서 저지른 실수는,

committed by ignorance, / in a virtuous disposition, /
덕망을 갖춘 사람이,

would never be of such fatal consequence / to the public
치명적인 영향을 끼치지는 않을 것이라고 　　　　　　　　　　　　　대중들의 번영에,

weal, / as the practices of a man, / whose inclinations
사람들의 행동보다. 　　　　　　　　　　　　성향이 부도덕하고,

led him to be corrupt, / and who had great abilities to
이를 운영하는데 뛰어나서

manage, / to multiply, and defend his corruptions.
자신의 부정을 옹호하고 증폭시키는.

In like manner, / the disbelief of a Divine Providence
마찬가지로 　　　　　신의 섭리를 믿지 않는 사람은

renders / a man incapable of holding / any public station;
가질 수 없게 되어 있다 　　　　　　　　어떤 공직도;

/ for, / since kings avow themselves / to be the deputies of
왜냐하면, 황제가 스스로 공언하고 있는 이상 　　　　신의 대리인이라고,

Providence, / the Lilliputians think / nothing can be more
릴리펏인들은 생각하기 때문에 　　더 어리석은 일은 없다고

absurd / than for a prince to employ such men / as disown
황제가 그런 사람을 채용하는 일보다

the authority / under which he acts.
공직자로서 　　　　자신의 행동에 기반하여.

In relating these and the following laws, / I would only
이런 법률들과 다음에 얘기할 법률과 관련해서, 　　　　　　단지 이해해 주길 바란다

be understood / to mean the original institutions, / and
본래의 제도를 말하는 것이지,

not the most scandalous corruptions, / into which these
극히 창피스러운 부패를 뜻하는 것이 아니라고, 　　　사람들이 빠져버린

people are fallen / by the degenerate nature of man.
인간의 타락한 본성 때문에.

For, / as to that infamous practice / of acquiring great
왜냐하면, 이 수치스러운 제도는 　　　　　고위직은 얻는다거나

employments / by dancing on the ropes, / or badges
줄타기 춤에 의해,

of favor and distinction / by leaping over sticks / and
혹은 직위나 총애를 얻는 　　　　막대기를 뛰어넘거나

creeping under them, / the reader is to observe, / that they
그 아래를 기어다니는 행동을 통해. 　　그러니 독자 여러분은 알아야 한다,

were first introduced / by the grandfather of the emperor
그 제도들은 처음 도입되었으며   지금 황제의 할아버지에 의해

/ now reigning, / and grew to the present height / by the
현재 널리 퍼져서,   현재와 같이 극대화되었음을

gradual increase of party and faction.
정당과 파벌이 점차 많아짐에 따라.

Ingratitude is among them a capital crime, / as we read /
배은망덕은 이 나라에서 중죄 중의 하나이다.　　　　　　　우리가 읽은 바처럼

it to have been in some other countries: / for they reason
다른 나라에서도 그렇다고:　　　　　　　　　왜냐하면 그들은 생각한다;

thus; / that whoever makes ill returns to his benefactor, /
은인에게도 악으로 보답하는 자는 누구나,

must needs be a common enemy / to the rest of mankind, /
공통의 원수일 수밖에 없다고　　　　　　　　그 나머지 인류에게도,

from whom he has received no obligation, / and therefore /
그들에게 아무런 의무도 부여받지 않은,　　　　　　　따라서

such a man is not fit to live.
그런 인간은 사는 것이 옳지 않다는 것이다.

Their notions / relating to the duties of parents and
그들의 생각은　　　부모와 자식 간의 의무에 대한

children / differ extremely from ours. For, / since the
우리와는 전혀 다르다.　　　　　왜냐하면,

conjunction of male and female / is founded upon the
수컷과 암컷의 결합은　　　　　　대자연의 법칙에 근거한 것이므로,

great law of nature, / in order to propagate and continue
그 종을 증식시키고 유지시키기 위해,

the species, / the Lilliputians will needs have it, / that men
그래서 릴리펏인들의 생각으로는 필요했다.

and women are joined together, / like other animals, / by
남자와 여자도 결합하는 것이라는 주장이.　　　다른 동물처럼,

the motives of concupiscence; / and that their tenderness
성적 충족이라는 동기에 의해;　　　　　그리고 그들의 애정도

/ towards their young proceeds / from the like natural
자식에 대한　　　　　　마찬가지로 자연의 섭리에서 비롯되었다고:

principle: / for which reason / they will never allow /
그래서 그들의 논리로는　　그들은 허용하지 않는다

that a child is under any obligation / to his father / for
자식이 어떤 의무감을 가져야 한다는 것을　　아버지에 대해　　자신을 낳아

begetting him, / or to his mother / for bringing him into
주었다는 이유로,　　　혹은 어머니에게　　자신을 이 세상에 나오게 해 주었다는

Ingratitude 배은망덕 | benefactor 은인 | notion 생각 | propagate 증식시키다 | concupiscence 성적 욕구
| obligation 의무 | misery 불행 | otherwise 다르게 | nursery 보육원 | cottagers 농민 | rudiment 기초 |
docility 유순함

the world; / which, / considering the miseries of human
이유로; 그것은, 인생의 불행을 고려해 볼 때,

life, / was neither a benefit in itself, / nor intended so by his
그 자체가 혜택도 아니며, 부모의 의도도 아니라는 것이다,

parents, / whose thoughts, / in their love encounters, / were
그들의 생각은, 사랑의 교합을 이룰 때,

otherwise employed. Upon these, and the like reasonings,
전혀 다른 데 있었다는 것이다. 이런 저런 논리에 의해,

/ their opinion is, / that parents are the last of all others
그들의 의견은, 부모는 결코 믿을 만한 사람이 아니라는 것이다

to be trusted / with the education of their own children; /
자녀 교육에 있어서;

and therefore / they have in every town public nurseries,
따라서 그들에게는 모든 마을마다 공립 보육원이 있어서,

/ where all parents, / except cottagers and laborers, / are
그곳에서 모든 부모는, 농민과 노동자를 제외한,

obliged to send / their infants of both sexes / to be reared
보낼 의무가 있다 자신들의 아들 딸들을

and educated, / when they come to the age of twenty
양육되고 교육 받도록, 아이가 생후 20개월이 되면,

moons, / at which time / they are supposed to have / some
이 시기에 갖는다고 여겨지기 때문이다

rudiments of docility. These schools are of several kinds,
순종적인 성격의 기초를. 이런 학교들은 여러 종류가 있다,

Key Expression

the last person to ~ : 결코 ~할 사람이 아니다

the last person to는 어떤 일을 할만한 마지막 사람, 즉 '결코 그런 일을 할 사람이 아니다'라는 뜻을 강조하기 위해 쓰는 말입니다.

ex) Parents are the last of all others to be trusted with the education of their own children.
부모는 자녀 교육에 있어서 결코 믿을 만한 사람이 아니다.

/ suited to different qualities, and both sexes. They have
각 신분과 성별에 맞게.

certain professors well skilled / in preparing children / for
학교들은 능력을 갖춘 교사들을 보유하고 있다   아이들을 준비시키는데 있어

such a condition of life / as befits the rank of their parents,
그런 삶의 조건에 따라   부모의 지위나,

/ and their own capacities, / as well as inclinations. I shall
아이들 본인의 능력과,   성향에 적합한.   먼저

first say / something of the male nurseries, / and then / of
이야기 하겠다   남자 보육원에 대해서,   그리고 나서

the female.
여자 보육원에 관해서도.

The nurseries for males / of noble or eminent birth, / are
남자 아이들의 보육원에는   귀족이나 저명한 집안 출신의,

provided / with grave and learned professors, / and their
갖춰져 있다   근엄하고 학식 있는 교사들과,

several deputies. The clothes and food of the children /
보조 교사들이.   아이들의 의복과 음식은

are plain and simple. They are bred up / in the principles
소박하고 단순하다.   그들은 양육된다   원칙에 의해

/ of honor, justice, courage, modesty, clemency, religion,
명예, 정의, 용기, 겸손, 관용, 신앙,

/ and love of their country; / they are always employed in
그리고 조국에 대한 사랑의;   그들은 항상 무엇인가를 해야 한다.

some business, / except in the times of eating and sleeping,
식사 시간과 자는 시간 외에는,

/ which are very short, / and two hours for diversions /
매우 짧은.   그리고 두 시간의 오락 시간은

consisting of bodily exercises. They are dressed by men
신체 단련 과정으로 구성된다.   그들은 남자 하인들이 옷을 입혀 준다

/ till four years of age, / and then / are obliged to dress
4살이 될 때까지.   그리고 그 후로는 혼자 옷을 입어야만 한다.

themselves, / although their quality be ever so great; /
아무리 높은 신분이라 하더라고;

and the women attendant, / who are aged proportionably
그리고 시중 드는 하녀들이,   우리 나라로 치면 50세 정도 되는,

to ours at fifty, / perform only the most menial offices.
대부분의 허드렛일을 한다.

They are never suffered / to converse with servants, / but
아이들은 절대로 해서는 안 되고   하인들과 대화하는 것을,

go together / in smaller or greater numbers / to take their
같이 다녀야 한다   소규모나 대규모의 그룹으로   오락 시간에 참석할 때,

diversions, / and always / in the presence of a professor, /
그리고 항상   교사가 자리한 상태에서,

or one of his deputies; / whereby they avoid / those early
혹은 보조 교사가;   그렇게 해서 그들은 피한다   어린

bad impressions of / folly and vice, / to which our children
어린 시절의 나쁜 영향을   어리석고 악한 행동에 의한,

are subject.
우리 아이들이 빠지곤 하는.

capacity 능력 | inclination 성향 | deputy 조교 | modesty 겸손 | clemency 관용 | diversion 놀이 |
proportionably 비례하게 | menial 하찮은

Their parents are suffered to see them / only twice a year;
부모들은 아이들을 만날 수 있다   일 년에 한두 번 만;

/ the visit is to last but an hour; / they are allowed to / kiss
그리고 그 방문은 한 시간이 채 되지 않는다;   부모는 허용된다   아이에게

the child / at meeting and parting; / but a professor, / who
입맞추는 것이   만날 때와 헤어질 때에만;   그리고 교사가,

always stands by / on those occasions, / will not suffer
항상 옆에 서 있는   이런 경우,   못하도록 했다

them / to whisper, / or use any fondling expressions, / or
       귓속말을 하거나,   다른 애정 표현들을 사용하거나,

bring any presents / of toys, sweetmeats, and the like.
혹은 선물을 주는 것을   장난감이나, 과자 등과 같은.

The pension from each family / for the education and
수업료는 각 가정으로부터 받았으며   자녀의 교육과 오락을 위한,

entertainment of a child, / upon failure of due payment, /
                              제때 지불하지 않으면,

is levied by the emperor's officers.
황제의 관리들이 수금한다.

The nurseries for children / of ordinary gentlemen,
아이들을 위한 보육원은   일반적인 신사와

/ merchants, traders, and handicrafts, / are managed
상인, 무역업자, 그리고 수공업자의

proportionably / after the same manner; / only those
적절하게 운영된다   같은 방식을 따라;   다만 무역에 종사하게

designed for trades / are put out apprentices / at eleven
될 아이들은   견습생으로 보내진다   11세 때,

years old, / whereas those of persons of quality / continue
반면에 높은 신분의 자녀들은

in their exercises / till fifteen, / which answers to twenty-
계속 공부한다   15세가 될 때까지,   우리로 치면 21세에 해당하는:

one with us: / but the confinement is gradually lessened /
                그러나 제약은 점차 줄어든다

for the last three years.
마지막 3년 간은.

sweetmeat 사탕과자 | confinement 제한, 갇힘 | frightful 무서운 | folly 어리석은 행동 | chambermaid 하녀
| coward 비겁한 | decency 단정함

In the female nurseries, / the young girls of quality / are
여자 아이들의 보육원에서는,   신분이 높은 여자 아이들은

educated much like the males, / only they are dressed /
남자 아이들과 비슷한 교육을 받는다.   다만 그들은 입혀 준다

by orderly servants of their own sex; / but always in the
자신과 성별이 같은 하녀들이;

presence of a professor or deputy, / till they come to dress
그러나 언제나 교사나 조교가 있는 곳에서,   그들이 혼자서 옷을 입을 수 있을

themselves, / which is at five years old. And if it be found
때까지,   즉 5살까지.   그리고 만약 발견된다면

/ that these nurses ever presume / to entertain the girls /
보모들이 시도하는 것이   여자 아이들을 즐겁게 해 주려고

with frightful or foolish stories, / or the common follies
무섭거나 바보 같은 이야기로,   또는 어리석은 장난을 친다면

practised / by chambermaids among us, / they are publicly
영국에서 하녀들이 하듯이,   그들은 공개적으로 채찍질을

whipped thrice / about the city, / imprisoned for a year,
세 번 당하고   시내에서,   1년 동안 투옥되며,

/ and banished for life / to the most desolate part of the
평생 동안 추방당한다   제일 먼 변두리로,

country. Thus the young ladies are / as much ashamed /
그래서 젊은 숙녀들은   부끄러워하고

of being cowards and fools / as the men, / and despise all
겁쟁이나 바보가 되는 것을   남자들처럼,   모든 몸치장도 경멸한다,

personal ornaments, / beyond decency and cleanliness: /
단정하고 깨끗하지 못한:

neither did I perceive any difference / in their education /
나는 어떤 차이점도 보지 못했다   교육에 있어서

made by their difference of sex, / only that the exercises
성별로 인한,   단지 여성들의 체육은

of the females / were not altogether so robust; / and that
그렇게 심하지 않았고;

some rules were given them / relating to domestic life, /
또한 몇 가지 규칙을 가르쳤다   가정 생활에 관한,

and a smaller compass of learning / was enjoined them:
그리고 더 적은 범위의 학문이   그들에게 부과되었다:

/ for their maxim is, / that among peoples of quality, /
왜냐하면 그들의 격언에 의하면,   신분이 높은 사람들에 있어서,

a wife should be always / a reasonable and agreeable
아내는 늘   분별 있고 상냥한 반려자여야 하기 때문이다.

companion, / because she cannot always be young. When
아내는 항상 젊을 수 없으니까.

the girls are twelve years old, / which among them is
여자 아이들이 12세가 되면,   이 나라에서 결혼 할 나이인,

the marriageable age, / their parents or guardians take
부모나 후견인이 집으로 데려간다.

them home, / with great expressions of gratitude / to the
큰 감사를 표하고

professors, / and seldom without tears / of the young lady
교사들에게,   눈물을 흘리지 않는 일은 거의 없다

and her companions.
떠나는 아이들과 친구들이.

In the nurseries of females of the meaner sort, / the
신분이 낮은 집안의 여자 아이들의 보육원에서는,

children are instructed / in all kinds of works / proper for
여자 아이들은 배운다   모든 종류의 일을   자신의 성별에

their sex, / and their several degrees: / those intended for
알맞은,   그리고 각자의 신분에: 수습생으로 예정된 여자 아이들은

apprentices / are dismissed at seven years old, / the rest
7세에 그곳을 나가고,

are kept to eleven.
나머지는 11세까지 남는다.

The meaner families / who have children at these
낮은 신분의 집안들은   자녀를 보육원에 맡긴,

nurseries, / are obliged, / besides their annual pension, /
해야 한다,   매년 교육비 외에도,

which is as low as possible, / to return to the steward of
최대한 적은 액수인,   보육원 간사에게 보내야 한다

the nursery / a small monthly share of their gettings, / to
자신들의 월 수입의 일부를,

be a portion for the child; / and therefore / all parents are
자녀 몫으로 되게 하려고; 그러므로 모든 부모들은 제한 받는다

limited / in their expenses / by the law. For the Lilliputians
비용을 쓰는데 있어서 법률에 의해. 왜냐하면 릴리펏인들은 생각한다

think / nothing can be more unjust, / than for people, / in
더 부당한 일은 없다고, 사람들에게 있어서,

subservience to their own appetites, / to bring children into
자신들이 욕정에 따라, 자녀를 낳고,

the world, / and leave the burthen of supporting them / on
양육의 부담을 떠 맡기는 것보다

the public. As to persons of quality, / they give security / to
국가에. 신분이 높은 사람들의 경우는, 적당한 액수의 보증금을 낸

appropriate a certain sum / for each child, / suitable to their
적절한 금액의 아이들을 위해, 각자의 사정에 맞게:

condition; / and these funds are always managed / with
그리고 이 기금은 항상 운영된다

good husbandry and the most exact justice.
매우 효율적이며 아주 공정하게.

The cottagers and laborers / keep their children at home,
농민과 노동자들은 자녀를 집에서 양육한다,

/ their business being / only to till and cultivate the earth,
그들의 일은 오직 밭을 갈고 경작하는 것뿐이라,

/ and therefore their education is / of little consequence /
따라서 그들의 교육은 별로 중요하지 않기 때문이다

to the public: / but the old and diseased among them, / are
사회에: 그러나 늙고 병든 사람들은,

supported by hospitals; / for begging is a trade unknown /
병원에서 부양 받는다: 거지라는 직업은 알려지지 않았기 때문이다

in this empire.
이 나라에는.

And here it may, perhaps, / divert the curious reader, / to
이쯤에서, 아마도,   호기심 많은 독자를 기쁘게 하는 것일 것이다,

give some account of my domestics, / and my manner of
내 집안 환경에 대해 설명하는 것이,   그리고 생활 방식에 대해

living / in this country, / during a residence of nine months,
이 나라에서의,   9개월하고, 13일 간 거주하는 동안,

and thirteen days. Having a head mechanically turned, /
기계에 재능이 있었고,

and being likewise forced by necessity, / I had made for
꼭 필요한 것이기도 해서,   나는 혼자서 만들었다

myself / a table and chair / convenient enough, / out of the
탁자와 의자를   충분히 편안한,   가장 큰 나무

largest trees / in the royal park. Two hundred sempstresses
몇 그루를 베어서   황실 공원에서.   200명의 재봉사들이 동원되었다

were employed / to make me shirts, / and linen for my bed
내 셔츠를 만들기 위해,   그리고 침대와 탁자를 덮을 보자기를,

and table, / all of the strongest and coarsest kind / they
가장 튼튼하고 거친 종류의 천으로

could get; / which, however, / they were forced to quilt
그들이 구할 수 있는;   그러나,   그것을 한꺼번에 꿰매야 했다

together / in several folds, / for the thickest was / some
여러 겹으로,   제일 두꺼운 천도

degrees finer than lawn. Their linen is usually three inches
우리 면포보다 훨씬 얇았기 때문이다.   그들의 리넨은 보통 폭이 3인치이고,

wide, / and three feet make a piece. The sempstresses
길이가 3피트인 조각이었다.   재봉사들이 내 몸 치수를 쟀는데

took my measure / as I lay on the ground, / one standing
내가 땅에 누워 있을 때,   한 사람이 목 근처에 서고,

at my neck, / and another at my mid-leg, / with a strong
또 한 사람이 다리 중간에 서서,   튼튼한 밧줄의 끝을,

cord extended, / that each held by the end, / while a third
각각 팽팽히 잡고 있는 동안,

measured the length of the cord / with a rule of an inch
세 번째 사람이 밧줄의 길이를 쟀다   1인치 길이의 자로,

long. Then they measured my right thumb, / and desired
그리고 나서 그들은 내 오른쪽 엄지 손가락을 재고,   더 이상 요구하지 않았다:

no more; / for by a mathematical computation, / that twice
왜냐하면 수학적인 계산에 의해.

round the thumb is once round the wrist, / and so on to
엄지 둘레의 두 배가 손목 둘레이며,　　　　　　　그렇게 목과 허리도

the neck and the waist, / and by the help of my old shirt,
알 수 있다는 것이다.　　　　또 내 낡은 셔츠를 이용하여.

/ which I displayed on the ground before them / for a
내가 그들 앞에 땅 위에 펼쳐놓은.

pattern, / they fitted me exactly. Three hundred tailors were
본을 위해서.　　그리고 그것들은 내게 정확히 맞았다. 300명의 재봉사가 동원되었다

employed / in the same manner / to make me clothes; / but
같은 방식으로　　　　　　　내 옷을 만들기 위해;

they had another contrivance / for taking my measure. I
그러나 그들은 또 다른 방법을 썼다　　　　내 치수를 재기 위해.

kneeled down, / and they raised a ladder / from the ground
나는 무릎을 꿇었고.　　　그러면 그들이 사다리를 놓았다

to my neck; / upon this ladder / one of them mounted, / and
땅에서 내 목까지;　　사다리 위에　　　그들 중 한 사람이 올라가서.

let fall a plumb-line / from my collar to the floor, / which
추가 달린 줄을 땅에 늘어뜨렸다　　내 셔츠 깃에서 땅바닥까지.

just answered the length of my coat: / but my waist and
이것이 내 상의 길이에 해당했다:　　　　　그러나 허리와 팔은

arms / I measured myself. When my clothes were finished,
내가 직접 쟀다.　　　　내 옷이 다 완성되었을 때,

/ which was done in my house / (for the largest of theirs /
그것은 내 집에서 만들어졌는데　　　(그들의 가장 큰 집도

would not have been able to hold them), / they looked like
내 옷들을 수용할 수 없었으므로).　　　　　그것은 마치 조각보 같았다

the patch-work / made by the ladies in England, / only that
　　　　　　　영국 여성들이 만든.

mine were all of a color.
단지 내 옷은 모든 같은 색이었지만.

---

mechanically 기계적인 I sempstresses 재봉사 I coarsest 거친 I finer 엷은, 아주 가는 I lawn 한랭사, 론 천(엷은
면포) I contrivance 장치, 방법 I kneel down 무릎 꿇다

I had three hundred cooks / to dress my victuals, / in
내게는 300명의 요리사가 있었다   내 음식을 준비하기 위한,

little convenient huts / built about my house, / where they
편리한 오두막에 사는   내 집 주위에 지어진,

and their families lived, / and prepared me two dishes
여기에서 그들은 가족들과 살면서,   각자 두 가지씩 음식을 만들어 주었다.

a-piece. I took up twenty waiters in my hand, / and placed
나는 20명의 웨이터들을 손으로 집어서,

them on the table: / a hundred more attended below /
탁자에 올려 놓았다: 100여 명은 기다리며

on the ground, / some with dishes of meat, / and some
아래쪽 바닥에서,   몇 명은 고기 접시를 든 채,

with barrels of wine and other liquors / slung on their
또 몇 명은 포도주 통이나 다른 술통을   어깨에 맨 채;

shoulders; / all which the waiters above drew up, / as I
이 모든 것을 웨이터들이 끌어 올렸다.   내 주문에

wanted, / in a very ingenious manner, / by certain cords,
따라,   매우 교묘한 방법으로,   일종의 밧줄을 이용해,

/ as we draw the bucket up a well / in Europe. A dish of
두레박으로 우물물을 길어 올리듯   유럽에서.

their meat was a good mouthful, / and a barrel of their
한 접시의 고기는 한 입에 충분한 양이었고,   술 한 통도

liquor / a reasonable draught. Their mutton yields to ours,
한 모금으로 적당했다.   그들의 양고기는 우리 것에 못하지만,

/ but their beef is excellent. I have had a sirloin so large, /
소고기는 훌륭했다.   나는 매우 큰 등심을 받았는데,

that I have been forced to make three bites of it; / but this
세 입에 나눠 먹어야 했다;   그러나 이것은

is rare. My servants were astonished / to see me eat it, /
드문 일이다. 하인들은 매우 놀라워했다   내가 먹는 것을 보고,

bones and all, / as in our country / we do the leg of a lark.
뼈까지 모조리,   우리 나라에서   종달새의 다리까지 먹어 치우듯이.

Their geese and turkeys / I usually ate at a mouthful, / and
그들의 거위와 칠면조는   보통 한 입에 먹었는데,

I confess they far exceed ours. Of their smaller fowl / I
우리 것보다 훨씬 맛이 좋았다고 고백한다.   더 작은 새들은

could take up twenty or thirty / at the end of my knife.
한 번에 2~30 마리를 집을 수 있었다   나이프 끝으로.

One day his imperial majesty, / being informed of my way
어느 날 황제 폐하는,   내 일상 생활을 듣고서는,

of living, / desired / "that himself and his royal consort, /
부탁했다   "자신과 황후,

with the young princes of the blood of both sexes, / might
황태자와 공주가,

have the happiness," / as he was pleased to call it, / "of
즐거움을 누리고 싶어 한다고,"   그는 기쁘게 이야기 하기를,

dining with me." They came accordingly, / and I placed
"나와 식사를 함께하는."   그들은 왔고,

them in chairs of state, / upon my table, / just over against
나는 그들을 귀빈석에 앉혔고,   식탁 위에,   나와 마주 보도록,

me, / with their guards about them. Flimnap, the lord high
그들 주변에는 호위병들이 지키고 있었다.   재무 대신인, 플랩넵도,

treasurer, / attended there likewise / with his white staff;
마찬가지로 동석했다   그의 흰 지팡이를 가지고;

Key Expression

음식의 양에 대한 표현

음식을 먹을 때 한 입, 한 모금, 한 접시 등의 표현을 쓰죠. 영어로는 어떻게 표현하는지 알아봅시다.

▶ 한 입 : a mouthful, a bite(한 입에 무는 양), a morsel(작은 조각)
▶ 한 모금 : a mouthful, a sip(아주 적은 양을 홀짝 홀짝 마실 때), a drop(한 방울)
▶ (단숨에) 한 모금 : a draught(죽 들이마시는 한 모금), a gulp(꿀꺽 한 모금)
▶ 한 접시 : a dish, a plate .

ex) A dish of their meat was a good mouthful, and a barrel of their liquor a
reasonable draught.
그들의 고기 한 접시는 한 입에 충분했고, 술 한 통도 한 모금에 적당했다.
Their geese and turkeys I usually ate at a mouthful.
그들의 거위와 칠면조 고기를 나는 보통 한 입에 먹었다.

---

victual 음식 | slung 매다(sling의 과거, 과거분사) | sirloin 소의 등심살

/ and I observed / he often looked on me / with a sour
그리고 나는 보았지만   그가 나를 자주 보는 것을

countenance, / which I would not seem to regard, / but ate
찌푸린 표정으로.   나는 모르는 척 했고.

more than usual, / in honor to my dear country, / as well
평소보다 더 많이 먹었다   내 조국의 명예를 위해,

as to fill the court with admiration. I have some private
또한 동석한 궁중 사람들을 놀라게 해 주려고.   나는 어떤 개인적인 이유로 믿었다.

reasons to believe, / that this visit from his majesty / gave
황제의 이번 방문이

Flimnap an opportunity / of doing me ill offices to his
플림냅에게는 기회를 주었다고   황제에게 나를 음해할.

master. That minister had always been my secret enemy,
그 대신은 항상 내 은밀한 적이었다.

/ though he outwardly caressed me / more than was usual
겉으로는 내게 다정했지만   평소보다 더

/ to the moroseness of his nature. He represented to the
퉁명스러운 성격에 어울리지 않게.   그는 황제에게 말했다

emperor / "the low condition of his treasury; / that he
"재정이 바닥나고 있어서;

was forced to take up money / at a great discount; / that
비용을 줄여야 한다고   많은 양을;

exchequer bills would not circulate / under nine per cent,
그리고 재무성 증권을 통용시키지 않겠다고   9% 이하로는,

/ below par; / that I had cost his majesty / above a million
액면가 이하인;   또한 내가 황제에게 비용 부담을 안겼다고

and a half of SPRUGS" / (their greatest gold coin, / about
150만 스프럭 이상의"   (스프럭은 그들이 가장 큰 금화 단위로,

the bigness of a spangle) / "and, / upon the whole, / that it
압정 정도의 크기이다)   "그래서, 이 모든 것을 볼 때,

would be advisable / in the emperor / to take the first fair
현명한 일이라고 했다   황제가   기회를 잡는 것이

occasion / of dismissing me."
나를 추방할.

I am here obliged to vindicate / the reputation of an
나는 여기에서 변명을 해야겠다   한 훌륭한 귀부인의 명예를 위해,

excellent lady, / who was an innocent sufferer / upon
                              무고하게 누명을 쓸 뻔한

my account. The treasurer took a fancy / to be jealous of
나 때문에.   재무 대신은 망상을 갖게 됐다   아내를 질투하는,

his wife, / from the malice of some evil tongues, / who
                    어떤 악한 자들의 밀고 때문에,

informed him / that her grace had taken a violent affection
그들은 그에게 알렸다   그녀가 열정을 품었다고

/ for my person; / and the court scandal ran / for some
        내 용모에 대해;   그리고 궁정의 추문은 퍼졌다   한동안,

time, / that she once came privately to my lodging. This
          그녀가 한 번 남몰래 내 거처에 찾아왔다는.   이것에 대해

/ I solemnly declare / to be a most infamous falsehood,
      내가 엄숙히 선언하건대,   가장 수치스러운 거짓말이다.

> ## Key Expression 🎯

> ### 양보의 접속사 though
> though는 '비록 ~이지만, 비록 ~일지라도'라는 의미를 가진 양보의 부사절을
> 이끄는 접속사입니다. though대신 although를 쓰기도 하지요. 양보의 의미
> 를 가지는 접속사를 정리해 볼까요.
> ▶ though / although : 비록 ~할지라도(기존의 사실)
> ▶ even though : though의 강조형(바꿀 수 없는 사실)
> ▶ even if : 설사 ~할지라도(조건·가정의 의미)
> ▶ in spite of / despite + 구 : ~에도 불구하고(*전치사)
> ▶ in spite of[despite] the fact that + 절 : ~에도 불구하고(*접속사처럼 사용)
>
> ex) That minister had always been my secret enemy, though he outwardly
>   caressed me more than was usual to the moroseness of his nature.
>   그 대신은 평소의 퉁명스런 성격과 달리 겉으로는 내게 다정했지만, 항상 나의
>   비밀스런 적이었다.

countenance 얼굴 | outwardly 겉으로는 | moroseness 뚱한, 시무룩한 | exchequer 국가 재정 | advisable
타당한, 이로운 | falsehood 거짓말

/ without any grounds, / further than that her grace was
아무 근거도 없는.　　　　　　　그녀는 기쁘게 나를 대했을 뿐이다

pleased to treat me / with all innocent marks of freedom
아주 순수한 우정의 표시로.

and friendship. I own / she came often to my house, / but
나는 인정한다　그녀가 자주 내 집에 왔다는 사실은.

always publicly, / nor ever without three more in the coach,
그러나 항상 공개적이었고,　언제나 세 명이 함께 마차를 타고 왔다.

/ who were usually her sister and young daughter, / and
대개는 여동생과 어린 딸과.

some particular acquaintance; / but this was common / to
그리고 어떤 친한 친구와;　　　　그러나 이것은 흔한 일이었다

many other ladies of the court. And I still appeal / to my
궁정의 다른 귀부인들도.　　　　그래서 여전히 물어 보고 싶다

servants round, / whether they at any time saw / a coach
내 주변 하인들에게.　　그들이 한 번이라도 본 적 있는지　　　마차가 내 집

at my door, / without knowing what persons were in it. On
앞에 있는 것을.　　어떤 사람이 안에 탔는지 알 수 없는.

those occasions, / when a servant had given me notice, /
이런 방문이 있을 때.　　하인이 내게 알려 주면.

my custom was to go immediately / to the door, / and, /
나는 즉시 가곤 했다　　　　　　　문 쪽으로,　　　　그리고.

after paying my respects, / to take up the coach and two
인사를 한 뒤.　　　　　　　　마차와 두 마리의 말을 들어서

horses / very carefully / in my hands / (for, / if there were
조심스럽게　　　　내 손 위에 올려 놓고　(왜냐하면, 여섯 마리 말이 끄는

six horses, / the postillion always unharnessed four,) / and
마차라도,　　　마부가 항상 네 마리 말의 마구는 풀어놓았기 때문에.)

place them on a table, / where I had fixed a movable rim
그리고 나서 탁자에 올려 놓았다.　　그곳에 나는 이동 가능한 테두리를 둘러놓았다.

quite round, / of five inches high, / to prevent accidents.
높이 5인치인.　　　　　사고를 막기 위해.

---

publicly 공공연하게 | acquaintance 아는 사람, 지인 | postillion 마부 | unharness 마구를 풀다

And I have often / had four coaches and horses / at once
그리고 종종   네 대의 마차와 말들이

on my table, / full of company, / while I sat in my chair, /
동시에 탁자에 올라,   가득 차기도 했다,   이때 나는 의자에 앉아서,

leaning my face towards them; / and when I was engaged
얼굴을 그들 쪽으로 기울였다;   그리고 내가 한 팀과 이야기 하고 있으면,

with one set, / the coachmen would gently / drive the others
마부는 부드럽게   다른 팀들의 마차를 몰곤 했다

/ round my table. I have passed many an afternoon / very
탁자 위를 돌며.   나는 여러 오후를 보냈다

agreeably / in these conversations. But I defy the treasurer,
즐겁게   이런 대화를 하면서.   그러나 나는 재무 대신에게 항변하는 바이다,

/ or his two informers / (I will name them, / and let them
혹은 두 밀고자에게   (그들의 이름을 밝히겠다.

make the best of it) / Clustril and Drunlo, / to prove / that
그들이 이를 기회로 활용하라며)   클러스트릴과 드런로에게,   증명해 보라고

any person ever came to me / INCOGNITO, / except the
누군가가 나를 찾아온 적이 있었는지   '은밀하게',

secretary Reldresal, / who was sent / by express command
렐드레살은 제외하고,   보내졌던   황제의 긴급명령으로,

of his imperial majesty, / as I have before related. I should
앞서 말했듯이.   나는 그렇게

not have dwelt so long / upon this particular, / if it had not
길게 곱씹지 않았을 것이다   이 일에 대해,   만약 이 일이 문제가

been a point / wherein the reputation of a great lady / is so
아니었다면   훌륭한 귀부인의 명예에

nearly concerned, / to say nothing of my own; / though I
그토록 깊이 관련된,   물론 내 자신의 명예도;

then had the honor to be a NARDAC, / which the treasurer
나는 영광스럽게도 나르닥의 작위를 가졌지만,   재무 대신은 그렇지 못했다;

himself is not; / for all the world knows, / that he is only
세상 사람이 다 알고 있듯이,   그는 단지 글럼글럼의

a GLUMGLUM, / a title inferior by one degree, / as that
지위를 갖고 있었다,   한 계급 아래인,

of a marquis is to a duke / in England; / yet I allow / he
마치 후작이 공작보다 한 계급 낮은 것처럼 영국에서;   그러나 나는 인정한다

preceded me / in right of his post. These false informations,
그가 나보다 앞서 있음을   직위의 권리에 있어서는.   이런 거짓된 정보가,

/ which I afterwards came to the knowledge of / by an
내가 나중에 알게 된   한 사건을 계기로

accident / not proper to mention, / made the treasurer
말하기에 적절치 않은,   재무 대신으로 하여금 자기 부인에게

show his lady / for some time / an ill countenance, / and
보이게 했다   한동안   험상궂은 표정을,   그리고

me a worse; / and although he was at last / undeceived and
내게는 더 심한 표정을; 그리고 그는 결국   오해를 풀고 부인과 화해했지만,

reconciled to her, / yet I lost all credit with him, / and found
               나는 그의 신뢰를 모두 잃었다.   그리고 알았다

/ my interest decline very fast / with the emperor himself, /
나에 대한 관심도 급속히 줄어들었음을   황제 자신의,

who was, indeed, / too much governed by that favorite.
그는 정말로,   그 신하에게 너무 많은 영향을 받고 있었다.

Key Expression ♥

to say nothing of ~ : ~는 말할 것도 없이, 물론

to say nothing of는 '~는 말할 것도 없이, ~는 제쳐두고, 물론'라는 의미를
가지며 문장 전체를 수식하는 부사적 용법으로 쓰이는 독립부정사의 일종입니다.
독립부정사는 숙어처럼 기억해서 사용하세요.

▶ to say nothing of = not to speak of = not to mention = let alone

ex) ···if it had not been a point wherein the reputation of a great lady is so nearly
concerned, to say nothing of my own.
만약 내 자신은 물론 이일이 훌륭한 귀부인의 명예에 그토록 깊이 관련된 문제
가 아니었다면, ···

coachman 마부 | defy 항변하다 | dwell upon ~을 곱씹다 | marquis 후작 | duke 공작 | undeceive 진실을
알다 | reconcile 화해하다

mini test 6

A. 다음 문장을 해석해 보세요.

(1) As the common size of the natives / is somewhat under six inches high, / so there is an exact proportion / in all other animals, / as well as plants and trees.
→

(2) If the person accused / makes his innocence plainly / to appear / upon his trial, / the accuser is immediately / put to an ignominious death.
→

(3) I could never observe / this maxim to be put in practice / by any nation except that of Lilliput.
→

(4) I should not have dwelt so long / upon this particular, / if it had not been a point / wherein the reputation of a great lady is so nearly concerned, / to say nothing of my own.
→

B. 다음 주어진 문구가 알맞은 문장이 되도록 순서를 맞춰보세요.

(1) 그들은 아주 정확하게 본다, 그러나 먼 거리는 잘 보지 못한다.
(great / see / They / exactness / with)

_____ , but at no great distance.

(2) 나는 요리사가 일반 파리보다도 작은 종달새의 깃털을 뽑는 것을 보고 매우 감탄했다.
(not / as / was / which / large / a / fly / common / so)
I have been much pleased with observing a cook pulling a lark, _____ .

Answer

A. (1) 주민들의 평균 키는 6인치보다 약간 작은 것에 따라, 식물과 나무뿐만 아니라 기타 모든 동물의 크기도 정확히 비례한다. (2) 만약 고발당한 사람이 재판에서 자신의 무죄를 명백히 입증하면, 고발한 사람이 즉시 불명예스런 사형에 처해진다. (3) 나는 이 말이 릴리펏처럼 철저하게 실천되는 나라를 본 적이 없었

(3) 그들의 제일 큰 나무는 높이가 약 7피트이다.
(tallest / seven / are / Their / feet / trees / about)
→

(4) 그들은 사기를 절도보다 더 큰 범죄로 여긴다.
(theft / look upon / They / than / as / greater crime / a / fraud)
→

C. 다음 주어진 문장이 본문의 내용과 맞으면 T, 틀리면 F에 동그라미 하세요.

(1) In Lilliput, they think highly of great abilities in choosing persons for employments.
(T / F)

(2) In Lilliput, parents are responsible for their children's education.
(T / F)

(3) In Lilliput, boys and girls are educated separately.
(T / F)

(4) The author had an affair with a lady in Lilliput.
(T / F)

D. 의미가 서로 비슷한 것끼리 연결해 보세요.

(1) gratify   ▶   ◀ ① assert
(2) allege   ▶   ◀ ② satisfy
(3) ignominious   ▶   ◀ ③ tendency
(4) inclinations ▶   ◀ ④ humiliating

7

The author, / being informed of a design / to accuse him of
저자가, 계획을 듣고는 그를 반역죄로 기소하려는,

high-treason, / makes his escape to Blefuscu. His reception
블레프스큐로 도피한다. 그곳에서의 환대.

there.

Before I proceed to give an account / of my leaving this
설명하기 전에 이 나라를 떠나는 된 것을,

kingdom, / it may be proper / to inform the reader / of a
적절할 것이다 독자에게 알리는 것이

private intrigue / which had been for two months forming /
비밀스런 음모에 대해 두 달 동안 꾸며진

against me.
나를 모함하려고.

I had been hitherto, / all my life, / a stranger to courts, / for
나는 그때까지, 평생 동안, 궁정과는 아무 상관없는 사람이었다,

which I was unqualified / by the meanness of my condition.
왜냐하면 자격이 없었기 때문이다 출생 신분이 낮아서.

I had indeed heard and read enough / of the dispositions
나는 물론 충분히 들었고 글도 읽었다

of great princes and ministers, / but never expected / to
군주와 대신들의 기질에 대해서는, 그러나 전혀 예상하지 못했다

have found such terrible effects of them, / in so remote
그것들이 그런 끔찍한 영향을 끼치리라고는, 이렇게 멀리 떨어진

a country, / governed, / as I thought, / by very different
나라에서도, 다스려지는, 내 생각으로, 전혀 다른 원칙에 의해

maxims / from those in Europe.
유럽과는.

high-treason 반역죄 | reception 환대 | intrigue 음모 | hitherto 그때까지 | unqualified 자격이 없는 | serviceable 도움이 되는 | indisposed 몸이 불편한

When I was just preparing / to pay my attendance / on
내가 막 준비하고 있을 때 / 방문하기 위해

the emperor of Blefuscu, / a considerable person at court
블레프스큐 황제를, / 궁정의 주요 인사 중 한 사람이

/ (to whom I had been very serviceable, / at a time when
(그에게 큰 도움을 준 적 있다, / 그가 상황에 놓였을 때

he lay / under the highest displeasure of his imperial
황제 폐하의 심한 노여움을 산)

majesty) / came to my house / very privately at night, / in
내 집에 왔다 / 밤에 매우 은밀하게, /

a close chair, / and, / without sending his name, / desired
가려진 가마를 타고, / 그리고, / 이름도 밝히지 않은 채,

admittance. The chairmen were dismissed; / I put the
들어오기를 청했다. / 가마꾼들은 물러갔다: / 그러자 나는 가마를

chair, / with his lordship in it, / into my coat-pocket: /
들어, / 그 귀족이 탄 채로, / 코트 호주머니 속으로 집어넣었다:

and, / giving orders to a trusty servant, / to say / I was
그리고, / 신임할 수 있는 하인에게 명령했다, / 말하라고

indisposed and gone to sleep, / I fastened the door of
내가 몸이 불편해서 잠자리에 들었다고, / 그리고 문을 걸어 잠근 후,

my house, / placed the chair on the table, / according
가마를 탁자 위에 놓고, /

to my usual custom, / and sat down by it. After the
평소 습관대로, / 그 옆에 앉았다.

common salutations were over, / observing his lordship's
의례적인 인사를 주고 받고 나서, / 그 귀족의 얼굴을 보고

countenance / full of concern, / and inquiring into the
근심으로 가득 찬, / 이유를 물었다.

reason, / he desired / "I would hear him with patience, / in
그러자 그는 부탁했다 "그의 말을 참을성 있게 들어 달라고,

a matter that highly concerned / my honor and my life."
매우 관련 있는 문제이므로 / 내 명예와 생명에."

His speech was to the following effect, / for I took notes of
그의 이야기는 다음과 같았다. / 기록해 두었기 때문에

it / as soon as he left me: /
그가 떠나자마자:

"You are to know, " / said he, / "that several committees
"당신은 알아야 합니다." 그가 말했다. "여러 번 비밀 회의가 최근 열렸습니다.

of council have been lately called, / in the most private
아주 은밀하게,

manner, / on your account; / and it is but two days / since
당신에 관한 문제로; 그리고 겨우 이틀이 지났습니다

his majesty came to a full resolution.
폐하가 중대한 결정을 내린지.

"You are very sensible / that Skyresh Bolgolam" /
"당신은 잘 알고 있다시피 스키레쉬 볼고람이"

(GALBET, or high-admiral) / "has been your mortal
(갈베트, 즉 해군 제독이다) "당신의 치명적인 적이 되어 왔습니다.

enemy, / almost ever since your arrival. His original
당신이 도착한 이래로 계속. 근원적인 이유는

reasons / I know not; / but his hatred is increased / since
나도 모릅니다; 그러나 그의 미움은 커졌습니다

your great success against Blefuscu, / by which / his glory
블레프스큐를 상대로 한 당신의 큰 승리 이후, 그것 때문에

as admiral is much obscured. This lord, / in conjunction
해군 제독으로서의 그의 명성이 가려졌습니다. 폐하께서는, 재무 대신인 플림냅과 함께,

with Flimnap the high-treasurer, / whose enmity against
당신에 대한 원한이 유명한

you is notorious / on account of his lady, / Limtoc the
그의 부인 문제로, 그리고 육군 대장 림톡과,

general, / Lalcon the chamberlain, / and Balmuff the
시종장 랄콘과, 대법관 발머프와 함께,

grand justiciary, / have prepared articles of impeachment /
몇 가지 조항을 작성했습니다

against you, / for treason and other capital crimes."
당신을 탄핵하는, 반역죄와 기타 중죄로."

This preface made me so impatient, / being conscious of
이렇게 시작하는 말은 나를 참을 수 없게 했다. 생각해 볼 때

/ my own merits / and innocence, / that I was going to
내가 세운 공적과 무죄임을, 그래서 그의 말을 가로막으려고 했다;

interrupt him; / when he entreated me to be silent, / and
하지만 그는 내게 침묵을 지켜달라고 간청하면서, 계속했다:—

thus proceeded: /—

Out of gratitude for the favors / you have done me, / I
은혜에 대한 보답으로   당신이 내게 베풀어 준,

procured information / of the whole proceedings, / and
나는 정보를 입수했습니다   모든 과정에 관한,

a copy of the articles; / wherein / I venture my head / for
그리고 탄핵문의 사본도;   이에 대해   내 목이 달아날 각오를 하고 있습니다

your service.
당신을 돕기 위해.

committee 회의 | conjunction 결합 | grand justiciary 대법관 | impeachment 탄핵

Articles of Impeachment / against QUINBUS FLESTRIN,
탄핵 조항들   퀸버스 플레스트린에 대한,

/ (the Man-Mountain.)
(인간산.)

ARTICLE I.
제1항.

Whereas, by a statute / made in the reign of his imperial
법에 의하여   칼린 데파르 플룬 황제의 폐하 치세 때 제정된,

majesty Calin Deffar Plune, / it is enacted, that, / whoever
규정되어 있다,

shall make water / within the precincts of the royal palace,
소변을 보는 사람은 누구나   궁궐의 경내에서,

/ shall be liable to the pains and penalties of high-treason;
대역죄의 처벌을 받게 될 것이라고;

/ notwithstanding, / the said Quinbus Flestrin, / in open
그럼에도 불구하고,   앞서 서술한 퀸버스 플레스트린은,

breach of the said law, / under color of extinguishing the
상기의 법을 공공연히 위반하여,   화재를 진압한다는 구실 하에

fire / kindled in the apartment / of his majesty's most
거처에서 발생한   황제 폐하의 배우자이신 황후 마마의,

dear imperial consort, / did maliciously, traitorously, and
악의적이고, 반역적으로, 흉악하게도,

devilishly, / by discharge of his urine, / put out the said fire
소변을 배설하여,

kindled in the said apartment, / lying and being within the
상기의 건물에서 발생한 화재를 진화했다,   상기의 궁궐의 경내에 위치한,

precincts of the said royal palace, / against the statute / in
법을 위반하고

that case provided, etc. / against the duty, etc.
이 경우에 정해져 있는,   의무 등을 저버렸다.

---

liable to ~ 있다 | notwithstanding 그럼에도 불구하고 | consort 거처 | maliciously 악의적인 | traitorously
반역적인 | devilishly 악귀 같은 | viceroy 총독 | forsake 포기하다 | heresy (특히 종교상의) 이단 | traitor
반역자 | auspicious 상서로운 | serene 위대한

ARTICLE II.
제2항.

That the said Quinbus Flestrin, / having brought the
앞서 서술한 퀸버스 플레스트린은,　　　　　　블레프스큐 제국 함대를 끌고 왔다

imperial fleet of Blefuscu / into the royal port, / and being
본국의 항구에,

afterwards commanded / by his imperial majesty / to
그리고 이후에 명령 받았다　　　　황제 폐하로부터

seize all the other ships / of the said empire of Blefuscu, /
나머지 함정을 전부 잡아오라는　　　상기의 블레프스큐 제국의,

and reduce that empire to a province, / to be governed by
그리고 그 제국을 속국으로 만들어서,　　　　그렇게 하여 총독이 통치하도록

a viceroy from hence, / and to destroy and put to death,
할 것을,　　　　　　　　또한 파괴하고 사형시킬 것을.

/ not only all the Big-endian exiles, / but likewise all the
　모든 큰 쪽 깨기 파의 망명자들 뿐만 아니라,　　　마찬가지로 그 나라의 모든 국민들을

people of that empire / who would not immediately forsake
큰 쪽 깨기라는 이단적인 주장을 즉시 포기하지 않는,

the Big-endian heresy, / he, / the said Flestrin, / like a
　　　　　　　　그러나 그는,　상기의 플레스트린은,

false traitor / against his most auspicious, serene, imperial
불충한 반역자처럼　가장 신성하고 위대하신 황제 폐하에 반대하며,

majesty, / did petition / to be excused from the said service,
　　　　청원을 올렸다　　상기의 임무를 면제 받고자,

/ upon pretence of unwillingness / to force the consciences,
　할 수 없다는 핑계를 대고　　　　　　　　양심을 강요하거나,

/ or destroy the liberties and lives of an innocent people.
　혹은 무고한 국민의 자유와 생명을 해치는 것을.

Key Expression❢

notwithstanding : 그럼에도 불구하고

notwithstanding이 부사로 쓰이면 '그럼에도 불구하고, 그렇기는 하지만'의 뜻으로, nonetheless, nevertheless, however 등과 같은 의미입니다. 문장 전체를 수식하며 콤마(,)와 함께 써서 문장과 분리해 줍니다.

ex) It is enacted, that, whoever shall make water within the precincts of the royal palace, shall be liable to the pains and penalties of high-treason; notwithstanding, the said Quinbus Flestrin…

궁궐의 경내에서 소변을 보는 사람은 누구나 대역죄의 처벌을 받게 된다고 규정되어 있다. 그럼에도 불구하고, 앞서 서술한 퀸버스 플레스트린은…

ARTICLE III.
제3항.

That, whereas certain ambassadors arrived / from the
몇 명의 대사가 도착했다

Court of Blefuscu, / to sue for peace / in his majesty's
블레프스큐의 궁정으로부터,　화친을 청원하기 위해　황제의 궁정에,

court, / he, the said Flestrin, / did, like a false traitor, /
그리고 상기의 플레스트린은,　불충한 반역자처럼 행동하며,

aid, abet, comfort, and divert, / the said ambassadors, /
돕고, 부추기고, 위로하고, 즐겁게 해 주었다,　상기의 대신들을,

although he knew / them to be servants to a prince / who
그는 알고 있었음에도　그들이 왕의 신하임을

was lately an open enemy / to his imperial majesty, / and
최근에도 공공연한 적이었던　황제 폐하의,　그리고

in an open war / against his said majesty.
공공연한 전쟁을 벌였던　상기의 황제와.

ARTICLE IV.
제4항.

That the said Quinbus Flestrin, / contrary to the duty of
상기 퀸버스 플레스트린은,　충실한 신하로서의 의무를 저버리고,

a faithful subject, / is now preparing / to make a voyage
현재 준비하는 중이다

/ to the court and empire of Blefuscu, / for which / he
블레프스큐의 궁정과 황제에게 여행을 떠날,　이에 대해

has received only verbal license / from his imperial
그는 단지 구두 허가만 얻었을 뿐이다　황제 폐하로부터;

majesty; / and, / under color of the said license, / does
그런데,　상기의 허가를 구실로,

falsely and traitorously intend to take / the said voyage,
불충하고 반역적으로 떠나려 한다　상기의 항해를,

/ and thereby / to aid, comfort, and abet / the emperor of
그럼으로써,　돕고, 위로하고, 부추기기 위해서　블레프스큐의 황제를,

Blefuscu, / so lately an enemy, / and in open war with his
최근까지도 우리의 적이며,　황제 폐하와 공공연한 전쟁을 벌이고 있는.

imperial majesty aforesaid.

There are some other articles; / but these are the most
그 외 다른 조항도 있었습니다;   그러나 이것들이 가장 중요해서,

important, / of which / I have read you an abstract.
그것들 중에서   요약해서 읽어드린 것입니다.

In the several debates / upon this impeachment, / it must
여러 차례의 토론 중에   이 탄핵문에 관한,   아셔야 합니다

be confessed / that his majesty gave many marks of his
폐하는 자비심을 보였다는 것을;

great lenity; / often urging / the services you had done
자주 강조하시면서   당신이 준 도움을,

him, / and endeavoring / to extenuate your crimes. The
애쓰셨습니다   당신의 죄를 가볍게 하려고.

treasurer and admiral insisted / that you should be put to /
재무 대신과 해군 제독은 주장했습니다   당신이 당해야 한다고

the most painful and ignominious death, / by setting fire to
가장 고통스럽고 비참한 사형을,   당신 집에 불을 지르고

your house / at night, / and the general was to attend / with
밤에,   장군이 들이닥치는 방법으로

twenty thousand men, / armed with poisoned arrows, / to
2만 명의 군사를 이끌고,   독화살로 무장한,

shoot you on the face and hands. Some of your servants /
당신의 얼굴과 손에 쏘기 위해.   당신의 하인 중 몇 명은

were to have private orders / to strew a poisonous juice / on
비밀스러운 명령을 받아   독극물을 뿌리게 하고

your shirts and sheets, / which would soon make / you tear
당신의 셔츠와 이불에,   그러면 그것이 곧 만들 것이라고   당신이 자신의

your own flesh, / and die in the utmost torture. The general
살을 쥐어뜯고,   가장 고통스럽게 죽도록.

came into the same opinion; / so that for a long time / there
육군 대장도 이 의견에 동조했습니다;   그래서 한동안

was a majority against you; / but his majesty resolving, /
대세는 당신에게 불리했습니다;   그러나 황제는 결심했고,

if possible, / to spare your life, / at last / brought off the
가능하면,   당신의 목숨을 살리기로,   마침내   시종장을 막아냈습니다.

chamberlain.

aforesaid 앞서 언급한 | lenity 자비로움 | urge 강조하다 | endeavor 노력하다 | extenuate 죄를 경감하다 |
ignominious 비참하게 | flesh 살 | chamberlain 시종장

Upon this incident, / Reldresal, / principal secretary for
이 일이 있은 후에, 렐드레살은, 궁내 대신이자,

private affairs, / who always approved himself your true
늘 당신의 진정한 친구였던,

friend, / was commanded by the emperor / to deliver
황제께 명령 받았습니다 의견을 말해 보라고,

his opinion, / which he accordingly did; / and therein /
그래서 그는 그렇게 했습니다; 그 내용은

justified the good thoughts / you have of him. He allowed
호의적인 의견을 입증했습니다 당신이 그에게 갖고 있는. 그는 당신의 죄가

your crimes to be great, / but that still there was room for
크다는 것은 인정했으나, 아직 자비를 베풀 여지가 있다고 했습니다,

mercy, / the most commendable virtue in a prince, / and for
자비는 군주에게 가장 훌륭한 덕목이며,

which his majesty was so justly celebrated. He said, / the
그 때문에 폐하는 정당함으로 명성이 높다고. 그가 말하길,

friendship between you and him / was so well known to the
당신과 그의 우정이 전 세계에 잘 알려져 있어서,

world, / that perhaps the most honorable board might think
최고 귀족들은 생각할지 모르지만

/ him partial; / however, / in obedience to the command / he
그가 편견을 갖고 있다고; 그러나, 명령에 순종하여

had received, / he would freely offer his sentiments. That
그가 받은, 자유롭게 자신의 생각을 밝히겠다고 했습니다.

if his majesty, / in consideration of your services, / and
만약 폐하께서, 당신의 도움을 헤아리시고,

pursuant to his own merciful disposition, / would please
또 폐하의 자비로우신 기질에 따라서, 당신의 목숨을 살리고,

to spare your life, / and only give orders / to put out both
다만 명령을 내린다면, 양쪽 눈을 못 보게 하라는

your eyes, / he humbly conceived, / that by this expedient
그가 겸손하게 생각하기에는, 이 명령으로

/ justice might / in some measure be satisfied, / and all the
정의도 구현될 것이며 어느 정도 만족하게 될 것이고, 모든 세상은 칭송할

world would applaud / the lenity of the emperor, / as well
것이라고 했습니다 황제의 관대함을,

as the fair and generous proceedings / of those who have
뿐만 아니라 공정함과 너그러운 조치를

the honor to be his counsellors. That the loss of your eyes
영광스럽게 조언자가 된 대신들의.   당신이 두 눈을 잃더라도

/ would be no impediment / to your bodily strength, / by
지장이 없을 것이라서   몸을 쓰는 데에는,

which / you might still be useful / to his majesty; / that
그 힘으로   당신은 여전히 유용할 것이며   폐하에게;

blindness is an addition to courage, / by concealing dangers
눈이 먼다는 것은 오히려 용기를 배가시킬 것이라고;   우리에 대한 위험을 가려주기 때문에;

from us; / that the fear you had / for your eyes, / was the
그리고 당신이 가졌던 공포감은   눈 때문에,

greatest difficulty / in bringing over the enemy's fleet, / and
가장 큰 어려움이었으니까,   적의 함대를 끌고 올 때,

it would be sufficient / for you to see / by the eyes of the
그리고 충분할 것이라고 했습니다   당신이 보는 것으로   신하들의 눈을 통해,

ministers, / since the greatest princes / do no more.
왜냐하면 가장 위대한 군주들도   그 이상 베풀지는 않으므로.

Key Expression

주장·요구·명령·제안 동사와 함께 쓰이는 should의 용법

주절에 주장·요구·명령·제안을 의미하는 동사가 쓰인 경우 그 목적어가 되는 종속절에서는 should + 동사원형을 사용합니다. 여기에 쓰이는 should는 '마땅히 그렇게 되어야만 한다'는 의미를 강조한 것으로 종종 should가 탈락되고 동사원형만 남기도 합니다.

또한 insist나 suggest의 경우 당위의 의미가 없이 단순히 사실을 진술할 때에는 이 규칙을 따르지 않는다는 사실도 기억하세요.

▶ (주장) insist
▶ (요구) demand, request, require   (that) + 주어 + (should) + 동사원형
▶ (명령) order, command
▶ (제안) suggest, propose, recommend

ex) The treasurer and admiral insisted that you should be put to the most painful and ignominious death.
재무 대신과 제독은 당신이 가장 고통스럽고 비참하게 처형되어야 한다고 주장했다.
It was strictly enjoined, that the project of starving you by degrees should be kept a secret.
당신을 점차 굶겨 죽인다는 계획은 비밀로 하라는 엄격한 명령이 내려졌다.

honorable 고귀하신 | partial 편애하는 | sentiment 생각 | merciful 자비로운 | applaud 박수를 보내다,
찬양하다 | counsellor 자문 의원

This proposal was received / with the utmost
이 제안은 받아들여졌습니다   극도의 불만과 함께

disapprobation / by the whole board. Bolgolam, the
            회의 참석자 전원의.   해군 제독인 볼고람은,

admiral, / could not preserve his temper, / but, rising up
화를 참지 못하고,   격노하며 일어서서,

in fury, / said, / he wondered / how the secretary durst
격분하여,   말했습니다, 궁금하다며   어떻게 궁내 대신이 감히 할 수 있는지

presume / to give his opinion / for preserving the life of
으로   의견을 내놓는 것을   반역자의 목숨을 살려 주자는;

a traitor; / that the services you had performed were, / by
그리고 당신이 이룬 공적들은,

all true reasons of state, / the great aggravation / of your
모든 진정한 상황을 고려해 본다면,   오히려 가중시키는 것이라고   당신의 범죄를;

crimes; / that you, / who were able to extinguish the fire /
당신이,   불을 끌 수 있었던 것은

by discharge of urine / in her majesty's apartment / (which
소변을 배설함으로써   황후 마마의 거처에서

he mentioned with horror), / might, at another time, / raise
(그는 치를 떨며 말했습니다),   다른 상황이었다면,   홍수를

an inundation / by the same means, / to drown the whole
일으킬 수 있기에   같은 방법으로,   온 궁전을 물에 잠기도록;

palace; / and the same strength / which enabled you to
그리고 그런 힘은   적의 함대를 끌고 올 수 있었던,

bring over the enemy's fleet, / might serve, / upon the first
                          사용될 수도 있다고,   불만이 생긴다면,

discontent, / to carry it back; / that he had good reasons /
          다시 적국으로 끌고 가는 데에; 그는 충분한 근거가 있다고 했습니다

to think you were a Big-endian / in your heart; / and, / as
당신이 큰 쪽 깨기 파라는   마음 속으로는;   그리고,

treason begins / in the heart, / before it appears in overt-
반역은 생겨난다고   마음 속으로부터,   행동으로 나타나기 전에,

acts, / so he accused you as a traitor / on that account, /
따라서 그는 당신을 반역자로 고발하고,   그런 이유로,

and therefore insisted / you should be put to death.
주장한다고 했습니다   당신이 처형되어야 한다고.

The treasurer was of the same opinion: / he showed to
재무 대신도 같은 생각이었습니다: 그는 보여 주었습니다

/ what straits / his majesty's revenue was reduced, / by
   얼마나 궁핍하게   황제의 재정이 줄어들었는지,

the charge of maintaining you, / which would soon /
당신을 부양하기 위해서,   그리고 곧

grow insupportable; / that the secretary's expedient / of
감당할 수 없게 될 것이라고;   궁내 대신의 방법은

putting out your eyes, / was so far from being a remedy /
당신의 눈을 멀게 한다는,   해결책과 거리가 먼 것이며

against this evil, / that it would probably increase it, / as is
이 악행에 대한,   아마도 문제를 악화시킬 것이라고,

manifest / from the common practice / of blinding some
분명한 것처럼   흔한 경험으로부터   새들의 눈을 멀게 하는 경우,

kind of fowls, / after which / they fed the faster, / and grew
                그에 따라,   새들은 먹이를 더 빨리 먹고,   더 빨리 살이

sooner fat; / that his sacred majesty and the council, / who
찌고 만다는;   거룩하신 폐하와 궁정 대신들도,

are your judges, were, / in their own consciences, / fully
당신을 심판하고 있는,   각자의 양심에 비추어,   당신의 유죄를

convinced of your guilt, / which was a sufficient argument
충분히 확신하고 있기 때문에,   이것이 충분한 근거가 된다는 것입니다

/ to condemn you to death, / without the formal proofs /
   당신을 사형에 처할,   공식적인 증거가 없이도

required by the strict letter of the law.
법률의 엄격한 조항들이 요구하는.

disapprobation 반대 | rise up 일어서다 | fury 분노, 화 | treason 반역 | strait 궁핍한 | insupportable 견딜
수 없는 | remedy 해결

But his imperial majesty, / fully determined against capital
그러나 황제께서는, 사형에 반대하는 의견을 굳히고,

punishment, / was graciously pleased to say, / that since the
자비롭게 말씀하셨습니다.

council thought / the loss of your eyes / too easy a censure,
대신들이 생각한다면 당신의 눈을 멀게 하는 것이 너무 가벼운 형벌이라고,

/ some other way may be inflicted / hereafter. And your
다른 추가적인 형벌을 부과할 수도 있다고 이후에. 그리고 당신의 친구인

friend the secretary, / humbly desiring to be heard again, /
궁내 대신이, 또 다시 발언하기를 공손히 청했습니다,

in answer to / what the treasurer had objected, / concerning
답변으로 재무 대신이 반대한 내용에 대한,

the great charge / his majesty was at / in maintaining you,
엄청난 비용에 대해 폐하가 부담하는 당신을 부양하는데 있어서,

/ said, / that his excellency, / who had the sole disposal / of
말하기를, 재무 대신께서, 전적으로 관할하고 있으니

the emperor's revenue, / might easily provide against that
황제의 수입을, 그 문제를 쉽게 해결할 수 있을 것이라고

evil, / by gradually lessening / your establishment; / by
점차적으로 줄여나감으로써 당신에 대한 급식을;

which, / for want of sufficient / for you would grow weak
그렇게 하면, 음식의 부족 때문에 당신은 점차 허약해지고 기절하여,

and faint, / and lose your appetite, / and consequently, /
식욕을 잃게 될 것입니다. 결과적으로,

decay, and consume / in a few months; / neither would
부패하여 없어져 버릴 것이라고 몇 달 안에;

the stench of your carcass / be then so dangerous, /
당신의 송장 냄새 또한 그때는 그다지 위험하지 않을 것이라고,

when it should become more than half diminished; / and
몸이 절반으로 줄어들었을 것이므로;

immediately upon your death / five or six thousand of his
그리고 당신이 죽자마자 5~6천 명의 폐하의 신하들이,

majesty's subjects might, / in two or three days, / cut your
2~3일 만에,

flesh from your bones, / take it away by cart-loads, / and
살을 뼈에서 발라내어, 수레에 실어서,

bury it in distant parts, / to prevent infection, / leaving the
멀리 떨어진 곳에 묻으면,   전염병 예방이 되고,   남겨진 해골은

skeleton / as a monument of admiration / to posterity.
경이로운 기념물이 될 것이라고 했습니다   후대에게.

graciously 자비스러운 | hereafter 후에 | revenue 수입 | establishment 고정된 수입(여기서는 음식) |
skeleton 해골 | monument 기념품 | posterity 후대

Thus, / by the great friendship of the secretary, / the whole
이와 같이, 궁내 대신의 큰 우정에 힘입어,

affair was compromised. It was strictly enjoined, / that
모든 일이 타협되었습니다.   엄격한 명령이 내려졌습니다

the project of starving you by degrees / should be kept a
당신을 점차 굶겨 죽이려는 계획은   비밀로 하도록;

secret; / but the sentence of putting out your eyes was /
              그러나 당신의 눈을 멀게 한다는 판결은

entered on the books; / none dissenting, / except Bolgolam
기록에 올렸습니다;   아무도 반대하지 않았습니다, 볼고람 제독을 제외하고는,

the admiral, / who, being a creature of the empress, / was
                  황후의 총신인 그는,

perpetually instigated / by her majesty / to insist upon your
항상 독촉을 받았습니다   황후에게   당신의 죽음을 주장하라고,

death, / she having borne perpetual malice against you, / on
황후는 늘 당신에게 반감을 품어왔습니다.

account of that infamous and illegal method / you took to
치욕스럽고 불법적인 방법 때문에   당신이 화재를 진화하

extinguish the fire / in her apartment.
기 위해 사용한   그녀의 거처에서.

Key Expression 🎵

the+비교급 ~, the+비교급 ~ : ~하면 할수록 더욱 더 ~하다
비교급을 사용한 특수 구문의 하나로 다음과 같은 방법으로 사용합니다. 또한 The
more, the better(많을수록 좋다)와 같이 간결하게 표현하는 경우도 있습니다.

▶ the + 비교급 + 주어 + 동사, the + 비교급 + 주어 + 동사
▶ the + 비교급 + 명사, the + 비교급 + 명사

ex) The more these praises were enlarged and insisted on, the more inhuman was
the punishment, and the sufferer more innocent.
이러한 찬사가 과장되고 강조될수록, 그 처벌은 더욱 비인도적이며, 그 희생자는 더
욱 무죄가 되어버린다.

In three days / your friend the secretary will be directed /
사흘 후에   당신의 친구인 궁내 대신이 명령을 받고

to come to your house, / and read before you / the articles
당신의 집을 찾아와서,   당신 앞에서 낭독할 것입니다

of impeachment; / and then / to signify the great lenity
탄핵문의 조항들을;   그리고 나서

and favor of his majesty and council, / whereby / you are
황제 폐하와 대신들의 자비심과 호의를 밝힐 것입니다.   그로 인해

only condemned / to the loss of your eyes, / which his
당신은 형벌만을 받게 된다고   두 눈을 잃는,

majesty does not question / you will gratefully and humbly
폐하는 의심하지 않습니다   당신이 감사하는 마음으로 겸허하게

/ submit to; / and twenty of his majesty's surgeons will
받아들일 것이라고;   그리고 폐하의 외과 의사 20명이 참석할 것입니다.

attend, / in order to see / the operation well performed, / by
보기 위해서   수술이 잘 되는지,

discharging very sharp-pointed arrows / into the balls of
매우 날카로운 화살을 쏘는 방법으로 하는   당신의 눈알에.

your eyes, / as you lie on the ground.
당신이 땅에 누워 있을 때.

I leave to your prudence / what measures you will take; /
당신의 판단에 맡기겠습니다   어떤 조치를 취할지는;

and to avoid suspicion, / I must immediately return / in as
그리고 의심을 피하기 위해서,   나는 당장 돌아가겠습니다

private a manner / as I came.
은밀한 방법으로   내가 왔을 때처럼.

His lordship did so; / and I remained alone, / under many
그 고관은 그렇게 돌아갔고;   나는 홀로 남아 있었다.

doubts and perplexities of mind.
수많은 의혹과 당혹감을 느낀 채.

It was a custom / introduced by this prince and his ministry
하나의 관습이 있었다   이 나라의 군주와 대신들이 만든

/ (very different, / as I have been assured, / from the practice
(매우 다른,   내가 알기로,   이전 시대의 관습과는,)

of former times,) / that after the court had decreed / any
궁정이 명한 후

cruel execution, / either to gratify the monarch's resentment,
어떤 잔혹한 집행을,   황제의 노여움을 달래 주거나,

/ or the malice of a favorite, / the emperor always made a
총신의 악의를 가라앉히기 위해,   황제는 항상 연설을 했다,

speech / to his whole council, / expressing his great lenity
모든 대신들에게,   그의 크나큰 자비심과 애정을 표현하면서,

and tenderness, / as qualities known and confessed by all the
온 세상 사람들이 알고 인정하는 자질들인,

world. This speech was immediately published / throughout
이 연설은 즉시 공표된다

the kingdom; / nor did anything terrify the people / so much
왕국 전체에;   그리고 어떤 것도 국민들을 두렵게 하는 것은 없었다

as those encomiums / on his majesty's mercy; / because it
이런 찬사보다 더   폐하의 자비심에 대한;   왜냐하면 그것은

was observed, / that the more these praises were enlarged
나타냈기 때문에,   이 찬사가 과장되고 강조될수록,

and insisted on, / the more inhuman was the punishment, /
그 처벌은 비인도적이고,

and the sufferer more innocent. Yet, / as to myself, / I must
희생자가 무죄라는 사실을.   그러나,   내 자신에 대해서는,

confess, / having never been designed for a courtier, / either
고백해야겠다,   궁정인이 될 계획이 전혀 없었기 때문에,

by my birth or education, / I was so ill a judge of things,
내 출신이나 교육으로나,   나는 사태를 분별하는데 서툴러서,

/ that I could not discover / the lenity and favor of this
전혀 알 수 없었다   이 판결의 자비와 호의라는 것을

sentence, / but conceived it / (perhaps erroneously) / rather
하지만 생각했다   (아마도 잘못 생각한 것일지 모르나)

encomium 찬사 | erroneously 잘못된 | rigorous 가혹한 | terminate 끝나다 | juncture 시점, 때 |
gratitude 감사

to be rigorous than gentle. I sometimes thought / of standing
관대하다기보다 오히려 가혹하다고.　　　　　나는 때때로 생각했다　　　　재판을 받을까 하고,

my trial, / for, / although I could not deny / the facts alleged
왜냐하면, 비록 내가 부인할 수 없더라도

in the several articles, / yet I hoped / they would admit / of
탄핵문의 조항 중 몇 가지 사실은,　　바랐기 때문이다　　그들이 인정할 것이라고

some extenuation.
다소 정상참작을.

But having in my life / perused many state-trials, / which
그러나 인생을 살아오면서　　많은 재판 기록을 정독한 후에,

I ever observed / to terminate / as the judges thought fit to
나는 알았다　　끝난다는 것을　　판사가 적절하다고 생각하는 대로.

direct, / I durst not rely on / so dangerous a decision, / in
그래서 나는 의존하지 않기로 했다　그렇게 위험한 결정에,

so critical a juncture, / and against such powerful enemies.
이토록 중대한 때에,　　　　그렇게 강력한 적에 대항하여.

Once / I was strongly bent upon resistance, / for, / while
한 번은　　강력하게 저항할 생각도 했다.　　　　왜냐하면,

I had liberty / the whole strength of that empire / could
내가 자유로운 동안　　온 국민의 힘으로도

hardly subdue me, / and I might easily / with stones / pelt
나를 꺾을 수 없을 것이기에,　그리고 나는 쉽게　　돌을 가지고

the metropolis to pieces; / but I soon rejected that project /
수도를 산산조각 낼 수 있을 것이기에;　그러나 나는 곧 계획을 접었다

with horror, / by remembering the oath / I had made to the
두려움에,　맹세를 떠올리고　　　　황제에게 했던,

emperor, / the favors I received from him, / and the high
그리고 황제에게서 받은 호의와,　　나르닥이라는 높은 작위를

title of NARDAC / he conferred upon me. Neither had I
떠올리고　　그가 내게 수여한.　　나는 그렇게 빨리 배우지

so soon learned / the gratitude of courtiers, / to persuade
못했다　　궁정인들의 감사를 표하는 법을,　　나 자신을 설득하기

myself, / that his majesty's present seventies / acquitted me
위해,　이번 황제의 가혹한 형벌이

of all past obligations.
내 모든 과거의 의무를 면제하는 것이라는.

At last, / I fixed upon a resolution, / for which it is
마침내, 나는 결심했다, 이로 인해

probable / I may incur some censure, / and not unjustly;
나는 비난을 초래할 수도 있고, 정당한 것일지도 모른다;

/ for I confess / I owe the preserving of mine eyes, / and
왜냐하면 나도 인정하니까 내가 두 눈을 보존하고,

consequently my liberty, / to my own great rashness and
자유를 누릴 수 있었던 것은, 내 경솔함과 경험 부족 탓이었음을:

want of experience; / because, / if I had then known /
때문에, 내가 그때 알았더라면

the nature of princes and ministers, / which I have since
군주와 대신들의 본성을, 이후에 알게 된

observed / in many other courts, / and their methods of
많은 다른 나라 궁정에서, 죄인을 다루는 그들의 방법이

treating criminals / less obnoxious than myself, / I should,
나보다 훨씬 죄가 덜한, 나는,

/ with great alacrity and readiness, / have submitted / to
신속하게 기꺼이, 받아들였을 것이다.

so easy a punishment. But hurried on / by the precipitancy
그렇게 가벼운 처벌을. 하지만 쫓겨서 젊음이 가진 성급함에,

of youth, / and having his imperial majesty's license / to
그리고 황제의 허가서를 가지고 있었기에

pay my attendance upon the emperor of Blefuscu, / I took
블레프스큐의 황제를 보러 가도 좋다는,

this opportunity, / before the three days were elapsed, /
나는 이것을 기회 삼아, 사흘도 채 지나지 않아,

to send a letter to my friend the secretary, / signifying
친구인 궁내 대신에게 편지를 보냈다, 결심을 나타내는

my resolution / of setting out that morning for Blefuscu,
그 날 아침 블레프스큐로 떠날 것이라는,

/ pursuant to the leave I had got; / and, / without waiting
내가 받은 허가서에 따라; 그리고, 답장을 기다리지도 않고,

for an answer, / I went to that side of the island / where
섬 쪽으로 갔다 우리 함대가

our fleet lay. I seized a large man of war, / tied a cable to
정박하고 있는. 나는 큰 군함을 붙잡아, 뱃머리에 밧줄을 감고,

the prow, / and, / lifting up the anchors, / I stripped myself,
그리고, 닻을 올렸다. 옷을 벗은 후,

/ put my clothes / (together with my coverlet, / which I
옷을 넣고 (침대보와 함께,

carried under my arm) / into the vessel, / and, / drawing
옆구리에 껴서 가져온) 배 안에. 그리고, 그것을 끌고,

it after me, / between wading and swimming / arrived at
걷거나 헤엄치면서

the royal port of Blefuscu, / where the people had long
블레프스큐의 항구에 도착했다. 거기에는 사람들이 나를 오랫동안 기다리고 있었다:

expected me: / they lent me two guides / to direct me to the
그들은 내게 두 명의 안내인을 붙여

capital city, / which is of the same name. I held them / in
수도로 인도했다 같은 이름을 가진. 나는 그들을 잡아

my hands, / till I came / within two hundred yards of the
손에 올려 놓았다, 당도할 때까지 성문에서 200야드 떨어진 곳에,

gate, / and desired them / "to signify my arrival / to one
그리고 그들에게 부탁했다 "내 도착을 알리고

of the secretaries, / and let him know, / I there waited his
대신들 중 한 사람에게, 그에게 전해 달라고, 그곳에서 황제의 지시를

majesty's command." I had an answer / in about an hour,
기다리겠다고." 나는 답변을 받았다 약 한 시간 후에,

Key Expression

부정주어를 이용한 최상급 표현

'가장 ~한'이라는 의미의 최상급을 표현하는 다양한 방법을 알아봅시다.
▶ ~ the + 최상급 + 명사
▶ 부정주어 ~ 비교급 + than ~
▶ 부정주어 ~ so + 원급 + as ~
▶ 긍정주어 ~ 비교급 + than + any other ~

ex) Nor did anything terrify the people so much as those encomiums on his majesty's mercy.
어떤 것도 폐하의 자비심에 대한 이런 찬사보다 더 국민들을 두렵게 하는 것은 없다.
= Nor did anything terrify the people more than those encomiums on his majesty's mercy.

rashness 경솔함 | obnoxious 나쁜 | alacrity 민첩 | precipitancy 성급함 | elapse 지나다 | pursuant ~에 따른 | wade (물, 진흙 속을) 힘겹게 헤치며 걷다

173

/ "that his majesty, / attended by the royal family, / and
"황제 폐하께서, 왕족을 대동하고,

great officers of the court, / was coming out to receive
궁정 고관들과, 나를 맞으러 오고 있다는."

me." I advanced a hundred yards. The emperor and his
나는 100야드를 더 나아갔다. 황제와 그의 수행원들이

train / alighted from their horses, / the empress and ladies
말에서 내리고, 황후와 귀부인들은

/ from their coaches, / and I did not perceive / they were
그들의 마차에서 내렸다. 그리고 나는 느끼지 못했다 그들이 조금도

in any fright or concern. I lay on the ground / to kiss his
무서워 하거나 걱정하는 기색을. 나는 땅에 누워서

majesty's and the empress's hands. I told his majesty, /
황제와 황후의 손에 입을 맞추었다. 나는 황제에게 말했다,

"that I was come / according to my promise, / and with
"저는 왔습니다 약속에 따라, 그리고 허락을 얻어

the license / of the emperor my master, / to have the honor
내 주인이신 릴리펏 황제의, 뵙는 영광을 갖기 위해

of seeing / so mighty a monarch, / and to offer him any
위대하신 황제를, 그리고 봉사를 해 드리기 위해

service / in my power, / consistent with my duty / to my
제가 할 수 있는, 의무에 어긋나지 않는다면 내 주인이신

own prince;" / not mentioning a word / of my disgrace, /
군주에 대한;" 한 마디도 하지 않은 채 나의 불명예에 관해서는,

because / I had hither / to no regular information of it, /
왜냐하면 나는 그때까지 정식 통보를 받지 않았고,

and might suppose myself wholly ignorant / of any such
내 자신이 전혀 모르는 것으로 되어 있었기 때문에 그런 계획에 대해;

design; / neither could I reasonably conceive / that the
또한 이성적으로 전혀 생각할 수 없었다 황제가 그 비밀을

emperor would discover the secret, / while I was out of
폭로하리라고는, 내가 그의 권한 밖에 있는 동안;

perceive 감지하다 | wholly 완전히, 전적으로

his power; / wherein, / however, / it soon appeared / I was
이 점에 있어서,   그러나,   곧 밝혀졌다

deceived.
내가 틀렸다는 것이.

I shall not trouble the reader / with the particular account
독자 여러분을 지루하게 하지는 않겠다   내 환대식에 대한 자세한 설명으로

of my reception / at this court, / which was suitable / to the
            궁정에서의,   알맞았던

generosity of so great a prince; / nor of the difficulties / I
위대한 군주의 자비에;   또한 고생했던 이야기도 하지 않겠다

was in for want of a house and bed, / being forced to lie / on
나는 집과 잠자리가 없어서,   땅바닥에 누워야만 했다,

the ground, / wrapped up in my coverlet.
            침대보로 몸을 감싼 채.

A. 다음 문장을 해석해 보세요.

(1) This preface made me so impatient, / being conscious of my own merits and innocence, / that I was going to interrupt him.
→

(2) He allowed your crimes to be great, / but that still there was room for mercy.
→

(3) Although I could not deny / the facts alleged in the several articles, / yet I hoped / they would admit of some extenuation.
→

(4) Neither could I reasonably conceive / that the emperor would discover the secret, / while I was out of his power; / wherein, / however, / it soon appeared / I was deceived.
→

B. 다음 주어진 문장이 되도록 빈칸에 써 넣으세요.

(1) 궁궐 경내에서 소변을 보는 사람은 누구나 대역죄의 처벌을 받게 된다.

_____ shall

be liable to the pains and penalties of high-treason.

(2) 재무 대신과 해군 제독은 <u>당신이 가장 고통스럽고 비참한 처벌을 받아야 한다고 주장했다</u>.

The treasurer and admiral _____

_____ .

(3) <u>어떤 조치를 취할지는</u> 당신의 판단에 맡기겠다.

I leave to your prudence _____ .

(4) <u>어떤 것도</u> 폐하의 자비심에 대한 이런 찬사보다 <u>국민들을 두렵게 하는 것은 없</u>었다.

A. (1) 이렇게 시작하는 말은 나의 공적과 무죄를 생각할 때 나를 참을 수 없게 해서 그의 말을 가로막으려고 했다. (2) 그는 당신의 죄가 크다는 것은 인정했으나, 아직 자비를 베풀 여지가 있다고 했다. (3) 비록 내가 탄핵문의 조항 중 몇 가지 사실을 부인할 수 없더라도, 나는 그들이 다소 정상참작을 인정할 것이라고 바랐다. (4) 나는 내가 그의 권한 밖에 있는 동안 황제가

                                                           those
encomiums on his majesty's mercy.

C.다음 주어진 문구가 알맞은 문장이 되도록 순서를 맞춰 보세요.

(1) 재무 대신도 같은 생각이었다.
    (the / of / The treasurer / opinion / was / same)
    →

(2) 이 찬사가 과장되고 강조될수록, 그 처벌은 더욱 비인도적이다.
    (The more / the more / inhuman / were / was / enlarged / and
    / the punishment / insisted on, / these praises)
    →

(3) 나는 궁정인들의 감사를 표하는 법을 그렇게 빨리 배우지도 못했다.
    (had / Neither / so soon / the gratitude / I / of / courtiers /
    learned)
    →

(4) 그는 그런 이유로 당신을 반역자로 고발하고, 따라서 당신이 사형 당해야 한다고
    주장했다.
    (you / insisted / put / e / should / death / to)
    He accused you as a traitor on that account, and therefore

D. 다음 단어에대한 맞는 설명과 연결해 보세요.

(1) rigorous   ▶   ◀ ① in spite of

(2) notwithstanding ▶   ◀ ② very thorough and strict

(3) forsake   ▶   ◀ ③ a formal expression of praise

(4) encomiums   ▶   ◀ ④ stop doing it

The author, / by a lucky accident, / finds means to leave
저자가,   행운의 사건에 의해,   블레프스큐에서 떠날 방법을 찾는다;

Blefuscu; / and, / after some difficulties, / returns safe to
그리고,   약간의 어려움을 겪은 후,

his native country.
무사히 고국으로 돌아온다.

Three days after my arrival, / walking out of curiosity / to
도착한지 사흘 후에,   호기심이 나서 걸어가다가

the north-east coast of the island, / I observed, / about half
섬의 북동쪽의 해안으로,   나는 보았다,

a league off in the sea, / somewhat that looked like a boat
약 반 리그 떨어진 바다에,   뒤집어진 보트처럼 보이는 어떤 물체를.

overturned. I pulled off my shoes and stockings, / and, /
신발과 양말을 벗었다,   그리고,

wailing two or three hundred yards, / I found the object /
2~3백 야드를 걸어가,   그 물체를 보았다

to approach nearer / by force of the tide; / and then plainly
좀 더 가까이 다가오는 것을   조류에 밀려;   그리고 나서 분명히 확인했다

saw / it to be a real boat, / which I supposed might / by
그것이 정말 보트라는 것을,   그것은 아마도

some tempest / have been driven from a ship.
폭풍에 의해   어떤 배에서 밀려온 것 같았다.

Key Expression♟

재귀대명사의 두 가지 용법

'~자신'을 뜻하는 ~self 형태의 대명사를 재귀대명사라고 부릅니다.
재귀대명사의 용법에는 두 가지가 있는데 주어와 목적어가 같을 때 쓰는 재귀용법과
주어나 목적어를 강조하기 위해 쓰는 강조용법입니다.

ex) I stripped myself, and waded. (재귀용법)
    나는 옷을 벗고 물 속을 걸었다.
    ···my waist and arms I measured myself. (강조용법)
    내 허리와 팔은 내가 직접 쟀다.

Whereupon, / I returned immediately / towards the city, /
그래서, 당장 돌아갔다 수도로,

and desired his imperial majesty / to lend me / twenty of
그리고 황제에게 간청했다 빌려 달라고

the tallest vessels / he had left, / after the loss of his fleet,
제일 큰 20척의 배를 그에게 남아 있는, 함대를 잃고 난 후,

/ and three thousand seamen, / under the command of his
그리고 300명의 해군도, 부제독이 지휘하는.

vice-admiral. This fleet sailed round, / while I went back
이 함대가 섬을 돌아 항해했고, 그 동안 제일 짧은 지름길로

the shortest way / to the coast, / where I first discovered the
해안으로 갔다, 처음 보트를 발견했던 곳으로.

boat. I found / the tide had driven it still nearer. The seamen
나는 발견했다 조류가 그것을 해안에 더 가깝게 떠민 것을.

were all provided with cordage, / which I had beforehand
모든 해군은 밧줄을 제공 받았다, 내가 미리 꼬아놓은

twisted / to a sufficient strength. When the ships came
충분히 튼튼하도록. 함정들이 도착했을 때,

up, / I stripped myself, / and waded / till I came / within a
나는 옷을 벗고, 물 속을 걸었다 도착할 때까지

hundred yards off the boat, / after which / I was forced to
보트에서 100야드 떨어진 곳에, 그 후에는 헤엄쳐야 했다

swim / till I got up to it. The seamen threw me / the end of
보트에 도달할 때까지. 해군들이 내게 던졌고 밧줄의 끝을,

the cord, / which I fastened to a hole / in the fore-part of the
나는 그것을 구멍에 묶었다 보트 앞부분에,

boat, / and the other end to a man of war; / but I found / all
그리고 다른 한 끝은 전함에; 그러나 나는 알았다

my labor / to little purpose; / for, / being out of my depth, /
내 모든 노력이 소용없음을; 왜냐하면, 내 키보다 깊어서,

vice-admiral 부제독 | beforehand 미리 | necessity 불가피한 일

I was not able to work. In this necessity / I was forced to
일할 수 없었기 때문에.   이런 절박한 상황에서   나는 뒤로 헤엄쳐야만 했고,

swim behind, / and push the boat forward, / as often as I
보트를 앞으로 밀며.   가능한 자주,

could, / with one of my hands; / and the tide favoring me,
한 손으로;   그리고 조류도 나를 도와줘서,

/ I advanced so far / that I could just hold up my chin /
나는 상당히 전진했고   턱을 위로 내밀어

and feel the ground. I rested two or three minutes, / and
바닥에 닿을 수 있었다.   나는 2~3분 쉬었다가,

then gave the boat another shove, / and so on, / till the
다시 보트를 밀었다.   그렇게 계속하여,

sea was no higher than my arm-pits; / and now, / the most
물의 깊이가 겨드랑이에 이르렀다;   그리고 이제,

laborious part being over, / I took out my other cables,
일의 제일 힘든 고비만 남았다.   나는 다른 밧줄을 꺼내어,

/ which were stowed in one of the ships, / and fastened
한 선박에 실렸던,   그리고 그것들을 묶었다

them / first to the boat, / and then to nine of the vessels
처음에는 보트에,   그리고 다음으로 9척의 선박에

/ which attended me; / the wind being favorable, / the
내 옆에 있던;   바람이 유리한 방향으로 불어서,

seamen towed, / and I shoved, / until we arrived / within
해군들이 끌고,   내가 밀면서,   마침내 우리는 도착했다

forty yards of the shore; / and, / waiting till the tide was
해안에서 40야드 떨어진 곳까지;   그리고,   조수가 밀려날 때까지 기다렸다가,

out, / I got dry to the boat, / and by the assistance of
몸을 말린 후에 보트에 다가갔다.   그리고 2,000명의 해군의 도움과,

two thousand men, / with ropes and engines, / I made a
밧줄과 연장들을 이용해,

shift to turn it on its bottom, / and found it was but little
나는 보트를 뒤집었고,   크게 망가진 곳이 없음을 알았다.

damaged.

laborious 힘든 | stow 집어넣다 | expostulation 충고

I shall not trouble the reader / with the difficulties I was
독자 여러분을 괴롭히진 않겠다   내가 겪은 고생들로,

under, / by the help of certain paddles, / which cost me
        노의 도움을 받아,   만드는 데 열흘이나 걸렸던.

ten days making, / to get my boat to the royal port of
        보트를 블레프스큐의 항구로 가져오기 위해,

Blefuscu, / where a mighty concourse of people appeared
        그곳에는 엄청난 무리의 군중들이 나타나서

/ upon my arrival, / full of wonder / at the sight of so
  내가 도착하자,   무척 놀랐다   그런 거대한 배를 보고.

prodigious a vessel. I told the emperor / "that my good
                나는 황제에게 말했다   "행운의 여신이 던져 줘서

fortune had thrown / this boat in my way, / to carry me
                    내게 이 보트를,

to some place / whence I might return / into my native
나를 데려가게 되었다고 내가 돌아갈 곳   내 조국으로;

country; / and begged his majesty's orders / for getting
        그리고 황제에게 명령을 내려 줄 것을 간청했다   물자를 마련하도록

materials / to fit it up, / together with his license to
        보트에 갖출,   출국 허가와 함께;"

depart;" / which, / after some kind expostulations, / he
그 간청을,   충고의 말을 건넨 후,

was pleased to grant.
그는 흔쾌히 수락했다.

I did very much wonder, / in all this time, / not to have
나는 매우 궁금했다.　　　　　　　이 모든 일이 있는 동안,　　　들어보지 않은 것이

heard of / any express relating to me / from our emperor
　　　　　나에 관한 어떤 얘기도　　　　　　릴리펏 황제로부터

/ to the court of Blefuscu. But I was afterward / given
블레프스큐의 궁정으로.　　　　　　그러나 나는 나중에

privately to understand, / that his imperial majesty, / never
은밀하게 알게 되었다.　　　　　우리 황제는,

imagining / I had the least notice of his designs, / believed
상상하지 못했고　　내가 그의 계획을 조금이라도 알고 있다고,　　　　믿었다는 것을

/ I was only gone to Blefuscu / in performance of my
　내가 블레프스큐로 간 것이라고　　　　오직 내 약속을 지키기 위해서,

promise, / according to the license / he had given me, /
허가에 따라서　　　　　　　그가 내게 준,

which was well known at our court, / and would return /
그것은 우리 궁정에 잘 알려져 있었고,　　　　　　돌아올 거라고 믿었다는 것을

in a few days, / when the ceremony was ended. But he was
며칠 내로,　　　의식이 끝나면.　　　　　　　그러나 그는 마침내

at last in pain / at my long absence; / and after consulting
불안해졌고　　　내 오랜 부재에;　　　　그래서 재무 대신과 상의한 후

with the treasurer / and the rest of that cabal, / a person
　　　　　　기타 각료들과,

of quality was dispatched / with the copy of the articles
한 고관을 파견했다　　　　　나에 대한 탄핵문의 사본을 지참시켜.

against me. This envoy had instructions / to represent to
　　　　　　이 사신은 지시 받았다

the monarch of Blefuscu, / "the great lenity of his master,
블레프스큐의 황제에게 전하라고　　"매우 자비심 깊은 군주는,

/ who was content to punish me / no farther than with the
　나를 처벌하는데 만족했다고,　　　　내 두 눈을 없애는 것만으로;

loss of mine eyes; / that I had fled from justice; / and if
　　　　　　나는 재판으로부터 도망쳤으며;　　　만약 내가

I did not return / in two hours, / I should be deprived of
돌아오지 않는다면　　두 시간 안에,　　나르닥 작위를 박탈당하고,

envoy 특사 | insupportable 유지하기 힘든 | encumbrance 부담

my title of NARDAC, / and declared a traitor." The envoy
반역자로 선포될 것이다'라고. 이 특사는 여기에

further added, / "that in order to maintain the peace and
덧붙였다. "평화와 우애를 유지하기 위하여

amity / between both empires, / his master expected / that
두 제국 간의. 황제는 기대한다고

his brother of Blefuscu would give orders / to have me sent
형제의 나라인 블레프스큐 황제가 명령을 내려 줄 것이라고 나를 릴리펏으로 돌려보내

back to Lilliput, / bound hand and foot, / to be punished as
라는. 손과 발을 묶어서. 반역자로 처벌되도록."

a traitor."

The emperor of Blefuscu, / having taken three days to
블레프스큐 황제는. 사흘 동안 협의한 후,

consult, / returned an answer / consisting of many civilities
답변을 보냈다 대단히 정중한 인사와 변명 담은.

and excuses. He said, / "that as for sending me bound, /
그는 말하기를. "나를 묶어서 보내는 것은,

his brother knew / it was impossible; / that, although I had
형제인 폐하도 알 것이라고 했다 불가능 하다는 사실을; 비록 그의 함대를 빼앗았지만,

deprived him of his fleet, / yet he owed great obligations
그는 내게 큰 은혜를 입고 있다고

to me / for many good offices / I had done him / in making
많은 선행들로 인해 내가 그에게 해 준 평화를 조성하기

the peace. That, however, / both their majesties would soon
위해. 그러나, 곧 두 제국은 안심할 수 있을 것이라고;

be made easy; / for I had found a prodigious vessel / on the
왜냐하면 내가 엄청나게 큰 배를 발견했기 때문에

shore, / able to carry me on the sea, / which he had given
해안에서. 바다에 타고 갈 수 있으며, 그는 장비를 갖추도록 명령을

orders to fit up, / with my own assistance and direction; /
내렸다고. 내 도움과 요청에 따라;

and he hoped, / in a few weeks, / both empires would be
그리고 그는 기대한다고 했다. 몇 주 후면, 두 제국은 벗어날 수 있을 것이라고

freed / from so insupportable an encumbrance."
이토록 감당하기 힘든 부담으로부터."

With this answer / the envoy returned to Lilliput; / and the
이 답장을 가지고   특사는 릴리펏으로 돌아갔다;

monarch of Blefuscu related to me / all that had passed;
그리고 블레프스큐의 황제는 내게 말해 주었다   그간 있었던 모든 일을;

/ offering me at the same time / (but under the strictest
그리고 동시에 내게 제안했다   (하지만 절대 비밀로)

confidence) / his gracious protection, / if I would continue
그의 자비로운 보호를,   만약 내가 계속 그를 위해 봉사

in his service; / wherein, / although I believed him
하겠다면;   이에 대해,   나는 그가 진심임을 믿었지만,

sincere, / yet I resolved / never more to put any confidence
나는 결심했다   더 이상 신뢰하지 않겠다고

/ in princes or ministers, / where I could possibly avoid it;
군주나 대신들을,   피할 수만 있다면;

/ and therefore, / with all due acknowledgments / for his
그래서,   충분히 감사를 표하면서

favourable intentions, / I humbly begged to be excused.
그의 호의에,   나는 공손하게 거절했다.

I told him, / "that since fortune, / whether good or evil,
나는 그에게 말했다, "운명이,   좋은 쪽이든 나쁜 쪽이든,

/ had thrown a vessel in my way, / I was resolved / to
내게 배 한 척을 던져 주었으니,   나는 결심했다고

venture myself / on the ocean, / rather than be an occasion
모험을 하기로   바다로 나가는,   불화의 원인이 되기보다는

of difference / between two such mighty monarchs."
위대하신 두 군주들 간의".

Key Expression

whether A or B : A이든 B이든

접속사 whether는 명사절과 부사절을 이끄는 두 가지 용도로 사용됩니다. 부사절을 이끄는 whether는 '~이든 ~이든'의 뜻을 가지고 있답니다. 또한 whether ~ or not과 같이 사용하여 '~이든 아니든'이라는 의미로도 흔히 쓰여요.

ex) I told him, "that since fortune, whether good or evil, had thrown a vessel in my way, I was resolved to venture myself on the ocean."
나는 그에게 말했다. "운명이 좋은 쪽이든 나쁜 쪽이든 내게 배 한 척을 던져 주었으니, 나는 바다로 나가는 모험을 하기로 결심했다"라고.

hasten 재촉하다 | quilt 누벼 꿰매다 | grease 기름을 치다 | rough 대충한, 대강한

Neither did I find / the emperor at all displeased; / and I
나는 전혀 발견할 수 없었다   황제에게서 불만의 징후를;

discovered, / by a certain accident, / that he was very glad
그리고 알게 되었다,   어떤 사건에 의해,   그가 내 결심을 매우 반가워 했고,

of my resolution, / and so were most of his ministers.
대부분의 대신들도 그러했다는 것을.

These considerations moved me / to hasten my departure
이런 사항들이 나를 움직여   출발을 서두르게 했다

/ somewhat sooner than I intended; / to which the court,
의도했던 것보다 조금 빨리;   이에 대해서 궁정도,

/ impatient to have me gone, / very readily contributed.
내가 어서 가기를 바랐기 때문에,   기꺼이 협력해 주었다.

Five hundred workmen were employed / to make two sails
500명의 일꾼들이 고용되어   두 개의 돛을 만들었다

/ to my boat, / according to my directions, / by quilting
내 보트에 달,   내 지시에 따라,   13겹으로 겹쳐 누비는

thirteen folds / of their strongest linen together. I was at
방법으로   그들의 가장 튼튼한 리넨 천을.

the pains of / making ropes and cables, / by twisting ten,
나는 고생했다   새끼줄과 밧줄을 만드는데,   10개, 20개, 30개를 꼬아서

twenty, or thirty / of the thickest and strongest of theirs.
그 나라에서 가장 굵은 줄을.

A great stone / that I happened to find, / after a long
커다란 돌이   내가 우연히 발견한,   오랫동안 찾은 끝에,

search, / by the sea-shore, / served me for an anchor. I
해안가에서,   내게 닻이 되어 주었다.

had the tallow of three hundred cows, / for greasing my
나는 소 300마리의 기름을 가지게 되었고,   보트에 기름칠을 하기 위한,

boat, / and other uses. I was at incredible pains / in cutting
그리고 다른 용도로.   나는 엄청나게 고생했다   베는 데

down / some of the largest timber-trees, / for oars and
가장 큰 목재용 나무를,   노와 돛대를 위한,

masts, / wherein I was, / however, / much assisted / by his
이 일에 있어서,   그러나,   많은 도움을 받았다

majesty's ship-carpenters, / who helped me / in smoothing
황제의 선박 목수들에게,   나를 도와 준,   그것들을 다듬는데,

them, / after I had done the rough work.
내가 대충 작업을 마친 후.

In about a month, / when all was prepared, / I sent to
약 한 달 후,   모든 준비가 되었을 때,

receive his majesty's commands, / and to take my leave.
황제의 명령을 받으러 사람을 보냈다.   그리고 작별 인사를 드리겠다고.

The emperor and royal family came / out of the palace; /
황제와 왕족들이 나왔고   왕궁에서;

I lay down on my face / to kiss his hand, / which he very
나는 땅에 얼굴을 대고 누웠다   그의 손에 입맞추기 위해,   그가 매우 자비롭게

graciously gave me: / so did / the empress and young
내게 내밀어 준: 그렇게 했다 황후와 황태자들도.

princes of the blood. His majesty presented me / with
황제는 내게 주었다

fifty purses / of two hundred SPRUGS a-piece, / together
50개의 지갑을   각각 200스프럭씩 들어 있는,

with his picture at full length, / which I put immediately
그의 전신 초상화와 함께,   나는 그것을 즉시 넣었다

/ into one of my gloves, / to keep it from being hurt. The
내 장갑 한 쪽에,   다치지 않도록.

ceremonies at my departure / were too many / to trouble the
출발 의식들이   너무 많아서   독자를 지루하게 할 것

reader with / at this time.
이니 생략하겠다   이번에는.

I stored the boat / with the carcases of a hundred oxen, / and
나는 보트에 실었다   100마리 분의 소고기와,

three hundred sheep, / with bread and drink proportionable,
300마리 분의 양고기,   이에 상응하는 빵과 음료,

/ and as much meat ready dressed / as four hundred cooks
그리고 요리된 고기들을   400여 명의 요리사가 제공한 만큼의.

could provide. I took with me / six cows and two bulls
나는 가졌다   살아 있는 암소 여섯 마리와 황소 두 마리를,

alive, / with as many ewes and rams, / intending to carry
같은 수의 암양과 숫양도 함께,   내 조국에 데려갈 생각으로,

them into my own country, / and propagate the breed. And
그리고 번식시키려고.   그리고

to feed them / on board, / I had a good bundle of hay, /
그것들을 먹이기 위해 배에 실었다.   충분한 양의 건초와,

and a bag of corn. I would gladly have taken a dozen of
옥수수 한 자루를.   나는 10여 명의 주민을 데려가고 싶었지만,

the natives, / but this was a thing / the emperor would by
            이 일은   황제가 절대로 허락하지 않았다;

no means permit; / and, / besides a diligent search / into
                    그리고,   샅샅이 조사했을 뿐만 아니라

my pockets, / his majesty engaged my honor / "not to
내 호주머니를,   황제는 내 명예를 걸고 맹세하도록 했다

carry away / any of his subjects, / although with their own
"데려가지 않겠다고   그의 백성을,   비록 그들이 동의하고 원하더라도."

consent and desire."

ewe 암양 | ram 숫양 | propagate 번식시키다

Having thus prepared all things / as well as I was able, /
이렇게 해서 모든 것을 준비한 후   내가 할 수 있는.

I set sail / on the twenty-fourth day of September 1701, /
나는 항해를 출발했다   1701년 9월 24일.

at six in the morning; / and when I had gone about four-
오전 6시에;   그리고 내가 4리그쯤 갔을 때

leagues / to the northward, / the wind being at south-east,
   북쪽으로,   남동풍이 불었고,

/ at six in the evening / I descryed a small island, / about
저녁 6시에   나는 작은 섬을 발견했다.

half a league to the north-west. I advanced forward, / and
북서쪽으로 약 반 리그쯤 되는 곳에서.   나는 그쪽으로 전진했고,

cast anchor / on the lee-side of the island, / which seemed
닻을 내렸다   섬의 바람이 불어가는 쪽으로,   그러나 그곳은 사람이

to be uninhabited. I then took some refreshment, / and
살지 않는 듯 했다.   그래서 나는 음식을 약간 먹고,

went to my rest. I slept well, / and as I conjectured at least
휴식을 취했다.   나는 푹 잤고,   적어도 6시간은 지났다고 추측했다.

six hours, / for I found the day broke / in two hours after
   왜냐하면 동이 트는 것을 봤기에   깨어난지 두 시간 후.

I awaked. It was a clear night. I ate my breakfast / before
   날씨가 맑은 밤이었다.   나는 아침을 먹었다

the sun was up; / and heaving anchor, / the wind being
해가 떠오르기 전에;   그리고 닻을 올리자,   순풍이 불어서,

favorable, / I steered the same course / that I had done
   나는 같은 방향으로 나아갔다   그 전 날 했던대로,

the day before, / wherein I was directed / by my pocket
   방향을 잡으며   휴대용 나침반으로.

compass. My intention was to reach, / if possible, / one of
내 의도는 도착하는 것이었다.   가능하다면,

those islands, / which I had reason to believe / lay to the
섬들 중 하나에,   믿을 근거가 있는

north-east of Van Diemen's Land. I discovered nothing / all
반 디멘 랜드의 북동쪽에 있다고.   나는 아무것도 발견하지 못했다

that day; / but upon the next, / about three in the afternoon,
그 날 하루 종일;   하지만 다음 날,   오후 3시 경에,

/ when I had by my computation / made twenty-four
내 계산으로는 블레프스큐로부터 24리그 정도

leagues from Blefuscu, / I descryed a sail / steering to the
왔을 때, 나는 배를 발견했다 남동쪽으로 항해하는;

south-east; / my course was due east. I hailed her, / but
내 배의 진로는 동쪽이었다. 나는 그 배에 소리쳤으나,

could get no answer; / yet I found I gained upon her, / for
아무런 대답도 듣지 못했다; 그러나 나는 그 배에 닿을 수 있음을 알았다.

the wind slackened. I made all the sail I could, / and in half
바람이 약해졌기 때문에. 나는 있는 대로 돛을 다 펼쳤고, 반 시간 후

an hour / she spied me, / then hung out her ancient, / and
그 배는 나를 알아채고, 깃발을 내걸며,

discharged a gun. It is not easy to express / the joy I was
총을 한 발 쏘았다. 표현하기는 쉬운 일이 아니다 내가 느낀 기쁨을,

in, / upon the unexpected hope / of once more seeing / my
예상치 못한 희망으로 다시 한 번 볼 수 있다는

beloved country, / and the dear pledges I left in it. The ship
내 사랑하는 조국과, 두고 온 사랑하는 아이들을. 그 배는 돛을 줄였고,

slackened her sails, / and I came up with her / between five
그 배는 돛을 줄였고, 나는 따라잡았다

and six in the evening, / September 26th; / but my heart
오후 5시와 6시 사이에, 9월 26일; 내 심장은 터질 듯 했다

leaped within me / to see her English colors. I put my cows
그 배의 영국 깃발을 보자. 나는 소와 양들을 넣고

and sheep / into my coat-pockets, / and got on board / with
코트 호주머니에, 배에 올랐다

all my little cargo of provisions. The vessel was an English
작은 짐들을 모두 가지고. 그 배는 영국 상선이었다.

merchantman, / returning from Japan / by the North and
일본으로부터 귀국 중인 북태평양과 남태평양을 거쳐;

South seas; / the captain, / Mr. John Biddel, / of Deptford, /
선장인, 존 비들 씨는, 뎁트포드 출신의,

a very civil man, / and an excellent sailor.
매우 예의 바르고, 능숙한 뱃사람이었다.

descry 보게 되다 | uninhabite 사람이 살지 않는 | slacken 약해지다 | pledge 약속

189

We were now / in the latitude of 30 degrees south; / there
우리는 그때 있었다   남위 30도에;

were about fifty men / in the ship; / and here / I met an old
50명의 선원이 있었다   배 안에는;   그리고 이곳에서

comrade of mine, / one Peter Williams, / who gave me a
나는 옛 동료를 만났다,   피터 윌리엄즈라는 이름의,   그는 나를 좋은 사람이라고

good character / to the captain. This gentleman treated
소개했다   선장에게.   이 신사는 나를 친절히 대해 주며,

me with kindness, / and desired I would let him know /
알려 달라고 요청했다

what place I came from last, / and whither I was bound; /
마지막에 어디에서 출발하여,   어느 방향으로 가고 있었는지;

which I did in a few words, / but he thought I was raving,
나는 대략 설명했으나,   그는 내가 미쳤다고 생각했다,

/ and that the dangers I underwent / had disturbed my
그리고 내가 겪은 위험이   내 머리를 이상하게 만들었다고

head; / whereupon I took my black cattle and sheep / out
생각했다;   그래서 나는 검은 소와 양을 꺼냈다

of my pocket, / which, / after great astonishment, / clearly
호주머니에서,   그러자,   매우 놀라고는,

convinced him of my veracity. I then showed him the gold
내 진실을 분명히 인정했다.   그리고 나서 나는 그에게 금을 보여 주었다

/ given me by the emperor of Blefuscu, / together with his
블레프스큐의 황제로부터 받은,   황제의 전신 초상화와,

majesty's picture at full length, / and some other rarities
그 나라의 몇 가지 진품과 함께,

of that country. I gave him two purses / of two hundreds
나는 그에게 지갑 두 개를 줬다   각각 200스프럭씩 들어 있는,

SPRUGS each, / and promised, / when we arrived / in
그리고 약속했다,   우리가 영국에 도착하면,

England, / to make him a present / of a cow and a sheep
그에게 선물로 주겠다고   소 한 마리와 새끼를 가진 양 한 마리를.

big with young.

---

veracity 진실 | rarity 진귀함 물건, 진품 | prosperous 평온한 | mingle 섞다 | constant 지속적인, 변함없는

I shall not trouble the reader / with a particular account
독자 여러분을 지루하게 하지는 않겠다   이 항해에 대한 자세한 이야기로,

of this voyage, / which was very prosperous / for the most
그 항해는 매우 평온했다   대부분,

part. We arrived in the Downs / on the 13th of April, 1702.
우리는 다운즈에 도착했다   1702년 4월 13일에,

I had only one misfortune, / that the rats on board carried
딱 한 번 불행한 사건이 있었는데,   배 안의 쥐들이 물어 가 버린 일이었다

away / one of my sheep; / I found her bones / in a hole, /
내 양 한 마리를;   나는 양의 뼈를 발견했다   구멍 속에서 보았다,

picked clean from the flesh. The rest of my cattle / I got
살을 깨끗이 뜯어 먹힌 채.   가축들 나머지는   무사히

safe ashore, / and set them a-grazing / in a bowling-green
육지로 데려갔고,   그것들을 방목했다   그리니치에 있는 볼링용 잔디밭에,

at Greenwich, / where the fineness of the grass / made
그곳의 가는 풀들은

them feed very heartily, / though I had always feared the
그들을 실컷 배부르게 했다.   항상 반대로 걱정했던 것과 달리:

contrary: / neither could I possibly have preserved them /
아마도 절대로 그것들을 보존하지 못했을 것이다

in so long a voyage, / if the captain had not allowed me /
그렇게 긴 항해 동안,   만약 선장이 내게 허락하지 않았다면

some of his best biscuit, / which, / rubbed to powder, / and
그의 최고급 비스킷을 약간,   그것을,   비벼서 가루로 만들어,

mingled with water, / was their constant food. The short
물과 섞으면,   그들의 음식이 되었다.   짧은 시간 동안

time / I continued in England, / I made a considerable
나는 영국에 머물렀고,   상당한 수익을 얻었다

profit / by showing my cattle / to many persons of quality
내 가축을 구경시켜서   수많은 상류층 및 기타 사람들에게;

and others: / and before I began my second voyage, / I sold
그리고 두 번째 항해를 시작하기 전에,   그것들을

them / for six hundred pounds. Since my last return / I find
팔았다   600파운드에,   마지막 항해에서 돌아온 후   나는 발견했다

/ the breed is considerably increased, / especially the sheep,
상당히 번식이 증가했음을,   특히 양이,

/ which I hope will prove / much to the advantage of the
나는 그것을 밝히는 바이다   양모 제조업에 큰 이익을 가져다 줄 것임을,

woollen manufacture, / by the fineness of the fleeces.
그 훌륭한 양털 때문에.

I stayed but two months / with my wife and family, / for
나는 단지 두 달 간 머물렀다   부인과 가족 곁에,

my insatiable desire / of seeing foreign countries, / would
멈출 수 없는 욕구 때문에   외국을 보고 싶다는,

suffer me to continue no longer. I left fifteen hundred
더 이상 계속하는 것이 괴로웠다.   나는 1,500파운드를 남겼고

pounds / with my wife, / and fixed her in a good house
아내에게,   그녀를 레드리프의 멋진 집에서 살게 했다.

/ at Redriff. My remaining stock / I carried with me, /
나머지 재산은   내가 가져온,

part in money and part in goods, / in hopes to improve
일부는 현금으로 일부는 물건들로 바꿨다,   내 운을 높여 보겠다는 희망으로.

my fortunes. My eldest uncle John had left / me an estate
큰아버지인 존이 남겨 주었다   내게 토지를,

in land, / near Epping, / of about thirty pounds a year; /
에핑 근처에,   매년 30파운드 가량 수입이 되는;

and I had a long lease / of the Black Bull in Fetter-Lane,
또한 나는 장기 임차권을 갖고 있었고 페터레인의 블랙불에,

/ which yielded me / as much more; / so that I was not
내게 수입을 주는   그 이상의;   그래서 나는 아무런 위험이 없었다

in any danger / of leaving my family upon the parish.
가족을 두고 떠나야 하는.

My son Johnny, / named so after his uncle, / was at the
내 아들 조니는,   숙부를 따서 이름 지은,

grammar-school, / and a towardly child. My daughter
중학교에 다니고 있었는데,   유망한 아이였다.   딸인 베티는

Betty / (who is now well married, / and has children) /
(지금은 잘 결혼해서,   아이도 있는)

was then at her needle-work. I took leave of my wife,
그때 바느질을 배우고 있었다.   나는 아내, 아들과 딸을 남겨 두고 떠났고,

---

manufacture 제조업 | fineness 섬세함 | fleece 양털 | towardly 유순한, 충실한

and boy and girl, / with tears on both sides, / and went on
모두 눈물로 작별 인사를 하며,

board the Adventure, / a merchant ship of three hundred
어드벤처 호에 올랐다.   그것은 300톤의 상선으로,

tons, / bound for Surat, / captain John Nicholas, / of
수라트로 향하는,   존 니콜라스 선장이,

Liverpool, / commander. But my account of this voyage /
리버풀 출신의,   지휘를 맡은.   그러나 이 항해에 대한 이야기는

must be referred / to the Second Part of my Travels.
넘겨야겠다   내 여행기의 제2부로.

mini test 8

A. 다음 문장을 해석해 보세요.

(1) But I found / all my labor to little purpose; / for, / being out of my depth, / I was not able to work.
→

(2) I did very much wonder, / in all this time, / not to have heard of / any express relating to me / from our emperor / to the court of Blefuscu.
→

(3) I told him, / "that since fortune, / whether good or evil, / had thrown a vessel in my way, / I was resolved / to venture myself / on the ocean, / rather than be an occasion of difference between two such mighty monarchs.
→

(4) I would gladly have taken a dozen of the natives, / but this was a thing / the emperor would by no means permit.
→

B. 다음 주어진 문구가 알맞은 문장이 되도록 순서를 맞춰 보세요.

(1) 나는, <u>피할 수만 있다면</u>, 군주나 대신들을 더 이상 신뢰하지 않겠다고 결심했다.
(it / could / where / avoid / I / possibly)
I resolved never more to put any confidence in princes or ministers, _____.

(2) 그가 내 결심을 매우 반가워 했고, <u>대부분의 대신들 또한 그랬다.</u>
(were / his ministers / most of / so)
He was very glad of my resolution, _____
_____

Answer

A. (1) 그러나 나는 내 모든 노력이 효과가 없음을 알았다: 왜냐하면, 내 키보다 깊어서, 일을 할 수 없었기 때문이다. (2) 나는 이 모든 일이 벌어지는 동안, 릴리펏 황제로부터 블레프스큐의 궁정에 나에 관한 어떤 소식도 듣지 못한 것이 매우 궁금했다. (3) 나는 그에게 말했다, '좋은 일이든 나쁜 일이든, 운명이 내게 배 한 척을 던져 주었으니, 나

(3) 내가 느낀 기쁨을 표현하기는 쉬운 일이 아니다.
(I was / to express / easy / in / It is / the joy / not)
→

(4) 외국을 보고 싶다는 멈출 수 없는 욕구 때문에, 더 이상 계속하는 것이
힘들었다.
(to / suffer / no / me / would / longer / continue)
My insatiable desire of seeing foreign countries

C. 다음 주어진 문장이 본문의 내용과 맞으면 T, 틀리면 F에 동그라미 하세요.

(1) The emperor of Blefuscu helped the author leave the country.
(T / F)

(2) At last, the author succeeded in returning to his home.
(T / F)

(3) The author could take a dozen of the natives to his home.
(T / F)

(4) His cattle taken from Blefuscu made him very rich.
(T / F)

D. 의미가 비슷한 것끼리 서로 연결해 보세요.

(1) encumbrance   ▶   ◀ ① loosen

(2) slacken   ▶   ◀ ② truth

(3) veracity   ▶   ◀ ③ burden

(4) rarity   ▶   ◀ ④ treasure

Answer

195

Gulliver's Travels를 다시 읽어 보세요.

⟁ 1 ⟁

The author gives some account of himself and family. His first
inducements to travel. He is shipwrecked, and swims for his life. Gets
safe on shore in the country of Lilliput; is made a prisoner, and carried
up the country.

My father had a small estate in Nottinghamshire: I was the third of five
sons. He sent me to Emanuel College in Cambridge at fourteen years old,
where I resided three years, and applied myself close to my studies; but
the charge of maintaining me, although I had a very scanty allowance,
being too great for a narrow fortune, I was bound apprentice to Mr. James
Bates, an eminent surgeon in London, with whom I continued four years.
My father now and then sending me small sums of money, I laid them out
in learning navigation, and other parts of the mathematics, useful to those
who intend to travel, as I always believed it would be, some time or other,
my fortune to do. When I left Mr. Bates, I went down to my father: where,
by the assistance of him and my uncle John, and some other relations, I
got forty pounds, and a promise of thirty pounds a year to maintain me
at Leyden: there I studied physic two years and seven months, knowing it
would be useful in long voyages.
Soon after my return from Leyden, I was recommended by my good
master, Mr. Bates, to be surgeon to the Swallow, Captain Abraham
Pannel, commander; with whom I continued three years and a half,
making a voyage or two into the Levant, and some other parts. When I
came back I resolved to settle in London; to which Mr. Bates, my master,
encouraged me, and by him I was recommended to several patients. I
took part of a small house in the Old Jewry; and being advised to alter my
condition, I married Mrs. Mary Burton, second daughter to Mr. Edmund
Burton, hosier, in Newgate-street, with whom I received four hundred
pounds for a portion.
But my good master Bates dying in two years after, and I having few

friends, my business began to fail; for my conscience would not suffer
me to imitate the bad practice of too many among my brethren. Having
therefore consulted with my wife, and some of my acquaintance, I
determined to go again to sea. I was surgeon successively in two ships,
and made several voyages, for six years, to the East and West Indies, by
which I got some addition to my fortune. My hours of leisure I spent in
reading the best authors, ancient and modern, being always provided
with a good number of books; and when I was ashore, in observing
the manners and dispositions of the people, as well as learning their
language; wherein I had a great facility, by the strength of my memory.
The last of these voyages not proving very fortunate, I grew weary of the
sea, and intended to stay at home with my wife and family. I removed
from the Old Jewry to Fetter Lane, and from thence to Wapping, hoping
to get business among the sailors; but it would not turn to account.
After three years expectation that things would mend, I accepted an
advantageous offer from Captain William Prichard, master of the
Antelope, who was making a voyage to the South Sea. We set sail from
Bristol, May 4, 1699, and our voyage was at first very prosperous.
It would not be proper, for some reasons, to trouble the reader with the
particulars of our adventures in those seas; let it suffice to inform him,
that in our passage from thence to the East Indies, we were driven by a
violent storm to the north-west of Van Diemen's Land. By an observation,
we found ourselves in the latitude of 30 degrees 2 minutes south. Twelve
of our crew were dead by immoderate labor and ill food; the rest were in a
very weak condition. On the 5th of November, which was the beginning
of summer in those parts, the weather being very hazy, the seamen spied a
rock within half a cable's length of the ship; but the wind was so strong,
that we were driven directly upon it, and immediately split. Six of the
crew, of whom I was one, having let down the boat into the sea, made a
shift to get clear of the ship and the rock. We rowed, by my computation,
about three leagues, till we were able to work no longer, being already
spent with labor while we were in the ship. We therefore trusted ourselves

to the mercy of the waves, and in about half an hour the boat was overset by a sudden flurry from the north. What became of my companions in the boat, as well as of those who escaped on the rock, or were left in the vessel, I cannot tell; but conclude they were all lost. For my own part, I swam as fortune directed me, and was pushed forward by wind and tide. I often let my legs drop, and could feel no bottom; but when I was almost gone, and able to struggle no longer, I found myself within my depth; and by this time the storm was much abated. The declivity was so small, that I walked near a mile before I got to the shore, which I conjectured was about eight o'clock in the evening. I then advanced forward near half a mile, but could not discover any sign of houses or inhabitants; at least I was in so weak a condition, that I did not observe them. I was extremely tired, and with that, and the heat of the weather, and about half a pint of brandy that I drank as I left the ship, I found myself much inclined to sleep. I lay down on the grass, which was very short and soft, where I slept sounder than ever I remembered to have done in my life, and, as I reckoned, about nine hours; for when I awaked, it was just day-light. I attempted to rise, but was not able to stir: for, as I happened to lie on my back, I found my arms and legs were strongly fastened on each side to the ground; and my hair, which was long and thick, tied down in the same manner. I likewise felt several slender ligatures across my body, from my arm-pits to my thighs. I could only look upwards; the sun began to grow hot, and the light offended my eyes. I heard a confused noise about me; but in the posture I lay, could see nothing except the sky. In a little time I felt something alive moving on my left leg, which advancing gently forward over my breast, came almost up to my chin; when, bending my eyes downwards as much as I could, I perceived it to be a human creature not six inches high, with a bow and arrow in his hands, and a quiver at his back. In the mean time, I felt at least forty more of the same kind (as I conjectured) following the first. I was in the utmost astonishment, and roared so loud, that they all ran back in a fright; and some of them, as I was afterwards told, were hurt with the falls they got by leaping from my sides upon the ground. However, they soon returned, and one of them, who ventured so far as to get a full sight of my face, lifting up his hands and eyes by way of admiration, cried out in a shrill but distinct voice, HEKINAH DEGUL: the others repeated the same words several times, but then I knew not what they meant. I lay all this while, as the reader may believe, in great uneasiness. At length, struggling to get loose, I had the fortune to break the strings, and wrench out the pegs that fastened my left arm to the ground; for, by lifting it up to my face, I discovered the methods they had taken to bind me, and at the same time with a violent pull, which gave me excessive pain, I a little loosened the strings that tied down my hair on the left side, so that I was just able to turn my head about two inches. But the creatures ran off a second time, before I could seize them; whereupon there was a great shout in a very shrill accent, and after it ceased I heard one of them cry aloud TOLGO PHONAC; when in an instant I felt above a hundred arrows discharged on my left hand, which, pricked me like so many needles; and besides, they shot another flight into the air, as we do bombs in Europe, whereof many, I suppose, fell on my body, (though I felt them not), and some on my face, which I immediately covered with my left hand. When this shower of arrows was over, I fell a groaning with grief and pain; and then striving again to get loose, they discharged another volley larger than the first, and some of them attempted with spears to stick me in the sides; but by good luck I had on a buff jerkin, which they could not pierce. I thought it the most prudent method to lie still, and my design was to continue so till night, when, my left hand being already loose, I could easily free myself: and as for the inhabitants, I had reason to believe I might be a match for the greatest army they could bring against me, if they were all of the same size with him that I saw. But fortune disposed otherwise of me. When the people observed I was quiet, they discharged no more arrows; but, by the noise I heard, I knew their numbers increased; and about four yards from me, over against my right ear, I heard a knocking for above an hour, like that of people at work; when turning my head that way, as well as the pegs and strings would permit me, I saw a stage erected about a foot and a half from the ground, capable of holding four of the inhabitants, with two or three ladders to mount it: from whence one of them, who seemed to be a person of quality, made me a long speech, whereof I understood not one syllable. But I should have mentioned, that before the principal person began his oration, he cried out three times, LANGRO DEHUL SAN (these words and the former were afterwards repeated and explained to me); whereupon, immediately, about fifty of the inhabitants came and cut the strings that fastened the left side of my head, which gave me the liberty of turning it to the right, and of observing the person and gesture of him that was to speak. He appeared to be of a middle age, and taller than any of the other three who attended him, whereof one was a page that held up his train, and seemed to be somewhat longer than my middle finger; the other two stood one on each side to support him. He acted every part of an orator, and I could observe many periods of threatenings, and others of promises, pity, and kindness. I answered in a few words, but in the most submissive manner, lifting up my left hand, and both my eyes to the sun, as calling him for a witness; and being almost famished with hunger, having not eaten a morsel for some hours before I left the ship, I found the demands of nature so strong upon me, that I could not forbear showing my impatience (perhaps against the strict rules of decency) by putting my finger frequently to my mouth, to signify that I wanted food. The HURGO (for so they call a great lord, as I afterwards learnt) understood me very well. He descended from the stage, and commanded that several ladders should be applied to my sides, on which above a hundred of the inhabitants mounted and walked towards my mouth, laden with baskets full of meat, which had been provided and sent thither by the king's orders, upon the first intelligence he received of me. I observed there was the flesh of several animals, but could not distinguish them by the taste. There were shoulders, legs, and loins, shaped like those of mutton, and very well dressed, but smaller than the wings of a lark. I ate them by two or three at a mouthful, and took three loaves at a time, about the bigness of musket bullets.

They supplied me as fast as they could, showing a thousand marks of wonder and astonishment at my bulk and appetite. I then made another sign, that I wanted drink. They found by my eating that a small quantity would not suffice me; and being a most ingenious people, they slung up, with great dexterity, one of their largest hogsheads, then rolled it towards my hand, and beat out the top; I drank it off at a draught, which I might well do, for it did not hold half a pint, and tasted like a small wine of Burgundy, but much more delicious. They brought me a second hogshead, which I drank in the same manner, and made signs for more; but they had none to give me. When I had performed these wonders, they shouted for joy, and danced upon my breast, repeating several times as they did at first, HEKINAH DEGUL. They made me a sign that I should throw down the two hogsheads, but first warning the people below to stand out of the way, crying aloud, BORACH MEVOLAH; and when they saw the vessels in the air, there was a universal shout of HEKINAH DEGUL. I confess I was often tempted, while they were passing backwards and forwards on my body, to seize forty or fifty of the first that came in my reach, and dash them against the ground. But the remembrance of what I had felt, which probably might not be the worst they could do, and the promise of honor I made them — for so I interpreted my submissive behavior — soon drove out these imaginations. Besides, I now considered myself as bound by the laws of hospitality, to a people who had treated me with so much expense and magnificence. However, in my thoughts I could not sufficiently wonder at the intrepidity of these diminutive mortals, who durst venture to mount and walk upon my body, while one of my hands was at liberty, without trembling at the very sight of so prodigious a creature as I must appear to them. After some time, when they observed that I made no more demands for meat, there appeared before me a person of high rank from his imperial majesty. His excellency, having mounted on the small of my right leg, advanced forwards up to my face, with about a dozen of his retinue; and producing his credentials under the signet royal, which he applied close to my eyes, spoke about ten minutes without any signs of anger, but with a kind of determinate resolution, often pointing forwards, which, as I afterwards found, was towards the capital city, about half a mile distant; whither it was agreed by his majesty in council that I must be conveyed. I answered in few words, but to no purpose, and made a sign with my hand that was loose, putting it to the other (but over his excellency's head for fear of hurting him or his train) and then to my own head and body, to signify that I desired my liberty. It appeared that he understood me well enough, for he shook his head by way of disapprobation, and held his hand in a posture to show that I must be carried as a prisoner. However, he made other signs to let me understand that I should have meat and drink enough, and very good treatment. Whereupon I once more thought of attempting to break my bonds; but again, when I felt the smart of their arrows upon my face and hands, which were all in blisters, and many of the darts still sticking in them, and observing likewise that the number of my enemies increased, I gave tokens to let them know that they might do with me what they pleased. Upon this, the HURGO and his train withdrew, with much civility and cheerful countenances. Soon after I heard a general shout, with frequent repetitions of the words PEPLOM SELAN; and I felt great numbers of people on my left side relaxing the cords to such a degree, that I was able to turn upon my right, and to ease myself with making water; which I very plentifully did, to the great astonishment of the people; who, conjecturing by my motion what I was going to do, immediately opened to the right and left on that side, to avoid the torrent, which fell with such noise and violence from me. But before this, they had daubed my face and both my hands with a sort of ointment, very pleasant to the smell, which, in a few minutes, removed all the smart of their arrows. These circumstances, added to the refreshment I had received by their victuals and drink, which were very nourishing, disposed me to sleep. I slept about eight hours, as I was afterwards assured; and it was no wonder, for the physicians, by the emperor's order, had mingled a sleepy potion in the hogsheads of wine.

It seems, that upon the first moment I was discovered sleeping on the ground, after my landing, the emperor had early notice of it by an express; and determined in council, that I should be tied in the manner I have related, (which was done in the night while I slept;) that plenty of meat and drink should be sent to me, and a machine prepared to carry me to the capital city.

This resolution perhaps may appear very bold and dangerous, and I am confident would not be imitated by any prince in Europe on the like occasion. However, in my opinion, it was extremely prudent, as well as generous: for, supposing these people had endeavored to kill me with their spears and arrows, while I was asleep, I should certainly have awaked with the first sense of smart, which might so far have roused my rage and strength, as to have enabled me to break the strings wherewith I was tied; after which, as they were not able to make resistance, so they could expect no mercy.

These people are most excellent mathematicians, and arrived to a great perfection in mechanics, by the countenance and encouragement of the emperor, who is a renowned patron of learning. This prince has several machines fixed on wheels, for the carriage of trees and other great weights. He often builds his largest men of war, whereof some are nine feet long, in the woods where the timber grows, and has them carried on these engines three or four hundred yards to the sea. Five hundred carpenters and engineers were immediately set at work to prepare the greatest engine they had. It was a frame of wood raised three inches from the ground, about seven feet long, and four wide, moving upon twenty-two wheels. The shout I heard was upon the arrival of this engine, which, it seems, set out in four hours after my landing. It was brought parallel to me, as I lay. But the principal difficulty was to raise and place me in this vehicle. Eighty poles, each of one foot high, were erected for this purpose, and very strong cords, of the bigness of packthread, were fastened by hooks to many bandages, which the workmen had girt round my neck, my hands, my body, and my legs. Nine hundred of the strongest men were employed to draw up these cords, by many pulleys fastened on the poles; and thus, in less than three hours, I was raised and slung into the engine, and there tied fast. All this I was told; for, while the operation was performing, I lay in a profound sleep, by the force of that soporiferous medicine infused into my liquor. Fifteen hundred of the emperor's largest horses, each about four inches and a half high, were employed to draw me towards the metropolis, which, as I said, was half a mile distant.

About four hours after we began our journey, I awaked by a very ridiculous accident; for the carriage being stopped a while, to adjust something that was out of order, two or three of the young natives had the curiosity to see how I looked when I was asleep; they climbed up into the engine, and advancing very softly to my face, one of them, an officer in the guards, put the sharp end of his half-pike a good way up into my left nostril, which tickled my nose like a straw, and made me sneeze violently; whereupon they stole off unperceived, and it was three weeks before I knew the cause of my waking so suddenly. We made a long march the remaining part of the day, and, rested at night with five hundred guards on each side of me, half with torches, and half with bows and arrows, ready to shoot me if I should offer to stir. The next morning at sunrise we continued our march, and arrived within two hundred yards of the city gates about noon. The emperor, and all his court, came out to meet us; but his great officers would by no means suffer his majesty to endanger his person by mounting on my body.

At the place where the carriage stopped there stood an ancient temple, esteemed to be the largest in the whole kingdom; which, having been polluted some years before by an unnatural murder, was, according to the zeal of those people, looked upon as profane, and therefore had been applied to common use, and all the ornaments and furniture carried away. In this edifice it was determined I should lodge. The great gate fronting to the north was about four feet high, and almost two feet wide, through which I could easily creep. On each side of the gate was a small window, not above six inches from the ground: into that on the left side, the king's smith conveyed four-score and eleven chains, like those that hang to a lady's watch in Europe, and almost as large, which were locked to my left leg with six-and-thirty padlocks. Over against this temple, on the other side of the great highway, at twenty feet distance, there was a turret at least five feet high. Here the emperor ascended, with many principal lords of his court, to have an opportunity of viewing me, as I was told, for I could not see them. It was reckoned that above a hundred thousand inhabitants came out of the town upon the same errand; and, in spite of my guards, I believe there could not be fewer than ten thousand at several times, who mounted my body by the help of ladders. But a proclamation was soon issued, to forbid it upon pain of death. When the workmen found it was impossible for me to break loose, they cut all the strings that bound me; whereupon I rose up, with as melancholy a disposition as ever I had in my life. But the noise and astonishment of the people, at seeing me rise and walk, are not to be expressed. The chains that held my left leg were about two yards long, and gave me not only the liberty of walking backwards and forwards in a semicircle, but, being fixed within four inches of the gate, allowed me to creep in, and lie at my full length in the temple.

 2

The emperor of Lilliput, attended by several of the nobility, comes to see the author in his confinement. The emperor's person and habit described. Learned men appointed to teach the author their language. He gains favor by his mild disposition. His pockets are searched, and his sword and pistols taken from him.

When I found myself on my feet, I looked about me, and must confess I never beheld a more entertaining prospect. The country around appeared like a continued garden, and the enclosed fields, which were generally forty feet square, resembled so many beds of flowers. These fields were intermingled with woods of half a stang, and the tallest trees, as I could judge, appeared to be seven feet high. I viewed the town on my left hand, which looked like the painted scene of a city in a theatre.

I had been for some hours extremely pressed by the necessities of nature; which was no wonder, it being almost two days since I had last disburdened myself. I was under great difficulties between urgency and shame. The best expedient I could think of, was to creep into my house, which I accordingly did; and shutting the gate after me, I went as far as the length of my chain would suffer, and discharged my body of that uneasy load. But this was the only time I was ever guilty of so uncleanly an action; for which I cannot but hope the candid reader will give some allowance, after he has maturely and impartially considered my case, and the distress I was in. From this time my constant practice was, as soon as I rose, to perform that business in open air, at the full extent of my chain; and due care was taken every morning before company came, that the offensive matter should be carried off in wheel-barrows, by two servants appointed for that purpose. I would not have dwelt so long upon a circumstance that, perhaps, at first sight, may appear not very momentous, if I had not thought it necessary to justify my character, in point of cleanliness, to the world; which, I am told, some of my maligners have been pleased, upon this and other occasions, to call in question. When this adventure was at an end, I came back out of my house, having occasion for fresh air. The emperor was already descended from the tower, and advancing on horse-back towards me, which had like to have cost him dear; for the beast, although very well trained, yet wholly unused to such a sight, which appeared as if a mountain moved before him, reared up on its hinder feet: but that prince, who is an excellent horseman, kept his seat, till his attendants ran in, and held the bridle, while his majesty had time to dismount. When he alighted, he surveyed me round with great admiration; but kept beyond the length of my chain. He ordered his cooks and butlers, who were already prepared, to give me victuals and drink, which they pushed forward in a sort of vehicles upon wheels, till I could reach them. I took these vehicles and soon emptied them all; twenty of them were filled with meat, and ten with liquor; each of the former afforded me two or three good mouthfuls; and I emptied the liquor of ten vessels, which was contained in earthen vials, into one vehicle, drinking it off at a draught; and so I did with the rest. The empress, and young princes of the blood of both sexes, attended by many ladies, sate at some distance in their chairs; but upon the accident that happened to the emperor's horse, they alighted, and came near his person, which I am now going to describe. He is taller by almost the breadth of my nail, than any of his court; which alone is enough to strike an awe into the beholders. His features are strong and masculine, with an Austrian lip and arched nose, his complexion olive, his countenance erect, his body and limbs well proportioned, all his motions graceful, and his deportment majestic. He was then past his prime, being twenty-eight years and three quarters old, of which he had reigned about seven in great felicity, and generally victorious. For the better convenience of beholding him, I lay on my side, so that my face was parallel to his, and he stood but three yards off: however, I have had him since many times in my hand, and therefore cannot be deceived in the description. His dress was very plain and simple, and the fashion of it between the Asiatic and the European; but he had on his head a light helmet of gold, adorned with jewels, and a plume on the crest. He held his sword drawn in his hand to defend himself, if I should happen to break loose; it was almost three inches long; the hilt and scabbard were gold enriched with diamonds. His voice was shrill, but very clear and articulate; and I could distinctly hear it when I stood up. The ladies and courtiers were all most magnificently clad; so that the spot they stood upon seemed to resemble a petticoat spread upon the ground, embroidered with figures of gold and silver. His imperial majesty spoke often to me, and I returned answers: but neither of us could understand a syllable. There were several of his priests and lawyers present (as I conjectured by their habits), who were commanded to address themselves to me; and I spoke to them in as many languages as I had the least smattering of, which were High and Low Dutch, Latin, French, Spanish, Italian, and Lingua Franca, but all to no purpose. After about two hours the court retired, and I was left with a strong guard, to prevent the impertinence, and probably the malice of the rabble, who were very impatient to crowd about me as near as they durst; and some of them had the impudence to shoot their arrows at me, as I sat on the ground by the door of my house, whereof one very narrowly missed my left eye. But the colonel ordered six of the ringleaders to be seized, and thought no punishment so proper as to deliver them bound into my hands; which some of his soldiers accordingly did, pushing them forward with the butt-ends of their pikes into my reach. I took them all in my right hand, put five of them into my coat-pocket; and as to the sixth, I made a countenance as if I would eat him alive. The poor man squalled terribly, and the colonel and his officers were in much pain, especially when they saw me take out my penknife: but I soon put them out of fear; for, looking mildly, and immediately cutting the strings he was bound with, I set him gently on the ground, and away he ran. I treated the rest in the same manner, taking them one by one out of my pocket; and I observed both the soldiers and people were highly delighted at this mark of my clemency, which was represented very much to my advantage at court.

Towards night I got with some difficulty into my house, where I lay on the ground, and continued to do so about a fortnight; during which time, the emperor gave orders to have a bed prepared for me. Six hundred beds of the common measure were brought in carriages, and worked up in my house; a hundred and fifty of their beds, sewn together, made up the breadth and length; and these were four double: which, however, kept me but very indifferently from the hardness of the floor, that was of smooth stone. By the same computation, they provided me with sheets, blankets, and coverlets, tolerable enough for one who had been so long inured to hardships.

As the news of my arrival spread through the kingdom, it brought prodigious numbers of rich, idle, and curious people to see me; so that the villages were almost emptied; and great neglect of tillage and household affairs must have ensued, if his imperial majesty had not provided, by several proclamations and orders of state, against this inconveniency. He directed that those who had already beheld me should return home, and not presume to come within fifty yards of my house, without license from the court; whereby the secretaries of state got considerable fees.

In the mean time the emperor held frequent councils, to debate what course should be taken with me; and I was afterwards assured by a particular friend, a person of great quality, who was as much in the secret as any, that the court was under many difficulties concerning me. They apprehended my breaking loose; that my diet would be very expensive, and might cause a famine. Sometimes they determined to starve me; or at least to shoot me in the face and hands with poisoned arrows, which would soon dispatch me; but again they considered, that the stench of so large a carcass might produce a plague in the metropolis, and probably spread through the whole kingdom. In the midst of these consultations, several officers of the army went to the door of the great council-chamber, and two of them being admitted, gave an account of my behavior to the six criminals above-mentioned; which made so favorable an impression in the breast of his majesty and the whole board, in my behalf, that an imperial commission was issued out, obliging all the villages, nine hundred yards round the city, to deliver in every morning six beeves, forty sheep, and other victuals for my sustenance; together with a proportionable quantity of bread, and wine, and other liquors; for the due payment of which, his majesty gave assignments upon his treasury: — for this prince lives chiefly upon his own demesnes; seldom, except upon great occasions, raising any subsidies upon his subjects, who are bound to attend him in his wars at their own expense. An establishment was also made of six hundred persons to be my domestics, who had board-wages allowed for their maintenance, and tents built for them very conveniently on each side of my door. It was likewise ordered, that three hundred tailors should make me a suit of clothes, after the fashion of the country; that six of his majesty's greatest scholars should be employed to instruct me in their language; and lastly, that the emperor's horses, and those of the nobility and troops of guards, should be frequently exercised in my sight, to accustom themselves to me. All these orders were duly put in execution; and in about three weeks I made a great progress in learning their language; during which time the emperor frequently honored me with his visits, and was pleased to assist my masters in teaching me. We began already to converse together in some sort; and the first words I learnt, were to express my desire "that he would please give me my liberty;" which I every day repeated on my knees. His answer, as I could comprehend it, was, "that this must be a work of time, not to be thought on without the advice of his council, and that first I must LUMOS KELMIN PESSO DESMAR LON EMPOSO;" that is, swear a peace with him and his kingdom. However, that I should be used with all kindness; and he advised me to "acquire, by my patience and discreet behavior, the good opinion of himself and his subjects." He desired "I would not take it ill, if he gave orders to certain proper officers to search me; for probably I might carry about me several weapons, which must needs be dangerous things, if they answered the bulk of so prodigious a person." I said, "His majesty should be satisfied; for I was ready to strip myself, and turn up my pockets before him." This I delivered part in words, and part in signs. He replied, "that, by the laws of the kingdom, I must be searched by two of his officers; that he knew this could not be done without my consent and assistance; and he had so good an opinion of my generosity and justice, as to trust their persons in my hands; that whatever they took from me, should be returned when I left the country, or paid for at the rate which I would set upon them." I took up the two officers in my hands, put them first into my coat-pockets, and then into every other pocket about me, except my two fobs, and another secret pocket, which I had no mind should be searched, wherein I had some little necessaries that were of no consequence to any but myself. In one of my fobs there was a silver watch, and in the other a small quantity of gold in a purse. These gentlemen, having pen, ink, and paper, about them, made an exact inventory of everything they saw; and when they had done, desired I would set them down, that they might deliver it to the emperor. This inventory I afterwards translated into English, and is, word for word, as follows:

"IMPRIMIS, In the right coat-pocket of the great man-mountain" (for so I interpret the words QUINBUS FLESTRIN,) "after the strictest search, we found only one great piece of coarse-cloth, large enough to be a foot-cloth for your majesty's chief room of state. In the left pocket we saw a huge silver chest, with a cover of the same metal, which we, the searchers, were not able to lift. We desired it should be opened, and one of us stepping into it, found himself up to the mid leg in a sort of dust, some part whereof flying up to our faces set us both a sneezing for several times together. In his right waistcoat-pocket we found a prodigious bundle of white thin substances, folded one over another, about the bigness of three men, tied with a strong cable, and marked with black figures; which we humbly conceive to be writings, every letter almost half as large as the palm of our hands. In the left there was a sort of engine, from the back of which were extended twenty long poles, resembling the Pallisado's before your majesty's court: wherewith we conjecture the man-mountain combs his head; for we did not always trouble him with questions, because we found it a great difficulty to make him understand us. In the large pocket, on the right side of his middle cover" (so I translate the word RANFULO, by which they meant my breeches,) "we saw a hollow pillar of iron, about the length of a man, fastened to a strong piece of timber larger than the pillar; and upon one side of the pillar, were huge pieces of iron sticking out, cut into strange figures, which we know not what to make of. In the left pocket, another engine of the same kind. In the smaller pocket on the right side, were several round flat pieces of white and red metal, of different bulk; some of the white, which seemed to be silver, were so

large and heavy, that my comrade and I could hardly lift them. In the left
pocket were two black pillars irregularly shaped: we could not, without
difficulty, reach the top of them, as we stood at the bottom of his pocket.
One of them was covered, and seemed all of a piece: but at the upper
end of the other there appeared a white round substance, about twice the
bigness of our heads. Within each of these was enclosed a prodigious
plate of steel; which, by our orders, we obliged him to show us, because
we apprehended they might be dangerous engines. He took them out of
their cases, and told us, that in his own country his practice was to shave
his beard with one of these, and cut his meat with the other. There were
two pockets which we could not enter: these he called his fobs; they
were two large slits cut into the top of his middle cover, but squeezed
close by the pressure of his belly. Out of the right fob hung a great silver
chain, with a wonderful kind of engine at the bottom. We directed him
to draw out whatever was at the end of that chain; which appeared to
be a globe, half silver, and half of some transparent metal; for, on the
transparent side, we saw certain strange figures circularly drawn, and
though we could touch them, till we found our fingers stopped by the
lucid substance. He put this engine into our ears, which made an incessant
noise, like that of a water-mill: and we conjecture it is either some
unknown animal, or the god that he worships; but we are more inclined
to the latter opinion, because he assured us, (if we understood him right,
for he expressed himself very imperfectly) that he seldom did anything
without consulting it. He called it his oracle, and said, it pointed out the
time for every action of his life. From the left fob he took out a net almost
large enough for a fisherman, but contrived to open and shut like a purse,
and served him for the same use: we found therein several massy pieces
of yellow metal, which, if they be real gold, must be of immense value.
"Having thus, in obedience to your majesty's commands, diligently
searched all his pockets, we observed a girdle about his waist made of
the hide of some prodigious animal, from which, on the left side, hung a
sword of the length of five men; and on the right, a bag or pouch divided

into two cells, each cell capable of holding three of your majesty's subjects. In one of these cells were several globes, or balls, of a most ponderous metal, about the bigness of our heads, and requiring a strong hand to lift them: the other cell contained a heap of certain black grains, but of no great bulk or weight, for we could hold above fifty of them in the palms of our hands."

"This is an exact inventory of what we found about the body of the man-mountain, who used us with great civility, and due respect to your majesty's commission. Signed and sealed on the fourth day of the eighty-ninth moon of your majesty's auspicious reign.

CLEFRIN FRELOCK, MARSI FRELOCK."

When this inventory was read over to the emperor, he directed me, although in very gentle terms, to deliver up the several particulars. He first called for my scimitar, which I took out, scabbard and all. In the mean time he ordered three thousand of his choicest troops (who then attended him) to surround me at a distance, with their bows and arrows just ready to discharge; but I did not observe it, for mine eyes were wholly fixed upon his majesty. He then desired me to draw my scimitar, which, although it had got some rust by the sea water, was, in most parts, exceeding bright. I did so, and immediately all the troops gave a shout between terror and surprise; for the sun shone clear, and the reflection dazzled their eyes, as I waved the scimitar to and fro in my hand. His majesty, who is a most magnanimous prince, was less daunted than I could expect: he ordered me to return it into the scabbard, and cast it on the ground as gently as I could, about six feet from the end of my chain. The next thing he demanded was one of the hollow iron pillars; by which he meant my pocket pistols. I drew it out, and at his desire, as well as I could, expressed to him the use of it; and charging it only with powder, which, by the closeness of my pouch, happened to escape wetting in the sea (an inconvenience against which all prudent mariners take special care to provide,) I first cautioned the emperor not to be afraid, and then I let it off in the air. The astonishment here was much greater than at the sight of my scimitar. Hundreds fell down as if they had been struck dead; and even the emperor, although he stood his ground, could not recover himself for some time. I delivered up both my pistols in the same manner as I had done my scimitar, and then my pouch of powder and bullets; begging him that the former might be kept from fire, for it would kindle with the smallest spark, and blow up his imperial palace into the air. I likewise delivered up my watch, which the emperor was very curious to see, and commanded two of his tallest yeomen of the guards to bear it on a pole upon their shoulders, as draymen in England do a barrel of ale. He was amazed at the continual noise it made, and the motion of the minute-hand, which he could easily discern; for their sight is much more acute than ours: he asked the opinions of his learned men about it, which were various and remote, as the reader may well imagine without my repeating; although indeed I could not very perfectly understand them. I then gave up my silver and copper money, my purse, with nine large pieces of gold, and some smaller ones; my knife and razor, my comb and silver snuff-box, my handkerchief and journal-book. My scimitar, pistols, and pouch, were conveyed in carriages to his majesty's stores; but the rest of my goods were returned me.

I had as I before observed, one private pocket, which escaped their search, wherein there was a pair of spectacles (which I sometimes use for the weakness of mine eyes,) a pocket perspective, and some other little conveniences; which, being of no consequence to the emperor, I did not think myself bound in honor to discover, and I apprehended they might be lost or spoiled if I ventured them out of my possession.

 3

The author diverts the emperor, and his nobility of both sexes, in a very uncommon manner. The diversions of the court of Lilliput described. The author has his liberty granted him upon certain conditions.

My gentleness and good behavior had gained so far on the emperor and his court, and indeed upon the army and people in general, that I began to conceive hopes of getting my liberty in a short time. I took all possible methods to cultivate this favorable disposition. The natives came, by degrees, to be less apprehensive of any danger from me. I would sometimes lie down, and let five or six of them dance on my hand; and at last the boys and girls would venture to come and play at hide-and-seek in my hair. I had now made a good progress in understanding and speaking the language. The emperor had a mind one day to entertain me with several of the country shows, wherein they exceed all nations I have known, both for dexterity and magnificence. I was diverted with none so much as that of the rope-dancers, performed upon a slender white thread, extended about two feet, and twelve inches from the ground. Upon which I shall desire liberty, with the reader's patience, to enlarge a little.

This diversion is only practised by those persons who are candidates for great employments, and high favor at court. They are trained in this art from their youth, and are not always of noble birth, or liberal education. When a great office is vacant, either by death or disgrace (which often happens,) five or six of those candidates petition the emperor to entertain his majesty and the court with a dance on the rope; and whoever jumps the highest, without falling, succeeds in the office. Very often the chief ministers themselves are commanded to show their skill, and to convince the emperor that they have not lost their faculty. Flimnap, the treasurer, is allowed to cut a caper on the straight rope, at least an inch higher than any other lord in the whole empire. I have seen him do the summerset several times together, upon a trencher fixed on a rope which is no thicker than a common pack-thread in England. My friend Reldresal, principal secretary for private affairs, is, in my opinion, if I am not partial, the second after the treasurer; the rest of the great officers are much upon a par.

These diversions are often attended with fatal accidents, whereof great numbers are on record. I myself have seen two or three candidates break a limb. But the danger is much greater, when the ministers themselves are commanded to show their dexterity; for, by contending to excel themselves and their fellows, they strain so far that there is hardly one of them who has not received a fall, and some of them two or three. I was assured that, a year or two before my arrival, Flimnap would infallibly have broke his neck, if one of the king's cushions, that accidentally lay on the ground, had not weakened the force of his fall.

There is likewise another diversion, which is only shown before the emperor and empress, and first minister, upon particular occasions. The emperor lays on the table three fine silken threads of six inches long; one is blue, the other red, and the third green. These threads are proposed as prizes for those persons whom the emperor has a mind to distinguish by a peculiar mark of his favor. The ceremony is performed in his majesty's great chamber of state, where the candidates are to undergo a trial of dexterity very different from the former, and such as I have not observed the least resemblance of in any other country of the new or old world. The emperor holds a stick in his hands, both ends parallel to the horizon, while the candidates advancing, one by one, sometimes leap over the stick, sometimes creep under it, backward and forward, several times, according as the stick is advanced or depressed. Sometimes the emperor holds one end of the stick, and his first minister the other; sometimes the minister has it entirely to himself. Whoever performs his part with most agility, and holds out the longest in leaping and creeping, is rewarded with the blue-colored silk; the red is given to the next, and the green to the third, which they all wear girt twice round about the middle; and you see few great persons about this court who are not adorned with one of these girdles.

The horses of the army, and those of the royal stables, having been daily led before me, were no longer shy, but would come up to my very feet without starting. The riders would leap them over my hand, as I held it on the ground; and one of the emperor's huntsmen, upon a large courser, took my foot, shoe and all; which was indeed a prodigious leap. I had the good fortune to divert the emperor one day after a very extraordinary manner. I desired he would order several sticks of two feet high, and the thickness of an ordinary cane, to be brought me; whereupon his majesty commanded the master of his woods to give directions accordingly; and the next morning six woodmen arrived with as many carriages, drawn by eight horses to each. I took nine of these sticks, and fixing them firmly in the ground in a quadrangular figure, two feet and a half square, I took four other sticks, and tied them parallel at each corner, about two feet from the ground; then I fastened my handkerchief to the nine sticks that stood erect; and extended it on all sides, till it was tight as the top of a drum; and the four parallel sticks, rising about five inches higher than the handkerchief, served as ledges on each side. When I had finished my work, I desired the emperor to let a troop of his best horses twenty-four in number, come and exercise upon this plain. His majesty approved of the proposal, and I took them up, one by one, in my hands, ready mounted and armed, with the proper officers to exercise them. As soon as they got into order they divided into two parties, performed mock skirmishes, discharged blunt arrows, drew their swords, fled and pursued, attacked and retired, and in short discovered the best military discipline I ever beheld. The parallel sticks secured them and their horses from falling over the stage; and the emperor was so much delighted, that he ordered this entertainment to be repeated several days, and once was pleased to be lifted up and give the word of command; and with great difficulty persuaded even the empress herself to let me hold her in her close chair within two yards of the stage, when she was able to take a full view of the whole performance. It was my good fortune, that no ill accident happened in these entertainments; only once a fiery horse, that belonged to one of the captains, pawing with his hoof, struck a hole in my handkerchief, and his foot slipping, he overthrew his rider and himself; but I immediately relieved them both, and covering the hole with one hand, I set down the troop with the other, in the same manner as I took them up. The horse that fell was strained in the left shoulder, but the rider got no hurt; and I repaired my handkerchief as well as I could: however, I would not trust to the strength of it any more, in such dangerous enterprises.

About two or three days before I was set at liberty, as I was entertaining the court with this kind of feat, there arrived an express to inform his majesty, that some of his subjects, riding near the place where I was first taken up, had seen a great black substance lying on the around, very oddly shaped, extending its edges round, as wide as his majesty's bedchamber, and rising up in the middle as high as a man; that it was no living creature, as they at first apprehended, for it lay on the grass without motion; and some of them had walked round it several times; that, by mounting upon each other's shoulders, they had got to the top, which was flat and even, and, stamping upon it, they found that it was hollow within; that they humbly conceived it might be something belonging to the man-mountain; and if his majesty pleased, they would undertake to bring it with only five horses. I presently knew what they meant, and was glad at heart to receive this intelligence. It seems, upon my first reaching the shore after our shipwreck, I was in such confusion, that before I came to the place where I went to sleep, my hat, which I had fastened with a string to my head while I was rowing, and had stuck on all the time I was swimming, fell off after I came to land; the string, as I conjecture, breaking by some accident, which I never observed, but thought my hat had been lost at sea. I entreated his imperial majesty to give orders it might be brought to me as soon as possible, describing to him the use and the nature of it: and the next day the waggoners arrived with it, but not in a very good condition; they had bored two holes in the brim, within an inch and half of the edge, and fastened two hooks in the holes; these hooks were tied by a long cord to the harness, and thus my hat was dragged along for above half an English mile; but, the ground in that country being extremely smooth and level, it received less damage than I expected.

Two days after this adventure, the emperor, having ordered that part of his army which quarters in and about his metropolis, to be in readiness, took a fancy of diverting himself in a very singular manner. He desired I would stand like a Colossus, with my legs as far asunder as I conveniently could. He then commanded his general (who was an old experienced leader, and a great patron of mine) to draw up the troops in close order, and march them under me; the foot by twenty-four abreast, and the horse by sixteen, with drums beating, colors flying, and pikes advanced. This body consisted of three thousand foot, and a thousand horse. His majesty gave orders, upon pain of death, that every soldier in his march should observe the strictest decency with regard to my person; which however could not prevent some of the younger officers from turning up their eyes as they passed under me: and, to confess the truth, my breeches were at that time in so ill a condition, that they afforded some opportunities for laughter and admiration.

I had sent so many memorials and petitions for my liberty, that his majesty at length mentioned the matter, first in the cabinet, and then in a full council; where it was opposed by none, except Skyresh Bolgolam, who was pleased, without any provocation, to be my mortal enemy. But it was carried against him by the whole board, and confirmed by the emperor. That minister was GALBET, or admiral of the realm, very much in his master's confidence, and a person well versed in affairs, but of a morose and sour complexion. However, he was at length persuaded to comply; but prevailed that the articles and conditions upon which I should be set free, and to which I must swear, should be drawn up by himself. These articles were brought to me by Skyresh Bolgolam in person attended by two under-secretaries, and several persons of distinction. After they were read, I was demanded to swear to the performance of them; first in the manner of my own country, and afterwards in the method prescribed by their laws; which was, to hold my right foot in my left hand, and to place the middle finger of my right hand on the crown of my head, and my thumb on the tip of my right ear. But because the reader may be curious to have some idea of the style and manner of expression peculiar to that people, as well as to know the article upon which I recovered my liberty, I have made a translation of the whole instrument, word for word, as near as I was able, which I here offer to the public.

Golbasto Momarem Evlame Gurdilo Shefin Mully Ully Gue, most mighty Emperor of Lilliput, delight and terror of the universe, whose dominions extend five thousand BLUSTRUGS (about twelve miles in circumference) to the extremities of the globe; monarch of all monarchs, taller than the sons of men; whose feet press down to the centre, and whose head strikes against the sun; at whose nod the princes of the earth shake their knees; pleasant as the spring, comfortable as the summer, fruitful as autumn, dreadful as winter: his most sublime majesty proposes to the man-mountain, lately arrived at our celestial dominions, the following articles, which, by a solemn oath, he shall be obliged to perform: —

1st, The man-mountain shall not depart from our dominions, without our license under our great seal.

2d, He shall not presume to come into our metropolis, without our express order; at which time, the inhabitants shall have two hours warning to keep within doors.

3d, The said man-mountain shall confine his walks to our principal high roads, and not offer to walk, or lie down, in a meadow or field of corn.

4th, As he walks the said roads, he shall take the utmost care not to trample upon the bodies of any of our loving subjects, their horses, or carriages, nor take any of our subjects into his hands without their own consent.

5th, If an express requires extraordinary dispatch, the man-mountain shall be obliged to carry, in his pocket, the messenger and horse a six days journey, once in every moon, and return the said messenger back (if so required) safe to our imperial presence.

6th, He shall be our ally against our enemies in the island of Blefuscu, and do his utmost to destroy their fleet, which is now preparing to invade us.

7th, That the said man-mountain shall, at his times of leisure, be aiding and assisting to our workmen, in helping to raise certain great stones, towards covering the wall of the principal park, and other our royal buildings.

8th, That the said man-mountain shall, in two moons' time, deliver in an exact survey of the circumference of our dominions, by a computation of his own paces round the coast.

Lastly, That, upon his solemn oath to observe all the above articles, the said man-mountain shall have a daily allowance of meat and drink sufficient for the support of 1724 of our subjects, with free access to our royal person, and other marks of our favor. Given at our palace at Belfaborac, the twelfth day of the ninety-first moon of our reign.

I swore and subscribed to these articles with great cheerfulness and content, although some of them were not so honorable as I could have wished; which proceeded wholly from the malice of Skyresh Bolgolam, the high-admiral: whereupon my chains were immediately unlocked, and I was at full liberty. The emperor himself, in person, did me the honor to be by at the whole ceremony. I made my acknowledgements by prostrating myself at his majesty's feet: but he commanded me to rise; and after many gracious expressions, which, to avoid the censure of vanity, I shall not repeat, he added, "that he hoped I should prove a useful servant, and well deserve all the favors he had already conferred upon me, or might do for the future."

The reader may please to observe, that, in the last article of the recovery of my liberty, the emperor stipulates to allow me a quantity of meat and drink sufficient for the support of 1724 Lilliputians. Sometime after, asking a friend at court how they came to fix on that determinate number, he told me that his majesty's mathematicians, having taken the height of my body by the help of a quadrant, and finding it to exceed theirs in the proportion of twelve to one, they concluded from the similarity of their bodies, that mine must contain at least 1724 of theirs, and consequently would require as much food as was necessary to support that number of Lilliputians. By which the reader may conceive an idea of the ingenuity of that people, as well as the prudent and exact economy of so great a prince.

4

Mildendo, the metropolis of Lilliput, described, together with the emperor's palace. A conversation between the author and a principal secretary, concerning the affairs of that empire. The author's offers to serve the emperor in his wars.

The first request I made, after I had obtained my liberty, was, that I might have license to see Mildendo, the metropolis; which the emperor easily granted me, but with a special charge to do no hurt either to the inhabitants or their houses. The people had notice, by proclamation, of my design to visit the town. The wall which encompassed it is two feet and a half high, and at least eleven inches broad, so that a coach and horses may be driven very safely round it; and it is flanked with strong towers at ten feet distance. I stepped over the great western gate, and passed very gently, and sidling, through the two principal streets, only in my short waistcoat, for fear of damaging the roofs and eaves of the houses with the skirts of my coat. I walked with the utmost circumspection, to avoid treading on any stragglers who might remain in the streets, although the orders were very strict, that all people should keep in their houses, at their own peril. The garret windows and tops of houses were so crowded with spectators, that I thought in all my travels I had not seen a more populous place. The city is an exact square, each side of the wall being five hundred feet long. The two great streets, which run across and divide it into four quarters, are five feet wide. The lanes and alleys, which I could not enter, but only view them as I passed, are from twelve to eighteen inches. The town is capable of holding five hundred thousand souls: the houses are from three to five stories: the shops and markets well provided.
The emperor's palace is in the centre of the city where the two great streets meet. It is enclosed by a wall of two feet high, and twenty feet distance from the buildings. I had his majesty's permission to step over this wall; and, the space being so wide between that and the palace, I

could easily view it on every side. The outward court is a square of forty feet, and includes two other courts: in the inmost are the royal apartments, which I was very desirous to see, but found it extremely difficult; for the great gates, from one square into another, were but eighteen inches high, and seven inches wide. Now the buildings of the outer court were at least five feet high, and it was impossible for me to stride over them without infinite damage to the pile, though the walls were strongly built of hewn stone, and four inches thick. At the same time the emperor had a great desire that I should see the magnificence of his palace; but this I was not able to do till three days after, which I spent in cutting down with my knife some of the largest trees in the royal park, about a hundred yards distant from the city. Of these trees I made two stools, each about three feet high, and strong enough to bear my weight. The people having received notice a second time, I went again through the city to the palace with my two stools in my hands. When I came to the side of the outer court, I stood upon one stool, and took the other in my hand; this I lifted over the roof, and gently set it down on the space between the first and second court, which was eight feet wide. I then stept over the building very conveniently from one stool to the other, and drew up the first after me with a hooked stick. By this contrivance I got into the inmost court; and, lying down upon my side, I applied my face to the windows of the middle stories, which were left open on purpose, and discovered the most splendid apartments that can be imagined. There I saw the empress and the young princes, in their several lodgings, with their chief attendants about them. Her imperial majesty was pleased to smile very graciously upon me, and gave me out of the window her hand to kiss.

But I shall not anticipate the reader with further descriptions of this kind, because I reserve them for a greater work, which is now almost ready for the press; containing a general description of this empire, from its first erection, through a long series of princes; with a particular account of their wars and politics, laws, learning, and religion; their plants and animals; their peculiar manners and customs, with other matters very curious and useful; my chief design at present being only to relate such events and transactions as happened to the public or to myself during a residence of about nine months in that empire.

One morning, about a fortnight after I had obtained my liberty, Reldresal, principal secretary (as they style him) for private affairs, came to my house attended only by one servant. He ordered his coach to wait at a distance, and desired I would give him an hour's audience; which I readily consented to, on account of his quality and personal merits, as well as of the many good offices he had done me during my solicitations at court. I offered to lie down that he might the more conveniently reach my ear, but he chose rather to let me hold him in my hand during our conversation. He began with compliments on my liberty; said "he might pretend to some merit in it;" but, however, added, "that if it had not been for the present situation of things at court, perhaps I might not have obtained it so soon. For," said he, "as flourishing a condition as we may appear to be in to foreigners, we labor under two mighty evils: a violent faction at home, and the danger of an invasion, by a most potent enemy, from abroad. As to the first, you are to understand, that for about seventy moons past there have been two struggling parties in this empire, under the names of TRAMECKSAN and SLAMECKSAN, from the high and low heels of their shoes, by which they distinguish themselves. It is alleged, indeed, that the high heels are most agreeable to our ancient constitution; but, however this be, his majesty has determined to make use only of low heels in the administration of the government, and all offices in the gift of the crown, as you cannot but observe; and particularly that his majesty's imperial heels are lower at least by a DRURR than any of his court (DRURR is a measure about the fourteenth part of an inch). The animosities between these two parties run so high, that they will neither eat, nor drink, nor talk with each other. We compute the TRAMECKSAN, or high heels, to exceed us in number; but the power is wholly on our side. We apprehend his imperial highness, the heir to the crown, to have some tendency towards the high heels; at least we can plainly discover that one of his heels is higher than the other, which gives him a hobble in his gait. Now, in the midst of these intestine disquiets, we are threatened with an invasion from the island of Blefuscu, which is the other great empire of the universe, almost as large and powerful as this of his majesty. For as to what we have heard you affirm, that there are other kingdoms and states in the world inhabited by human creatures as large as yourself, our philosophers are in much doubt, and would rather conjecture that you dropped from the moon, or one of the stars; because it is certain, that a hundred mortals of your bulk would in a short time destroy all the fruits and cattle of his majesty's dominions: besides, our histories of six thousand moons make no mention of any other regions than the two great empires of Lilliput and Blefuscu. Which two mighty powers have, as I was going to tell you, been engaged in a most obstinate war for six-and-thirty moons past. It began upon the following occasion. It is allowed on all hands, that the primitive way of breaking eggs, before we eat them, was upon the larger end; but his present majesty's grandfather, while he was a boy, going to eat an egg, and breaking it according to the ancient practice, happened to cut one of his fingers. Whereupon the emperor his father published an edict, commanding all his subjects, upon great penalties, to break the smaller end of their eggs. The people so highly resented this law, that our histories tell us, there have been six rebellions raised on that account; wherein one emperor lost his life, and another his crown. These civil commotions were constantly fomented by the monarchs of Blefuscu; and when they were quelled, the exiles always fled for refuge to that empire. It is computed that eleven thousand persons have at several times suffered death, rather than submit to break their eggs at the smaller end. Many hundred large volumes have been published upon this controversy: but the books of the Big-endians have been long forbidden, and the whole party rendered incapable by law of holding employments. During the course of these troubles, the emperors of Blefusca did frequently expostulate by their ambassadors, accusing us of making a schism in religion, by offending against a fundamental doctrine of our great prophet Lustrog, in the fifty-fourth chapter of the Blundecral (which is their Alcoran). This, however, is thought to be a mere strain upon the text; for the words are these: 'that all true believers break their eggs at the convenient end.'

And which is the convenient end, seems, in my humble opinion to be left to every man's conscience, or at least in the power of the chief magistrate to determine. Now, the Big-endian exiles have found so much credit in the emperor of Blefuscu's court, and so much private assistance and encouragement from their party here at home, that a bloody war has been carried on between the two empires for six-and-thirty moons, with various success; during which time we have lost forty capital ships, and a much a greater number of smaller vessels, together with thirty thousand of our best seamen and soldiers; and the damage received by the enemy is reckoned to be somewhat greater than ours. However, they have now equipped a numerous fleet, and are just preparing to make a descent upon us; and his imperial majesty, placing great confidence in your valor and strength, has commanded me to lay this account of his affairs before you." I desired the secretary to present my humble duty to the emperor; and to let him know, "that I thought it would not become me, who was a foreigner, to interfere with parties; but I was ready, with the hazard of my life, to defend his person and state against all invaders."

 5

The author, by an extraordinary stratagem, prevents an invasion. A high title of honor is conferred upon him. Ambassadors arrive from the emperor of Blefuscu, and sue for peace. The empress's apartment on fire by an accident; the author instrumental in saving the rest of the palace.

The empire of Blefuscu is an island situated to the north-east of Lilliput, from which it is parted only by a channel of eight hundred yards wide.

I had not yet seen it, and upon this notice of an intended invasion, I avoided appearing on that side of the coast, for fear of being discovered, by some of the enemy's ships, who had received no intelligence of me; all intercourse between the two empires having been strictly forbidden during the war, upon pain of death, and an embargo laid by our emperor upon all vessels whatsoever. I communicated to his majesty a project I had formed of seizing the enemy's whole fleet; which, as our scouts assured us, lay at anchor in the harbor, ready to sail with the first fair wind. I consulted the most experienced seamen upon the depth of the channel, which they had often plumbed; who told me, that in the middle, at high-water, it was seventy GLUMGLUFFS deep, which is about six feet of European measure; and the rest of it fifty GLUMGLUFFS at most. I walked towards the north-east coast, over against Blefuscu, where, lying down behind a hillock, I took out my small perspective glass, and viewed the enemy's fleet at anchor, consisting of about fifty men of war, and a great number of transports: I then came back to my house, and gave orders (for which I had a warrant) for a great quantity of the strongest cable and bars of iron. The cable was about as thick as packthread and the bars of the length and size of a knitting-needle. I trebled the cable to make it stronger, and for the same reason I twisted three of the iron bars together, bending the extremities into a hook. Having thus fixed fifty hooks to as many cables, I went back to the north-east coast, and putting off my coat, shoes, and stockings, walked into the sea, in my leathern jerkin, about half an hour before high water. I waded with what haste I could, and swam in the middle about thirty yards, till I felt ground. I arrived at the fleet in less than half an hour. The enemy was so frightened when they saw me, that they leaped out of their ships, and swam to shore, where there could not be fewer than thirty thousand souls. I then took my tackling, and, fastening a hook to the hole at the prow of each, I tyed all the cords together at the end. While I was thus employed, the enemy discharged several thousand arrows, many of which stuck in my hands and face, and, beside the excessive smart, gave me much disturbance in my work. My greatest apprehension was for mine eyes, which I should have infallibly lost, if I had not suddenly thought of an expedient. I kept, among other little necessaries, a pair of spectacles in a private pocket, which, as I observed before, had escaped the emperor's searchers. These I took out and fastened as strongly as I could upon my nose, and thus armed, went on boldly with my work, in spite of the enemy's arrows, many of which struck against the glasses of my spectacles, but without any other effect, further than a little to discompose them. I had now fastened all the hooks, and, taking the knot in my hand, began to pull; but not a ship would stir, for they were all too fast held by their anchors, so that the boldest part of my enterprise remained. I therefore let go the cord, and leaving the looks fixed to the ships, I resolutely cut with my knife the cables that fastened the anchors, receiving about two hundred shots in my face and hands; then I took up the knotted end of the cables, to which my hooks were tied, and with great ease drew fifty of the enemy's largest men of war after me.

The Blefuscudians, who had not the least imagination of what I intended, were at first confounded with astonishment. They had seen me cut the cables, and thought my design was only to let the ships run adrift or fall foul on each other: but when they perceived the whole fleet moving in order, and saw me pulling at the end, they set up such a scream of grief and despair as it is almost impossible to describe or conceive. When I had got out of danger, I stopped awhile to pick out the arrows that stuck in my hands and face; and rubbed on some of the same ointment that was given me at my first arrival, as I have formerly mentioned. I then took off my spectacles, and waiting about an hour, till the tide was a little fallen, I waded through the middle with my cargo, and arrived safe at the royal port of Lilliput.

The emperor and his whole court stood on the shore, expecting the issue of this great adventure. They saw the ships move forward in a large half-moon, but could not discern me, who was up to my breast in water. When I advanced to the middle of the channel, they were yet more in pain, because I was under water to my neck. The emperor concluded me to be drowned, and that the enemy's fleet was approaching in a hostile manner: but he was soon eased of his fears; for the channel growing shallower every step I made, I came in a short time within hearing, and holding up the end of the cable, by which the fleet was fastened, I cried in a loud voice, "Long live the most puissant king of Lilliput!" This great prince received me at my landing with all possible encomiums, and created me a NARDAC upon the spot, which is the highest title of honor among them. His majesty desired I would take some other opportunity of bringing all the rest of his enemy's ships into his ports. And so unmeasureable is the ambition of princes, that he seemed to think of nothing less than reducing the whole empire of Blefuscu into a province, and governing it, by a viceroy; of destroying the Big-endian exiles, and compelling that people to break the smaller end of their eggs, by which he would remain the sole monarch of the whole world. But I endeavoured to divert him from this design, by many arguments drawn from the topics of policy as well as justice; and I plainly protested, "that I would never be an instrument of bringing a free and brave people into slavery." And, when the matter was debated in council, the wisest part of the ministry were of my opinion. This open bold declaration of mine was so opposite to the schemes and politics of his imperial majesty, that he could never forgive me. He mentioned it in a very artful manner at council, where I was told that some of the wisest appeared, at least by their silence, to be of my opinion; but others, who were my secret enemies, could not forbear some expressions which, by a side-wind, reflected on me. And from this time began an intrigue between his majesty and a junto of ministers, maliciously bent against me, which broke out in less than two months, and had like to have ended in my utter destruction. Of so little weight are the greatest services to princes, when put into the balance with a refusal to gratify their passions.

About three weeks after this exploit, there arrived a solemn embassy from Blefuscu, with humble offers of a peace, which was soon concluded, upon conditions very advantageous to our emperor, wherewith I shall not trouble the reader. There were six ambassadors, with a train of about five hundred persons, and their entry was very magnificent, suitable to the grandeur of their master, and the importance of their business. When their treaty was finished, wherein I did them several good offices by the credit I now had, or at least appeared to have, at court, their excellencies, who were privately told how much I had been their friend, made me a visit in form. They began with many compliments upon my valour and generosity, invited me to that kingdom in the emperor their master's name, and desired me to show them some proofs of my prodigious strength, of which they had heard so many wonders; wherein I readily obliged them, but shall not trouble the reader with the particulars. When I had for some time entertained their excellencies, to their infinite satisfaction and surprise, I desired they would do me the honor to present my most humble respects to the emperor their master, the renown of whose virtues had so justly filled the whole world with admiration, and whose royal person I resolved to attend, before I returned to my own country. Accordingly, the next time I had the honor to see our emperor, I desired his general license to wait on the Blefuscudian monarch, which he was pleased to grant me, as I could perceive, in a very cold manner; but could not guess the reason, till I had a whisper from a certain person, "that Flimnap and Bolgolam had represented my intercourse with those ambassadors as a mark of disaffection;" from which I am sure my heart was wholly free. And this was the first time I began to conceive some imperfect idea of courts and ministers.

It is to be observed, that these ambassadors spoke to me, by an interpreter, the languages of both empires differing as much from each other as any two in Europe, and each nation priding itself upon the antiquity, beauty, and energy of their own tongue, with an avowed contempt for that of their neighbor; yet our emperor, standing upon the advantage he had got by the seizure of their fleet, obliged them to deliver their credentials, and make their speech, in the Lilliputian tongue. And it must be confessed, that from the great intercourse of trade and commerce between both realms, from the continual reception of exiles which is mutual among them, and from the custom, in each empire, to send their young nobility and richer gentry to the other, in order to polish themselves by seeing the world, and understanding men and manners; there are few persons of distinction, or merchants, or seamen, who dwell in the maritime parts, but what can hold conversation in both tongues; as I found some weeks after, when I went to pay my respects to the emperor of Blefuscu, which, in the midst of great misfortunes, through the malice of my enemies, proved a very happy adventure to me, as I shall relate in its proper place.

The reader may remember, that when I signed those articles upon which I recovered my liberty, there were some which I disliked, upon account of their being too servile; neither could anything but an extreme necessity have forced me to submit. But being now a NARDAC of the highest rank in that empire, such offices were looked upon as below my dignity, and the emperor (to do him justice), never once mentioned them to me. However, it was not long before I had an opportunity of doing his majesty, at least as I then thought, a most signal service. I was alarmed at midnight with the cries of many hundred people at my door; by which, being suddenly awaked, I was in some kind of terror. I heard the word BURGLUM repeated incessantly: several of the emperor's court, making their way through the crowd, entreated me to come immediately to the palace, where her imperial majesty's apartment was on fire, by the carelessness of a maid of honor, who fell asleep while she was reading a romance. I got up in an instant; and orders being given to clear the way before me, and it being likewise a moonshine night, I made a shift to get to the palace without trampling on any of the people. I found they had already applied ladders to the walls of the apartment, and were well provided with buckets, but the water was at some distance. These buckets were about the size of large thimbles, and the poor people supplied me with them as fast as they could: but the flame was so violent that they did little good. I might easily have stifled it with my coat, which I unfortunately left behind me for haste, and came away only in my leathern jerkin. The case seemed wholly desperate and deplorable; and this magnificent palace would have infallibly been burnt down to the ground, if, by a presence of mind unusual to me, I had not suddenly thought of an expedient. I had, the evening before, drunk plentifully of a most delicious wine called GLIMIGRIM, (the Blefuscudians call it FLUNEC, but ours is esteemed the better sort,) which is very diuretic. By the luckiest chance in the world, I had not discharged myself of any part of it. The heat I had contracted by coming very near the flames, and by laboring to quench them, made the wine begin to operate by urine; which I voided in such a quantity, and applied so well to the proper places, that in three minutes the fire was wholly extinguished, and the rest of that noble pile, which had cost so many ages in erecting, preserved from destruction.

It was now day-light, and I returned to my house without waiting to congratulate with the emperor: because, although I had done a very eminent piece of service, yet I could not tell how his majesty might resent the manner by which I had performed it: for, by the fundamental laws of the realm, it is capital in any person, of what quality soever, to make water within the precincts of the palace. But I was a little comforted by a message from his majesty, "that he would give orders to the grand justiciary for passing my pardon in form:" which, however, I could not obtain; and I was privately assured, "that the empress, conceiving the greatest abhorrence of what I had done, removed to the most distant side of the court, firmly resolved that those buildings should never be repaired for her use: and, in the presence of her chief confidents could not forbear vowing revenge."

6

Of the inhabitants of Lilliput; their learning, laws, and customs; the manner of educating their children. The author's way of living in that country. His vindication of a great lady.

Although I intend to leave the description of this empire to a particular treatise, yet, in the mean time, I am content to gratify the curious reader with some general ideas. As the common size of the natives is somewhat under six inches high, so there is an exact proportion in all other animals, as well as plants and trees: for instance, the tallest horses and oxen are between four and five inches in height, the sheep an inch and half, more or less: their geese about the bigness of a sparrow, and so the several gradations downwards till you come to the smallest, which to my sight, were almost invisible; but nature has adapted the eyes of the Lilliputians to all objects proper for their view: they see with great exactness, but at no great distance. And, to show the sharpness of their sight towards objects that are near, I have been much pleased with observing a cook pulling a lark, which was not so large as a common fly; and a young girl threading an invisible needle with invisible silk. Their tallest trees are about seven feet high: I mean some of those in the great royal park, the tops whereof I could but just reach with my fist clenched. The other vegetables are in the same proportion; but this I leave to the reader's imagination.

I shall say but little at present of their learning, which, for many ages, has flourished in all its branches among them: but their manner of writing is very peculiar, being neither from the left to the right, like the Europeans, nor from the right to the left, like the Arabians, nor from up to down, like the Chinese, but aslant, from one corner of the paper to the other, like ladies in England.

They bury their dead with their heads directly downward, because they hold an opinion, that in eleven thousand moons they are all to rise again; in which period the earth (which they conceive to be flat) will turn upside down, and by this means they shall, at their resurrection, be found ready standing on their feet. The learned among them confess the absurdity of this doctrine; but the practice still continues, in compliance to the vulgar.

There are some laws and customs in this empire very peculiar; and if they were not so directly contrary to those of my own dear country, I should be tempted to say a little in their justification. It is only to be wished they were as well executed. The first I shall mention, relates to informers. All crimes against the state, are punished here with the utmost severity; but, if the person accused makes his innocence plainly to appear upon his trial, the accuser is immediately put to an ignominious death; and out of his goods or lands the innocent person is quadruply recompensed for the loss of his time, for the danger he underwent, for the hardship of his imprisonment, and for all the charges he has been at in making his defence; or, if that fund be deficient, it is largely supplied by the crown. The emperor also confers on him some public mark of his favor, and proclamation is made of his innocence through the whole city.

They look upon fraud as a greater crime than theft, and therefore seldom fail to punish it with death; for they allege, that care and vigilance, with a very common understanding, may preserve a man's goods from thieves, but honesty hath no fence against superior cunning; and, since it is necessary that there should be a perpetual intercourse of buying and selling, and dealing upon credit, where fraud is permitted and connived at, or has no law to punish it, the honest dealer is always undone, and the knave gets the advantage. I remember, when I was once interceding with the emperor for a criminal who had wronged his master of a great sum of money, which he had received by order and ran away with; and happening to tell his majesty, by way of extenuation, that it was only a breach of trust, the emperor thought it monstrous in me to offer as a defence the greatest aggravation of the crime; and truly I had little to say in return, farther than the common answer, that different nations had different customs; for, I confess, I was heartily ashamed.

Although we usually call reward and punishment the two hinges upon which all government turns, yet I could never observe this maxim to be put in practice by any nation except that of Lilliput. Whoever can there bring sufficient proof, that he has strictly observed the laws of his country for seventy-three moons, has a claim to certain privileges, according to his quality or condition of life, with a proportionable sum of money out of a fund appropriated for that use: he likewise acquires the title of SNILPALL, or legal, which is added to his name, but does not descend to his posterity. And these people thought it a prodigious defect of policy among us, when I told them that our laws were enforced only by penalties, without any mention of reward. It is upon this account that the image of Justice, in their courts of judicature, is formed with six eyes, two before, as many behind, and on each side one, to signify circumspection; with a bag of gold open in her right hand, and a sword sheathed in her left, to show she is more disposed to reward than to punish.

In chusing persons for all employments, they have more regard to good morals than to great abilities; for, since government is necessary to mankind, they believe, that the common size of human understanding is fitted to some station or other; and that Providence never intended to make the management of public affairs a mystery to be comprehended only by a few persons of sublime genius, of which there seldom are three born in an age: but they suppose truth, justice, temperance, and the like, to be in every man's power; the practice of which virtues, assisted by experience and a good intention, would qualify any man for the service of his country, except where a course of study is required. But they thought the want of moral virtues was so far from being supplied by superior endowments of the mind, that employments could never be put into such dangerous hands as those of persons so qualified; and, at least, that the mistakes committed by ignorance, in a virtuous disposition, would never be of such fatal consequence to the public weal, as the practices of a man, whose inclinations led him to be corrupt, and who had great abilities to manage, to multiply, and defend his corruptions.

In like manner, the disbelief of a Divine Providence renders a man incapable of holding any public station; for, since kings avow themselves to be the deputies of Providence, the Lilliputians think nothing can be more absurd than for a prince to employ such men as disown the authority under which he acts.

In relating these and the following laws, I would only be understood to mean the original institutions, and not the most scandalous corruptions, into which these people are fallen by the degenerate nature of man. For, as to that infamous practice of acquiring great employments by dancing on the ropes, or badges of favor and distinction by leaping over sticks and creeping under them, the reader is to observe, that they were first introduced by the grandfather of the emperor now reigning, and grew to the present height by the gradual increase of party and faction.

Ingratitude is among them a capital crime, as we read it to have been in some other countries: for they reason thus; that whoever makes ill returns to his benefactor, must needs be a common enemy to the rest of mankind, from whom he has received no obligation, and therefore such a man is not fit to live.

Their notions relating to the duties of parents and children differ extremely from ours. For, since the conjunction of male and female is founded upon the great law of nature, in order to propagate and continue the species, the Lilliputians will needs have it, that men and women are joined together, like other animals, by the motives of concupiscence; and that their tenderness towards their young proceeds from the like natural principle: for which reason they will never allow that a child is under any obligation to his father for begetting him, or to his mother for bringing him into the world; which, considering the miseries of human life, was neither a benefit in itself, nor intended so by his parents, whose thoughts, in their love encounters, were otherwise employed. Upon these, and the like reasonings, their opinion is, that parents are the last of all others to be trusted with the education of their own children; and therefore they have in every town public nurseries, where all parents, except cottagers and laborers, are obliged to send their infants of both sexes to be reared and educated, when they come to the age of twenty moons, at which time they are supposed to have some rudiments of docility. These schools are of several kinds, suited to different qualities, and both sexes. They have certain professors well skilled in preparing children for such a condition of life as befits the rank of their parents, and their own capacities, as well as inclinations. I shall first say something of the male nurseries, and then of the female.

The nurseries for males of noble or eminent birth, are provided with grave and learned professors, and their several deputies. The clothes and food of the children are plain and simple. They are bred up in the principles of honor, justice, courage, modesty, clemency, religion, and love of their country; they are always employed in some business, except in the times of eating and sleeping, which are very short, and two hours for diversions consisting of bodily exercises. They are dressed by men till four years of age, and then are obliged to dress themselves, although their quality be ever so great; and the women attendant, who are aged proportionably to ours at fifty, perform only the most menial offices. They are never suffered to converse with servants, but go together in smaller or greater numbers to take their diversions, and always in the presence of a professor, or one of his deputies; whereby they avoid those early bad impressions of folly and vice, to which our children are subject.

Their parents are suffered to see them only twice a year; the visit is to last but an hour; they are allowed to kiss the child at meeting and parting; but a professor, who always stands by on those occasions, will not suffer them to whisper, or use any fondling expressions, or bring any presents of toys, sweetmeats, and the like.

The pension from each family for the education and entertainment of a child, upon failure of due payment, is levied by the emperor's officers. The nurseries for children of ordinary gentlemen, merchants, traders, and handicrafts, are managed proportionably after the same manner; only those designed for trades are put out apprentices at eleven years old, whereas those of persons of quality continue in their exercises till fifteen, which answers to twenty-one with us: but the confinement is gradually lessened for the last three years.

In the female nurseries, the young girls of quality are educated much like the males, only they are dressed by orderly servants of their own sex; but always in the presence of a professor or deputy, till they come to dress themselves, which is at five years old. And if it be found that these nurses ever presume to entertain the girls with frightful or foolish stories, or the common follies practised by chambermaids among us, they are publicly whipped thrice about the city, imprisoned for a year, and banished for life to the most desolate part of the country. Thus the young ladies are as much ashamed of being cowards and fools as the men, and despise all personal ornaments, beyond decency and cleanliness: neither did I perceive any difference in their education made by their difference of sex, only that the exercises of the females were not altogether so robust; and that some rules were given them relating to domestic life, and a smaller compass of learning was enjoined them: for their maxim is, that among peoples of quality, a wife should be always a reasonable and agreeable companion, because she cannot always be young. When the girls are twelve years old, which among them is the marriageable age, their parents or guardians take them home, with great expressions of gratitude to the professors, and seldom without tears of the young lady and her companions.

In the nurseries of females of the meaner sort, the children are instructed in all kinds of works proper for their sex, and their several degrees: those intended for apprentices are dismissed at seven years old, the rest are kept to eleven.

The meaner families who have children at these nurseries, are obliged, besides their annual pension, which is as low as possible, to return to the steward of the nursery a small monthly share of their gettings, to be a portion for the child; and therefore all parents are limited in their expenses by the law. For the Lilliputians think nothing can be more unjust, than for people, in subservience to their own appetites, to bring children into the world, and leave the burthen of supporting them on the public. As to persons of quality, they give security to appropriate a certain sum for each child, suitable to their condition; and these funds are always managed with good husbandry and the most exact justice.

The cottagers and laborers keep their children at home, their business being only to till and cultivate the earth, and therefore their education is of little consequence to the public: but the old and diseased among them, are supported by hospitals; for begging is a trade unknown in this empire. And here it may, perhaps, divert the curious reader, to give some account of my domestics, and my manner of living in this country, during a residence of nine months, and thirteen days. Having a head mechanically turned, and being likewise forced by necessity, I had made for myself a table and chair convenient enough, out of the largest trees in the royal park. Two hundred sempstresses were employed to make me shirts, and linen for my bed and table, all of the strongest and coarsest kind they could get; which, however, they were forced to quilt together in several folds, for the thickest was some degrees finer than lawn. Their linen is usually three inches wide, and three feet make a piece. The sempstresses took my measure as I lay on the ground, one standing at my neck, and another at my mid-leg, with a strong cord extended, that each held by the end, while a third measured the length of the cord with a rule of an inch long. Then they measured my right thumb, and desired no more; for by a mathematical computation, that twice round the thumb is once round the wrist, and so on to the neck and the waist, and by the help of my old shirt, which I displayed on the ground before them for a pattern, they fitted me exactly. Three hundred tailors were employed in the same manner to make me clothes; but they had another contrivance for taking my measure. I kneeled down, and they raised a ladder from the ground to my neck; upon this ladder one of them mounted, and let fall a plumb-line from my collar to the floor, which just answered the length of my coat: but my waist and arms I measured myself. When my clothes were finished, which was done in my house (for the largest of theirs would not have been able to hold them), they looked like the patch-work made by the ladies in England, only that mine were all of a color.

I had three hundred cooks to dress my victuals, in little convenient huts built about my house, where they and their families lived, and prepared me two dishes a-piece. I took up twenty waiters in my hand, and placed them on the table: a hundred more attended below on the ground, some with dishes of meat, and some with barrels of wine and other liquors slung on their shoulders; all which the waiters above drew up, as I wanted, in a very ingenious manner, by certain cords, as we draw the bucket up a well in Europe. A dish of their meat was a good mouthful, and a barrel of their liquor a reasonable draught. Their mutton yields to ours, but their beef is excellent. I have had a sirloin so large, that I have been forced to make three bites of it; but this is rare. My servants were astonished to see me eat it, bones and all, as in our country we do the leg of a lark. Their geese and turkeys I usually ate at a mouthful, and I confess they far exceed ours. Of their smaller fowl I could take up twenty or thirty at the end of my knife. One day his imperial majesty, being informed of my way of living, desired "that himself and his royal consort, with the young princes of the blood of both sexes, might have the happiness," as he was pleased to call it, "of dining with me." They came accordingly, and I placed them in chairs of state, upon my table, just over against me, with their guards about them. Flimnap, the lord high treasurer, attended there likewise with his white staff; and I observed he often looked on me with a sour countenance, which I would not seem to regard, but ate more than usual, in honor to my dear country, as well as to fill the court with admiration. I have some private reasons to believe, that this visit from his majesty gave Flimnap an opportunity of doing me ill offices to his master. That minister had always been my secret enemy, though he outwardly caressed me more than was usual to the moroseness of his nature. He represented to the emperor "the low condition of his treasury; that he was forced to take up money at a great discount; that exchequer bills would not circulate under nine per cent. below par; that I had cost his majesty above a million and a half of SPRUGS" (their greatest gold coin, about the bigness of a spangle) "and, upon the whole, that it would be advisable in the emperor to take the first fair occasion of dismissing me."

I am here obliged to vindicate the reputation of an excellent lady, who was an innocent sufferer upon my account. The treasurer took a fancy to be jealous of his wife, from the malice of some evil tongues, who informed him that her grace had taken a violent affection for my person; and the court scandal ran for some time, that she once came privately to my lodging. This I solemnly declare to be a most infamous falsehood, without any grounds, further than that her grace was pleased to treat me with all innocent marks of freedom and friendship. I own she came often to my house, but always publicly, nor ever without three more in the coach, who were usually her sister and young daughter, and some particular acquaintance; but this was common to many other ladies of the court. And I still appeal to my servants round, whether they at any time saw a coach at my door, without knowing what persons were in it. On those occasions, when a servant had given me notice, my custom was to go immediately to the door, and, after paying my respects, to take up the coach and two horses very carefully in my hands (for, if there were six horses, the postillion always unharnessed four,) and place them on a table, where I had fixed a movable rim quite round, of five inches high, to prevent accidents. And I have often had four coaches and horses at once on my table, full of company, while I sat in my chair, leaning my face towards them; and when I was engaged with one set, the coachmen would gently drive the others round my table. I have passed many an afternoon very agreeably in these conversations. But I defy the treasurer, or his two informers (I will name them, and let them make the best of it) Clustril and Drunlo, to prove that any person ever came to me INCOGNITO, except the secretary Reldresal, who was sent by express command of his imperial majesty, as I have before related. I should not have dwelt so long upon this particular, if it had not been a point wherein the reputation of a great lady is so nearly concerned, to say nothing of my own; though I then had the honor to be a NARDAC, which the treasurer himself is not; for all the world knows, that he is only a GLUMGLUM, a title inferior by one degree, as that of a marquis is to a duke in England; yet I allow he preceded me in right of his post. These false informations, which I afterwards came to the knowledge of by an accident not proper to mention, made the treasurer show his lady for some time an ill countenance, and me a worse; and although he was at last undeceived and reconciled to her, yet I lost all credit with him, and found my interest decline very fast with the emperor himself, who was, indeed, too much governed by that favorite.

7

The author, being informed of a design to accuse him of high-treason, makes his escape to Blefuscu. His reception there.

Before I proceed to give an account of my leaving this kingdom, it may be proper to inform the reader of a private intrigue which had been for two months forming against me.

I had been hitherto, all my life, a stranger to courts, for which I was unqualified by the meanness of my condition. I had indeed heard and read enough of the dispositions of great princes and ministers, but never expected to have found such terrible effects of them, in so remote a country, governed, as I thought, by very different maxims from those in Europe.

When I was just preparing to pay my attendance on the emperor of Blefuscu, a considerable person at court (to whom I had been very serviceable, at a time when he lay under the highest displeasure of his imperial majesty) came to my house very privately at night, in a close chair, and, without sending his name, desired admittance. The chairmen were dismissed; I put the chair, with his lordship in it, into my coat-pocket: and, giving orders to a trusty servant, to say I was indisposed and gone to sleep, I fastened the door of my house, placed the chair on the table, according to my usual custom, and sat down by it. After the common salutations were over, observing his lordship's countenance full of concern, and inquiring into the reason, he desired "I would hear him with patience, in a matter that highly concerned my honor and my life." His speech was to the following effect, for I took notes of it as soon as he left me.

"You are to know," said he, "that several committees of council have been lately called, in the most private manner, on your account; and it is but two days since his majesty came to a full resolution.

"You are very sensible that Skyresh Bolgolam" (GALBET, or high-admiral) "has been your mortal enemy, almost ever since your arrival. His original reasons I know not; but his hatred is increased since your great success against Blefuscu, by which his glory as admiral is much obscured. This lord, in conjunction with Flimnap the high-treasurer, whose enmity against you is notorious on account of his lady, Limtoc the general, Lalcon the chamberlain, and Balmuff the grand justiciary, have prepared articles of impeachment against you, for treason and other capital crimes."

This preface made me so impatient, being conscious of my own merits and innocence, that I was going to interrupt him; when he entreated me to be silent, and thus proceeded:—

"Out of gratitude for the favors you have done me, I procured information of the whole proceedings, and a copy of the articles; wherein I venture my head for your service.

Articles of Impeachment against QUINBUS FLESTRIN, (the Man-Mountain.)

ARTICLE I.

Whereas, by a statute made in the reign of his imperial majesty Calin Deffar Plune, it is enacted, that, whoever shall make water within the precincts of the royal palace, shall be liable to the pains and penalties of high-treason; notwithstanding, the said Quinbus Flestrin, in open breach of the said law, under color of extinguishing the fire kindled in the apartment of his majesty's most dear imperial consort, did maliciously, traitorously, and devilishly, by discharge of his urine, put out the said fire kindled in the said apartment, lying and being within the precincts of the said royal palace, against the statute in that case provided, etc. against the duty, etc.

ARTICLE II.

That the said Quinbus Flestrin, having brought the imperial fleet of Blefuscu into the royal port, and being afterwards commanded by his imperial majesty to seize all the other ships of the said empire of Blefuscu, and reduce that empire to a province, to be governed by a viceroy from hence, and to destroy and put to death, not only all the Big-endian exiles, but likewise all the people of that empire who would not immediately forsake the Big-endian heresy, he, the said Flestrin, like a false traitor against his most auspicious, serene, imperial majesty, did petition to be excused from the said service, upon pretence of unwillingness to force the consciences, or destroy the liberties and lives of an innocent people.

ARTICLE III.

That, whereas certain ambassadors arrived from the Court of Blefuscu, to sue for peace in his majesty's court, he, the said Flestrin, did, like a false traitor, aid, abet, comfort, and divert, the said ambassadors, although he knew them to be servants to a prince who was lately an open enemy to his imperial majesty, and in an open war against his said majesty.

ARTICLE IV.

That the said Quinbus Flestrin, contrary to the duty of a faithful subject, is now preparing to make a voyage to the court and empire of Blefuscu, for which he has received only verbal license from his imperial majesty;

and, under color of the said license, does falsely and traitorously intend to take the said voyage, and thereby to aid, comfort, and abet the emperor of Blefuscu, so lately an enemy, and in open war with his imperial majesty aforesaid.

There are some other articles; but these are the most important, of which I have read you an abstract.

In the several debates upon this impeachment, it must be confessed that his majesty gave many marks of his great lenity; often urging the services you had done him, and endeavoring to extenuate your crimes. The treasurer and admiral insisted that you should be put to the most painful and ignominious death, by setting fire to your house at night, and the general was to attend with twenty thousand men, armed with poisoned arrows, to shoot you on the face and hands. Some of your servants were to have private orders to strew a poisonous juice on your shirts and sheets, which would soon make you tear your own flesh, and die in the utmost torture. The general came into the same opinion; so that for a long time there was a majority against you; but his majesty resolving, if possible, to spare your life, at last brought off the chamberlain.

Upon this incident, Reldresal, principal secretary for private affairs, who always approved himself your true friend, was commanded by the emperor to deliver his opinion, which he accordingly did; and therein justified the good thoughts you have of him. He allowed your crimes to be great, but that still there was room for mercy, the most commendable virtue in a prince, and for which his majesty was so justly celebrated. He said, the friendship between you and him was so well known to the world, that perhaps the most honorable board might think him partial; however, in obedience to the command he had received, he would freely offer his sentiments. That if his majesty, in consideration of your services, and pursuant to his own merciful disposition, would please to spare your life, and only give orders to put out both your eyes, he humbly conceived, that by this expedient justice might in some measure be satisfied, and all the world would applaud the lenity of the emperor, as well as the fair and generous proceedings of those who have the honor to be his counsellors. That the loss of your eyes would be no impediment to your bodily strength, by which you might still be useful to his majesty; that blindness is an addition to courage, by concealing dangers from us; that the fear you had for your eyes, was the greatest difficulty in bringing over the enemy's fleet, and it would be sufficient for you to see by the eyes of the ministers, since the greatest princes do no more.

This proposal was received with the utmost disapprobation by the whole board. Bolgolam, the admiral, could not preserve his temper, but, rising up in fury, said, he wondered how the secretary durst presume to give his opinion for preserving the life of a traitor; that the services you had performed were, by all true reasons of state, the great aggravation of your crimes; that you, who were able to extinguish the fire by discharge of urine in her majesty's apartment (which he mentioned with horror), might, at another time, raise an inundation by the same means, to drown the whole palace; and the same strength which enabled you to bring over the enemy's fleet, might serve, upon the first discontent, to carry it back; that he had good reasons to think you were a Big-endian in your heart; and, as treason begins in the heart, before it appears in overt-acts, so he accused you as a traitor on that account, and therefore insisted you should be put to death.

The treasurer was of the same opinion: he showed to what straits his majesty's revenue was reduced, by the charge of maintaining you, which would soon grow insupportable; that the secretary's expedient of putting out your eyes, was so far from being a remedy against this evil, that it would probably increase it, as is manifest from the common practice of blinding some kind of fowls, after which they fed the faster, and grew sooner fat; that his sacred majesty and the council, who are your judges, were, in their own consciences, fully convinced of your guilt, which was a sufficient argument to condemn you to death, without the formal proofs required by the strict letter of the law.

"But his imperial majesty, fully determined against capital punishment, was graciously pleased to say, that since the council thought the loss of your eyes too easy a censure, some other way may be inflicted hereafter. And your friend the secretary, humbly desiring to be heard again, in answer to what the treasurer had objected, concerning the great charge his majesty was at in maintaining you, said, that his excellency, who had the sole disposal of the emperor's revenue, might easily provide against that evil, by gradually lessening your establishment; by which, for want of sufficient for you would grow weak and faint, and lose your appetite, and consequently, decay, and consume in a few months; neither would the stench of your carcass be then so dangerous, when it should become more than half diminished; and immediately upon your death five or six thousand of his majesty's subjects might, in two or three days, cut your flesh from your bones, take it away by cart-loads, and bury it in distant parts, to prevent infection, leaving the skeleton as a monument of admiration to posterity.

Thus, by the great friendship of the secretary, the whole affair was compromised. It was strictly enjoined, that the project of starving you by degrees should be kept a secret; but the sentence of putting out your eyes was entered on the books; none dissenting, except Bolgolam the admiral, who, being a creature of the empress, was perpetually instigated by her majesty to insist upon your death, she having borne perpetual malice against you, on account of that infamous and illegal method you took to extinguish the fire in her apartment.

In three days your friend the secretary will be directed to come to your house, and read before you the articles of impeachment; and then to signify the great lenity and favor of his majesty and council, whereby you are only condemned to the loss of your eyes, which his majesty does not question you will gratefully and humbly submit to; and twenty of his majesty's surgeons will attend, in order to see the operation well performed, by discharging very sharp-pointed arrows into the balls of your eyes, as you lie on the ground.

"I leave to your prudence what measures you will take; and to avoid suspicion, I must immediately return in as private a manner as I came." His lordship did so; and I remained alone, under many doubts and perplexities of mind.

It was a custom introduced by this prince and his ministry (very different, as I have been assured, from the practice of former times,) that after the court had decreed any cruel execution, either to gratify the monarch's resentment, or the malice of a favorite, the emperor always made a speech to his whole council, expressing his great lenity and tenderness, as qualities known and confessed by all the world. This speech was immediately published throughout the kingdom; nor did anything terrify the people so much as those encomiums on his majesty's mercy; because it was observed, that the more these praises were enlarged and insisted on, the more inhuman was the punishment, and the sufferer more innocent. Yet, as to myself, I must confess, having never been designed for a courtier, either by my birth or education, I was so ill a judge of things, that I could not discover the lenity and favor of this sentence, but conceived it (perhaps erroneously) rather to be rigorous than gentle. I sometimes thought of standing my trial, for, although I could not deny the facts alleged in the several articles, yet I hoped they would admit of some extenuation. But having in my life perused many state-trials, which I ever observed to terminate as the judges thought fit to direct, I durst not rely on so dangerous a decision, in so critical a juncture, and against such powerful enemies. Once I was strongly bent upon resistance, for, while I had liberty the whole strength of that empire could hardly subdue me, and I might easily with stones pelt the metropolis to pieces; but I soon rejected that project with horror, by remembering the oath I had made to the emperor, the favors I received from him, and the high title of NARDAC he conferred upon me. Neither had I so soon learned the gratitude of courtiers, to persuade myself, that his majesty's present seventies acquitted me of all past obligations.

At last, I fixed upon a resolution, for which it is probable I may incur some censure, and not unjustly; for I confess I owe the preserving of mine eyes, and consequently my liberty, to my own great rashness and want of experience; because, if I had then known the nature of princes and ministers, which I have since observed in many other courts, and their methods of treating criminals less obnoxious than myself, I should, with great alacrity and readiness, have submitted to so easy a punishment. But hurried on by the precipitancy of youth, and having his imperial majesty's license to pay my attendance upon the emperor of Blefuscu, I took this opportunity, before the three days were elapsed, to send a letter to my friend the secretary, signifying my resolution of setting out that morning for Blefuscu, pursuant to the leave I had got; and, without waiting for an answer, I went to that side of the island where our fleet lay. I seized a large man of war, tied a cable to the prow, and, lifting up the anchors, I stripped myself, put my clothes (together with my coverlet, which I carried under my arm) into the vessel, and, drawing it after me, between wading and swimming arrived at the royal port of Blefuscu, where the people had long expected me: they lent me two guides to direct me to the capital city, which is of the same name. I held them in my hands, till I came within two hundred yards of the gate, and desired them "to signify my arrival to one of the secretaries, and let him know, I there waited his majesty's command." I had an answer in about an hour, "that his majesty, attended by the royal family, and great officers of the court, was coming out to receive me." I advanced a hundred yards. The emperor and his train alighted from their horses, the empress and ladies from their coaches, and I did not perceive they were in any fright or concern. I lay on the ground to kiss his majesty's and the empress's hands. I told his majesty, "that I was come according to my promise, and with the license of the emperor my master, to have the honor of seeing so mighty a monarch, and to offer him any service in my power, consistent with my duty to my own prince;" not mentioning a word of my disgrace, because I had hitherto no regular information of it, and might suppose myself wholly ignorant of any such design; neither could I reasonably conceive that the emperor would discover the secret, while I was out of his power; wherein, however, it soon appeared I was deceived.

I shall not trouble the reader with the particular account of my reception at this court, which was suitable to the generosity of so great a prince; nor of the difficulties I was in for want of a house and bed, being forced to lie on the ground, wrapped up in my coverlet.

 8

The author, by a lucky accident, finds means to leave Blefuscu; and, after some difficulties, returns safe to his native country.

Three days after my arrival, walking out of curiosity to the northeast coast of the island, I observed, about half a league off in the sea, somewhat that looked like a boat overturned. I pulled off my shoes and stockings, and, wailing two or three hundred yards, I found the object to approach nearer by force of the tide; and then plainly saw it to be a real boat, which I supposed might by some tempest have been driven from a ship. Whereupon, I returned immediately towards the city, and desired his imperial majesty to lend me twenty of the tallest vessels he had left, after the loss of his fleet, and three thousand seamen, under the command of his vice-admiral. This fleet sailed round, while I went back the shortest way to the coast, where I first discovered the boat. I found the tide had driven it still nearer. The seamen were all provided with cordage, which I had beforehand twisted to a sufficient strength. When the ships came up, I stripped myself, and waded till I came within a hundred yards off the boat, after which I was forced to swim till I got up to it. The seamen threw me the end of the cord, which I fastened to a hole in the fore-part of the boat, and the other end to a man of war; but I found all my labor to little purpose; for, being out of my depth, I was not able to work. In this necessity I was forced to swim behind, and push the boat forward, as often as I could, with one of my hands; and the tide favoring me, I advanced so far that I could just hold up my chin and feel the ground. I rested two or three minutes, and then gave the boat another shove, and so on, till the sea was no higher than my arm-pits; and now, the most laborious part being over, I took out my other cables, which were stowed in one of the ships, and fastened them first to the boat, and then to nine of the vessels which attended me; the wind being favorable, the seamen towed, and I shoved, until we arrived within forty yards of the shore; and, waiting till the tide was out, I got dry to the boat, and by the assistance of two thousand men, with ropes and engines, I made a shift to turn it on its bottom, and found it was but little damaged.

I shall not trouble the reader with the difficulties I was under, by the help of certain paddles, which cost me ten days making, to get my boat to the royal port of Blefuscu, where a mighty concourse of people appeared upon my arrival, full of wonder at the sight of so prodigious a vessel. I told the emperor "that my good fortune had thrown this boat in my way, to carry me to some place whence I might return into my native country; and begged his majesty's orders for getting materials to fit it up, together with his license to depart;" which, after some kind expostulations, he was pleased to grant.

I did very much wonder, in all this time, not to have heard of any express relating to me from our emperor to the court of Blefuscu. But I was afterward given privately to understand, that his imperial majesty, never imagining I had the least notice of his designs, believed I was only gone to Blefuscu in performance of my promise, according to the license he had given me, which was well known at our court, and would return in a few days, when the ceremony was ended. But he was at last in pain at my long absence; and after consulting with the treasurer and the rest of that cabal, a person of quality was dispatched with the copy of the articles against me. This envoy had instructions to represent to the monarch of Blefuscu, "the great lenity of his master, who was content to punish me no farther than with the loss of mine eyes; that I had fled from justice;

and if I did not return in two hours, I should be deprived of my title of NARDAC, and declared a traitor." The envoy further added, "that in order to maintain the peace and amity between both empires, his master expected that his brother of Blefuscu would give orders to have me sent back to Lilliput, bound hand and foot, to be punished as a traitor."

The emperor of Blefuscu, having taken three days to consult, returned an answer consisting of many civilities and excuses. He said, "that as for sending me bound, his brother knew it was impossible; that, although I had deprived him of his fleet, yet he owed great obligations to me for many good offices I had done him in making the peace. That, however, both their majesties would soon be made easy; for I had found a prodigious vessel on the shore, able to carry me on the sea, which he had given orders to fit up, with my own assistance and direction; and he hoped, in a few weeks, both empires would be freed from so insupportable an encumbrance."

With this answer the envoy returned to Lilliput; and the monarch of Blefuscu related to me all that had passed; offering me at the same time (but under the strictest confidence) his gracious protection, if I would continue in his service; wherein, although I believed him sincere, yet I resolved never more to put any confidence in princes or ministers, where I could possibly avoid it; and therefore, with all due acknowledgments for his favourable intentions, I humbly begged to be excused. I told him, "that since fortune, whether good or evil, had thrown a vessel in my way, I was resolved to venture myself on the ocean, rather than be an occasion of difference between two such mighty monarchs." Neither did I find the emperor at all displeased; and I discovered, by a certain accident, that he was very glad of my resolution, and so were most of his ministers. These considerations moved me to hasten my departure somewhat sooner than I intended; to which the court, impatient to have me gone, very readily contributed. Five hundred workmen were employed to make two sails to my boat, according to my directions, by quilting thirteen folds of their strongest linen together. I was at the pains of making ropes and cables, by twisting ten, twenty, or thirty of the thickest and strongest of theirs. A great stone that I happened to find, after a long search, by the sea-shore, served me for an anchor. I had the tallow of three hundred cows, for greasing my boat, and other uses. I was at incredible pains in cutting down some of the largest timber-trees, for oars and masts, wherein I was, however, much assisted by his majesty's ship-carpenters, who helped me in smoothing them, after I had done the rough work.

In about a month, when all was prepared, I sent to receive his majesty's commands, and to take my leave. The emperor and royal family came out of the palace; I lay down on my face to kiss his hand, which he very graciously gave me: so did the empress and young princes of the blood. His majesty presented me with fifty purses of two hundred SPRUGS a-piece, together with his picture at full length, which I put immediately into one of my gloves, to keep it from being hurt. The ceremonies at my departure were too many to trouble the reader with at this time.

I stored the boat with the carcases of a hundred oxen, and three hundred sheep, with bread and drink proportionable, and as much meat ready dressed as four hundred cooks could provide. I took with me six cows and two bulls alive, with as many ewes and rams, intending to carry them into my own country, and propagate the breed. And to feed them on board, I had a good bundle of hay, and a bag of corn. I would gladly have taken a dozen of the natives, but this was a thing the emperor would by no means permit; and, besides a diligent search into my pockets, his majesty engaged my honor "not to carry away any of his subjects, although with their own consent and desire."

Having thus prepared all things as well as I was able, I set sail on the twenty-fourth day of September 1701, at six in the morning; and when I had gone about four-leagues to the northward, the wind being at south-east, at six in the evening I descryed a small island, about half a league to the north-west. I advanced forward, and cast anchor on the lee-side of the island, which seemed to be uninhabited. I then took some refreshment, and went to my rest. I slept well, and as I conjectured at least six hours, for I found the day broke in two hours after I awaked. It was a clear night. I ate my breakfast before the sun was up; and heaving anchor, the wind being favorable, I steered the same course that I had done the day before, wherein I was directed by my pocket compass. My intention was to reach, if possible, one of those islands. which I had reason to believe lay to the north-east of Van Diemen's Land. I discovered nothing all that day; but upon the next, about three in the afternoon, when I had by my computation made twenty-four leagues from Blefuscu, I descryed a sail steering to the south-east; my course was due east. I hailed her, but could get no answer; yet I found I gained upon her, for the wind slackened. I made all the sail I could, and in half an hour she spied me, then hung out her ancient, and discharged a gun. It is not easy to express the joy I was in, upon the unexpected hope of once more seeing my beloved country, and the dear pledges I left in it. The ship slackened her sails, and I came up with her between five and six in the evening, September 26th; but my heart leaped within me to see her English colors. I put my cows and sheep into my coat-pockets, and got on board with all my little cargo of provisions. The vessel was an English merchantman, returning from Japan by the North and South seas; the captain, Mr. John Biddel, of Deptford, a very civil man, and an excellent sailor.

We were now in the latitude of 30 degrees south; there were about fifty men in the ship; and here I met an old comrade of mine, one Peter Williams, who gave me a good character to the captain. This gentleman treated me with kindness, and desired I would let him know what place I came from last, and whither I was bound; which I did in a few words, but he thought I was raving, and that the dangers I underwent had disturbed my head; whereupon I took my black cattle and sheep out of my pocket, which, after great astonishment, clearly convinced him of my veracity. I then showed him the gold given me by the emperor of Blefuscu, together with his majesty's picture at full length, and some other rarities of that country. I gave him two purses of two hundreds SPRUGS each, and promised, when we arrived in England, to make him a present of a cow and a sheep big with young.

I shall not trouble the reader with a particular account of this voyage, which was very prosperous for the most part. We arrived in the Downs on the 13th of April, 1702. I had only one misfortune, that the rats on board carried away one of my sheep; I found her bones in a hole, picked clean from the flesh. The rest of my cattle I got safe ashore, and set them a-grazing in a bowling-green at Greenwich, where the fineness of the grass made them feed very heartily, though I had always feared the contrary: neither could I possibly have preserved them in so long a voyage, if the captain had not allowed me some of his best biscuit, which, rubbed to powder, and mingled with water, was their constant food. The short time I continued in England, I made a considerable profit by showing my cattle to many persons of quality and others: and before I began my second voyage, I sold them for six hundred pounds. Since my last return I find the breed is considerably increased, especially the sheep, which I hope will prove much to the advantage of the woollen manufacture, by the fineness of the fleeces.

I stayed but two months with my wife and family, for my insatiable desire of seeing foreign countries, would suffer me to continue no longer. I left fifteen hundred pounds with my wife, and fixed her in a good house at Redriff. My remaining stock I carried with me, part in money and part in goods, in hopes to improve my fortunes. My eldest uncle John had left me an estate in land, near Epping, of about thirty pounds a year; and I had a long lease of the Black Bull in Fetter-Lane, which yielded me as much more; so that I was not in any danger of leaving my family upon the parish. My son Johnny, named so after his uncle, was at the grammar-school, and a towardly child. My daughter Betty (who is now well married, and has children) was then at her needle-work. I took leave of my wife, and boy and girl, with tears on both sides, and went on board the Adventure, a merchant ship of three hundred tons, bound for Surat, captain John Nicholas, of Liverpool, commander. But my account of this voyage must be referred to the Second Part of my Travels.